The
Melding

by

Sharmai Amber

INNER EYE BOOKS
OUGHTEN HOUSE PUBLICATIONS
LIVERMORE, CA USA

The Melding
by
Sharmai Amber

Published in 1998

Copyright © 1998   Sharmai Amber

00 99 98   0 9 8 7 6 5 4 3 2 1

Published by
INNER EYE BOOKS
an imprint of
OUGHTEN HOUSE PUBLICATIONS
PO BOX 2008
LIVERMORE, CA 94551
PHONE: (510) 447-2332
FAX: (510) 447-2376
TOLL-FREE: 1-888-ORDERIT
E-MAIL: oughten@oughtenhouse.com
INTERNET: www.oughtenhouse.com

Cover art by Maurine Paishon, Ad Venture Designs
Cover design by Eric Akeson, Akeson Design

Library of Congress Cataloging in Publication

Amber, Sharmai, 1956 -
    The Melding / by Sharmai Amber.
        p.   cm.
    Includes bibliographical references.
    ISBN 1-880666-72-3
    1. Amber, Sharmai, 1956- 2. Spiritual biography--United States.
    I. Title.
BL73.A58A3   1998
291.4'092--dc21

                                                                97-49867
                                                                CIP
ISBN 1-880666-72-3
            Printed in the USA

Table of Contents

Disclaimer

The characters in this book are real but the names and identifying characteristics of most have been changed. Locations have been altered in order to protect the privacy of those involved.

The quotations for *Who Are Lightworkers?* are modified versions of Jack Clarke's *What is New Age, Anyway?, Who are New Agers, Anyway?,* and *Why a New Age, Anyway?*. This copyrighted material is printed with permission. Copies on poster stock of the original versions are available from Jack Clarke, 4015 Falls Ridge Drive, Alpharetta, GA 30202 (770) 410-1140.

Keith Amber's *Truth That Sets Us Free* is copyrighted material printed with permission. Copies of the expanded set are available on poster stock from Sambershar, 47-388 Hui Iwa Street, #14-305, Kaneohe, Hawai'i 96744-5440 (800) 211-7370.

Original Cover Art Concept and sketches done by Beverly Mukai.

Photo of Jesus/Sananda provided by ASSK.

Dedication

To Jesus-Sananda—to whom this book belongs. Your awesome, enduring commitment and profound love for Earth and her imperfect human beings inspire and guide me daily.

Acknowledgments

Thank you my beloved husband, Keith. You helped me heal my deep wounds. You listened endlessly with love and patience, and you supported this project unfailingly. My heart, in all its wholeness, is yours for our eternity.

Thank you, Beverly Lawler for multiple layers of endless support from your big precious heart.

Paul Wood, thank you for guiding the fledging writer within me along the path to competency.

To Marilyn Pesola. Your editorial assistance helped me find my way into becoming a more refined writer. Thank you.

To the staff at Oughten House. Thank you for giving *The Melding* a chance to be seen by the world.

And to the many other physical helpers who contributed in a vast array of ways, I thank you from the bottom of my heart for helping this book find its way into print.

To our non-physical creative Guide-of-Light, Shalina. Thank you for your ceaseless patience. It has been my greatest honor and privilege to work under your guidance and tutelage.

To my beloved ethereal Father. Thank you for your extraordinary, all-embracing, meticulous caring, and rigorous empowerment. As crystalline finds clarity, I am deeply and forever grateful for your unending wisdom, guidance, and unconditional love.

Finally, my eternal gratitude and love to Leviticus and all of the ethereal entities who have made this project possible.

Namasté

Sharmai

Introduction

For many Westerners, the idea that we *choose* the specific conditions and circumstances of our lives *before* we're born is a foreign, even inconceivable, concept. For some, it's even offensive. Contemporary authors such as Betty J. Eadie and T. Lobsang Rampa specifically talk about "pre-mortal" contracts or "plans" made before birth, as do the books delivering messages from such spirit guides as Hilarion and his peer Emmanuel. Yet even with increasing evidence and understanding of this concept, there are still many who find it hard to believe.

Actually, a more accurate statement might be that people resist taking full responsibility for the circumstances of their personal world. Sometimes their situations are downright awful and taking responsibility is distasteful or even embarrassing. Occasionally, it's hard to imagine that we could have placed ourselves into such dire situations and conditions. But we are in those conditions for a reason and, in the end, we must face our lessons and meet our challenges head on. True responsibility for all the circumstances of our lives, good or bad, easy or difficult, is the only path to total personal transformation and *freedom*.

In *Embraced By The Light*, Betty J. Eadie says on page 48:[1]

I saw that in the pre-mortal world, we knew about and even chose our missions in life. I understood that our stations in life are based upon the objectives of those missions. Through divine knowledge we knew what many of our tests and experiences would be, and we prepared accordingly. We bonded with others—family members and friends—to help us complete our missions.

T. Lobsang Rampa, a high ranking Tibetan Buddhist, and author of 22 books, says it slightly differently in *You Forever* on pages 103 and 104:[2]

So it is in the spirit world; before a human is born, several months before he is born, in fact, somewhere in the world of spirit there is a conference. The one who is going to enter into a human body discusses with advisors how certain lessons may be learned in much the same way as a student upon Earth will discuss how he or she may study to obtain the desired qualifications. The spirit advisors are able to say that the student about to enter into the school of the world shall become a son or daughter of a certain married couple, or even of an unmarried couple! There will be a discussion as to what has to be learned and what hardships have to be undergone, for it is a sad fact that hardship teaches one more quickly and more permanently than does kindness.

Maurice B. Cooke of Toronto, Canada, channels the spirit guide, Hilarion, in the book entitled *Symbols*.[3] On pages 4 and 5, Hilarion states:

But modern man does not believe that there is a timing and a control exerted upon him by the forces which created him. It is true that the human race has the gift of free will—a rarity in the created worlds— but this free will is largely an inner freedom, as we have explained in The Nature Of Reality; *that is, man has complete freedom as to how he will respond to the events and patterns of his life, but only limited ability to control the external circumstances which affect him. When a human soul comes into incarnation, it voluntarily (i.e., by virtue of its free will) gives up the right to completely order and control the external circumstances and patterns of the Earth life about to be lived. It gives up the right and, in effect, hands the decision-making power over to its Higher Self, and to the guides, guardians, and advisors of that Higher Self. For it well knows that the personality, or lower self, about to be developed at the Earth level and to occupy a physical body will be unable to perceive the whole panorama of its existence, that its field of view will narrow down and focus only upon the details and petty preoccupation of Earth life. It thus entrusts itself to guidance from a higher level, and this guidance must entail a manipulation of many of life's events in order to bring spiritualizing forces to bear upon the Earth personality.*

Hilarion goes on to say:

It is regrettable how many unenlightened human beings have the view that those who are "into" metaphysics, spirituality, esoteric studies, etc., are either weird, deluded, or fanatics. Few realize the joy and fullness of a life in which love and service to others are the keynotes. Indeed, a good part of the desperation and emptiness felt by so many individuals nowadays results precisely from the fact that they have forgotten how to love freely, or to serve others, simply out of the joy of bringing happiness.

Finally, on page 140 in *Emmanuel's Book,* Emmanuel states:[4]

Before an incarnation, all of the aspects of the soul's needs and desires are profoundly studied. By whom? By the soul itself, and by the teachers and companions, the loved ones that are not at this time encased in a human form.

Since the purpose of human life is to learn and grow, all manner of soul-design is incorporated, with great creativity, into the projected human birth. The time element, the cultural area, the sex, the race, the family, the capacities—physical, mental and emotional—are ordered. … this information is utilized in the blueprint of the soul.

In *The Melding*, I go one step further than my predecessors. Prebirth contracts influence the lives of every person on Earth. The prebirth contracts of Katrina, David, and myself (Roxy) are described in detail to help you grasp the depth and breadth of the contracts' influence in our lives.

Sometimes people do things that go beyond logic. They place themselves into painful or perilous circumstances for illogical reasons. But perhaps not. Perhaps behind the scenes there is a prebirth contract compelling the individual forward to embrace the lessons chosen by their soul.

The strategies and possibilities are endless. I know that there is no way that Katrina, David, or I would have gone forward if we weren't so compelled from within, and so thoroughly sure to the core of our knowing, that what we were about to do had been agreed to.

From there, all we had left was trusting that our souls, or Higher Selves, knew what they were doing. Looking back, it is crystal clear that my Higher Self knew exactly what it was doing and I'm grateful for the experience. Of course, that's in retrospect. At the time there were many moments of "hell" that we all persisted through because of the compelling inner force of our prebirth contracts.

Indeed, this bizarre true story, which has not been exaggerated or embellished, will tempt you to judge and doubt. Many will think that I have used creative writer's license to reel the reader in further. I did not need to. The story itself is extraordinary enough and every word is true. Suspend your limits, beliefs, judgments, fears, and skepticism as you journey through our saga. Engage in the possibility that I speak the truth. Then, *discern from your heart and soul, not your head*, what feels right for you. Feel free to apply to your own life that which fits and forwards your growth.

Remember that *God loves all* and is *all inclusive.* By the mighty wisdom of God, there are a million *right* paths. And each and every one, ultimately, leads back to the Almighty.

In Love & Light,

Sharmai Amber

Cast of Main Characters

Extraterrestrial

Of The Light:

- **Sananda**: Also known as Jesus, the ethereal Being who has personally committed to guiding Earth into the Light and the fourth dimension. Jesus' Higher Self's name.
- **Master Zoozer:** The Chief Medical Officer in charge of overseeing both medical advancements on Earth and a medical staff which performs all psychic or etheric surgery of the Light on humanity.
- **The Great White Brotherhood**: A group of souls available to offer protection to physical and non-physical souls in need of help against the dark.
- **Lord Archangel Michael**: Angel in charge of a battalion of Protection, or Warrior Angels, who protect physical and non-physical souls in need of assistance against troublesome dark souls.

Of The Light Channeling Through Katrina:

- **Commander Ashtar:** Of the Ashtar Command, Sananda's right-hand man and Commander in charge of all relief efforts of Space Beings who hover around Earth prepared to assist humanity and Earth at any moment.
- **Lady Commander Athena:** Sananda's left-hand woman; in charge of the Karmic Board; silver-tongued Guide to many on Earth.
- **Tenaiia:** Chosen as prime Trinity catalyst, monitor, and ethereal protector of Katrina.
- **Arianne:** Katrina's Higher Self and one of the six chosen Melded Souls.
- **Aria:** Arianne's ethereal father.
- **Antonomn:** Guide chosen for difficult ego work with Roxy.
- **Master Merlin:** Master reigning magician in the sector of the universe where Earth resides.

Of The Dark Channeling Through Katrina:

- **Zeeq:** Adversarial Soul contracted to attempt to prevent The Melding from anchoring on Earth. Necromancer anchored in the dark.

Of The Light Channeling Through David:

- Master Leviticus: Master Teacher.

Terrestrial

- **Katrina:** One of six people on Earth contracted to become Melded.
- **David:** Contracted to be a designated caretaker for Katrina.
- **Roxy:** Author of The Melding. Contracted to be a designated caretaker for Katrina.
- **Bill:** Katrina's Earth father.
- **Lanna:** Katrina's Earth mother.
- **Monica:** Roxy's first counseling client.
- **Grant:** Business associate of the Plumbs.
- **Samuel Wheaton:** Counseling client of Roxy.

Passage Through Portals

David and Roxy Plumb were in San Diego in June of 1986, searching for a roommate and a moderate rent. They weren't having much luck. It had been a long and grueling process until David came upon a ROOMMATE WANTED sign in the local grocery store. The next thing they knew, they were moving in with a voluptuous young college student named Katrina.

"Amazing," Katrina exclaimed a few days later when she opened the door to her spacious two-bedroom apartment. "My landlady approved you guys. I didn't think it was ever going to happen. She rejected everybody else."

"Yeah," Roxy said. "We had an unusually rough time, too! Curious, really. You know, there are no accidents," she offered as they walked inside the apartment.

"What do you mean, 'no accidents'?" Katrina asked, cocking her head.

"Everything happens for a reason," replied Roxy.

"There is purpose in it all," David said. "Nothing is accidental."

"The real trick is to figure out what the perfection is," Roxy pointed out.

"And what lesson is to be learned," David added.

"Hmmm ... interesting," Katrina mused, contemplating the notion. "Well, then, I wonder why I'm so driven to be a teacher."

David and Roxy smiled at each other as they hoofed their meager belongings up the flight of pink cement stairs to their new second floor apartment. The smell of sweet gladiolas filled their senses.

"Seems like second nature, doesn't it David?"

"Yeah. We're so used to looking for the perfection of everything we forget that others don't even know to look."

"Boy, am I ever glad that Katrina is open to this stuff—it'll make living together more interesting."

At twenty-one, Katrina was strong, competent, and efficient. Even when she was twenty, her boss of several months entrusted her with hundreds of thousands of dollars to invest in the stock market. She made him money. Since her youth, she had been driven to attend college. She was highly intelligent and, as was the family pattern, preferred not to deal with emotions in any capacity, though she could be moody when the pressure was on. Like her father, she was witty and funny when she wanted to be. Friends tended to flock to her for advice; she had always been wise and mature for her age. She was a natural-born leader.

Katrina had a six-foot-two-inch, well-rounded hour-glass figure, flaming red hair and vibrant green eyes. As a child, when it became evident that she was going to be large, her father had encouraged her to talk softly so as not to seem intimidating. She had taken this advice to heart and developed a soft, sensual presentation. She was capable of reeling in almost any man, though it's doubtful that's what her father had in mind.

David's mother used to take him to her friend's house to get their tea leaves read. He was raised on a farm in northern Wisconsin on a diet of science fiction books. David was 42, with blond hair and twinkling blue eyes, and a full aureole beard he'd taken to wearing in his mid-twenties after finishing a four-year stint in the Navy.

At six-four, David was lean, handsome, and pleasantly tanned and weathered from being outside. He had been taught to ask questions (which didn't help much in the Navy) and that most anything was possible. His father was a grumpy old German who encouraged cockiness and independence, and who had mischief glimmering in his eyes. David's science fiction background had been a natural foundation from which his spiritual quest grew. Pursuing life's spiritual lessons had been his priority for several years.

David's nature was like that of a chameleon; he was able to blend with the personality of others and he preferred flowing with the moment. While Katrina's intelligence was broad, David's was more selective; he was a follower. Once put on a specific task, he would tenaciously see it through to the end. Somewhat radical, he at times believed that extreme measures were needed to effect positive change.

Roxy was in between Katrina and David. At thirty years of age, she appeared half their size. With rich, deep brown eyes and hair and a medium build, Roxy blended into almost any crowd.

Her childhood was uneventful and boring until her mid-teens. She was strong and independent and began pursuing dream interpretation and the meaning of life with a friend, against her mother's preference. Despite her mother's incessant objections, Roxy began seeing her first "medium" before she was twenty. Evangeline got Roxy thinking in terms of life's lessons, that there were no accidents. This philosophy opened up a whole new world, one which Roxy brought into her relationship with David. David and Roxy had been together for seven years, both intimately and professionally.

In a small insurance office where the Plumbs both worked, Roxy was the most effective "phoner," setting enough appointments and selling enough insurance to earn MDRT (Million Dollar Round Table) status in her first year. David was her manager. When they married, they were inspired to relocate to the West Coast. There they took up with a company that sold transformational seminars to Fortune 500 companies.

As a team, Roxy and David were naturals. Roxy set appointments and David fielded interviews. Though Roxy set upwards of twenty-five to thirty appointments per week, their beckoning destinies blocked all but a meager number from closing. David and Roxy were once again inspired to relocate, this time to San Diego where, unknown to them, they were due to hook up with Katrina.

Once in San Diego, Roxy read volumes of spiritual material. Reading up on soul connections, she ran across a description of Twin Flames, a refined soul connection above that of souls or soul mates. Two souls chose to connect, or contract, to be Twin Flames for a specific number of lifetimes to learn a specific set of lessons. It resonated. She knew she and David were Twin Flames. Twin Flames rarely connected in Earth lifetimes but when they did, there was always a good reason for it.

The days sped by after the Plumbs moved in with Katrina. Cheerful frolic merged into metaphysical conversations that began to dominate their world. Roxy wondered if they'd been sent to help awaken Katrina. That's when it all began.

Half-dressed, Roxy rushed into their mix-and-match living room, heading in the direction of the blood-curdling scream that had just pierced the walls of their bedroom. She found Katrina lying in a fetal position on the old, scratchy, faded couch. Her eyes were scrunched shut, her long red hair flung in all directions. A musty sweat filled the air.

"What's wrong?" Roxy asked.

There was no answer as the screams continued.

"What's happening?" Roxy asked again.

A mysterious, unexpected wave of responsibility for Katrina washed over her but she didn't know how to help or what to do. Katrina's continuous screams awakened David, just home from his night shift job as a security officer at a local hotel. Wearing crumpled shorts from their basket of dirty clothes, David stumbled to Roxy's side.

"What's the problem? What's going on?" he asked, blurry-eyed but ready to help.

"I don't know. Jesus, it sounds like she's dying or something," Roxy said.

Unaware of their presence, Katrina continued screaming. Then all of a sudden her screaming stopped. Her body stretched out, her feet swung around, and she sat up. An unknown voice began to speak through her. "We are performing third-eye surgery," the deep, scratchy male voice announced.

David and Roxy flashed a look at each other, wondering if they both had heard the same thing.

"She has an extremely low pain threshold," the voice said, irritated, "which makes this process most difficult. There is really nothing to be concerned with. We will be finished shortly."

As if automated, Katrina's body resumed its fetal position. Her face scrunched up again and the screaming continued. The psychic surgery lasted fifteen minutes. When it was finished, Katrina sat up and rubbed her eyes. Roxy and David stared at her. They had no idea what to expect.

"What happened?" Katrina asked.

"You just had psychic surgery on your third eye," Roxy said, trying to hide the jealousy she felt over Katrina's experience.

Katrina squinted her eyes and cocked her head. "I had what?"

"Psychic surgery," David said.

"Right! Whatever that is. Well, it hurt." She rubbed her forehead and stomped off to her bedroom.

Twice over the next six days, the process—and the screaming—was repeated. After the final surgery was performed, Katrina sat up on the couch. Blinking and squinting, she adjusted her vision while her head swayed to and fro. Focusing on Roxy, she said, "Wow! I can see your aura!"

"Really! What color is it?" Roxy's face lit up.

"It's a mixture." Katrina refocused and rubbed her eyes as she got used to her exquisite gift. "You've got some blues, reds, and pale yellow in it."

"Cool. What else can you see?"

Katrina refocused her eyes and scanned the room. Her eyes wandered past their garage sale furnishings, past her fish tank nestled in the corner out of the light, and finally paused at the bushy schefflera plant. "There, in the plant!"

"What?" Roxy's heart raced in excitement.

"There's a fairy in the plant."

"Really? What does she look like? Or is it a he?"

"It's a she. She's got long blond hair, a green kind of pixie dress on, big pink wings, and cute—she's really cute!"

"How big is she? What's she doing?"

"Let's see … she's about six inches tall. She seems to be working with the plant somehow. She's looking at me funny. I guess she's not used to being seen. I'd better leave her alone."

"What else can you see?" Roxy urged.

"Hmmm … let's see." Katrina looked around. "Wow! There's a lady standing over there in the corner, next to the fish tank."

"What does she look like? Who is she? Will she talk to you?" Roxy's effervescence bounced off the walls of their comfortable living room.

Katrina was much cooler. To her, the experience seemed commonplace. Since Roxy had been in her teens, she had yearned for such experiences.

"She says her name is Athena. She says we'll be meeting her soon."

"What does that mean?"

"I don't know. I get the feeling that she's not going to answer."

"What does she look like?"

"She's about five feet tall, very petite. Her features are real fine, and her skin is creamy like. She's wearing a silver-white, form-fitted uniform that shimmers. You know, pants and a top. She has silver low-top boots that also shimmer. Her long brown hair is pulled back and she's wearing a sort of helmet that just covers the top of her head. The helmet looks like it should fall off but it doesn't. She's smiling and has a friendly energy about her. She says she needs to go now but she's reminding me that she'll be back soon. She's fading. Boy, am I tired." With that Katrina readjusted her vision to only the physical dimension.

"Thanks, Katrina. That was so cool."

"Yeah. I guess so. I'm going to go rest now before school."

The Plumbs began talking to Katrina about meditation, omens and what they meant, channeling, intuition, psychic abilities, past lives, numerology, astrology, and the like. Though it was all new to Katrina, she seemed to absorb the information the way people absorb oxygen. In all of Roxy's years on a spiritual path, she had never seen anyone go from total spiritual sleep to being totally awake within a period of one month.

Katrina began delving into the underlying causes of incidents in her life, both current and past, curious for the first time what lessons were there for her.

"I wonder why my dad died of AIDS," Katrina said to David one day while they enjoyed a quiet moment together.

"Good question, Katrina. That must have been rough."

"Yeah. You guys got me thinking about a lot of things lately. Like, why I'm so big and why I crave being a teacher, and why my parents adopted those awful boys. Got lots of questions and not many answers."

"Wish I could help you, Katrina. I have a hard time figuring out my own stuff," David smiled.

Roxy taught her how to meditate, which Katrina embraced with dedication. She took to it the way a young bird takes to flying; it seemed inborn. David and Roxy watched her soar. With this discipline in place, their unseen Guides were able to open the second portal, catching them all by surprise.

Roxy had a small home-based business writing creative résumés. She was busy working on one when it happened.

"Hello?" a strange deep male voice crackled. It clearly wasn't Katrina's soft voice so Roxy went to investigate.

Katrina was sitting cross-legged on the couch, her hands resting on her thighs, palms facing up, middle fingers touching thumbs. Only the whites of her eyes showed through half-open slits. When Roxy saw her, she knew at once what was happening: Katrina's meditation had evolved into channeling.

"Hello," Roxy answered. "Who are you?"

"Hello," the voice crackled again, then fell silent. Katrina's body began to gently sway to and fro.

"Who are you?" Roxy repeated. But the entity in Katrina was gone.

Katrina returned, disoriented and confused. "What happened?"

"You were channeling!" Roxy said, bursting.

"I was what?"

"You channeled. An entity, male I believe, came into your body and spoke to me!"

"*Spoke* to you?" Katrina squinted her eyes in disbelief.

"Well, barely. All he could say was 'hello.' Even that was pretty difficult. Isn't this incredibly thrilling?"

"How do you know it was somebody else? How do you know it wasn't just me?"

"I've been around channeling before. First, I noticed that your body language totally changed. Like, you know how you sort of slump your shoulders?"

"I didn't know it was that obvious."

"Oh. Well, anyway, your back was rigidly straight. Your energy was also totally different. And so was your voice. It clearly wasn't your voice. The voice was deep and firm, yours is high and soft."

"I see. Well, we'll see. I gotta go."

This process continued daily. Roxy conversed with the entity to give him practice with the voice apparatus.

"Hello," he would begin.

"Who is this?" Roxy asked.

"We are working to adjust this body," came the deep male reply.

"Can I help somehow?"

"Patience. It is still difficult to speak. Soon …." and his voice faded out.

With each attempt, the entity became more adept at manipulating Katrina's body. Each day he became more proficient with her vocal chords, and words became clearer, stronger.

Then, on day seven, the third portal opened.

The Guides came while Katrina was in her channeling trance and took Katrina's Light body on her first journey-while-in-trance to places out in the universe. Emerging from her trance, her Light body having rejoined her physical body, Katrina's face broke out into a grin, "Guess what?"

"What? What happened?" The Plumbs were swept up in Katrina's ecstasy.

"I was taken on a journey and given the name of the ethereal guide who was speaking through me."

"Who was it?" Roxy shrieked.

"His name is Aria."

"Who's he?" David smiled.

"He's my father—my ethereal father and my Earth father. Aria, that's who's been speaking through me!" Katrina beamed.

"I'm confused," Roxy said. "You say your ethereal father's been speaking through you, or your physical father?"

"That's just it! He's both! My ethereal father was my physical father in this lifetime. Aria *was* Bill." Katrina's glee filled their living room.

"You mean Bill, your physical father in this lifetime, is also your ethereal father?" Roxy grappled with the notion of Katrina sharing a physical lifetime with her ethereal father.

"Yes! *Now* I trust this channeling process!" Katrina declared. "My father would never deceive me. Now I really know that I am channeling!"

That night as the Plumbs snuggled in bed on David's night off, Roxy's excitement filled the air. "Isn't this thrilling, David? You know, Katrina channeling?"

"Yeah, I guess—but not as thrilling as you," he said, as he began kissing his wife.

Who Are Lightworkers?

They are people curious about
Extra-sensory-perception
And all it implies.
—Jack Clarke

Lady Commander Athena

2

A Spiritual Prodigy

Katrina's gift exploded overnight from channeling just Aria to channeling a wide variety of ethereal entities or extraterrestrial beings. True to her word, Athena—Lady Commander—visited often. And while Katrina's physical body channeled, her journeys-while-in-trance flourished as her Light body traveled to places out in the universe. The vividness and extraordinary detail she brought back made the journeys come alive.

"There are no road signs out there, Roxy," Katrina began one afternoon upon her return from a journey-while-in-trance. "I asked Athena where the road signs were but she just laughed at me." Katrina shrugged and tossed her wild red hair off her face. "I guess it was kind of a dumb question, but I didn't know where I was going."

The thought of Athena's whispery voice laughing at Katrina's confusion brought a smile to Roxy's face as she urged Katrina on.

"I was in a beautiful, calm forest," Katrina said. "There were purple, blue, and pink flowers that emanated a soft light from their very centers and smelled heavenly, like exotic gardenias, only sweeter. Their texture was silky soft, yet firm—well, sort of. The wispy exquisite birds sounded angelic as they flew into the distance. The bubbling creek glistened and danced; it *felt* pure. The trees were real tall and looked kinda like a cross between an elongated split-leaf philodendron and a palm tree. They were strange, but cool." Katrina's eyes grew wide. "The leaves—even the trunk—produced their own light, as though they glowed from the inside out. I've never seen anything like it on Earth. Everything had a visible aura exploding with vitality. The colors were a rainbow of deep transparent hues I've never seen before."

"God, I wish I could take a journey like that. I'd love to go to my ethereal home."

"Never know, maybe someday you can."

"Maybe," Roxy said, doubtful. "Anyway, tell me more."

"I found myself wondering how to get across the creek without getting wet when a fairy on the other side answered my thought. 'Use your wings,' she said. I looked and realized I *did* have wings. So I flew across and walked towards a cave, passing chipmunk-like creatures busily talking among themselves, fairies creating new plants and flowers, a beautiful creamy pair of deer-like creatures who were so in love, and a pair of cockatoo-type of birds that wished me a good journey.

"Finally, I reached the entrance of this cave where there was a huge crystal about six feet tall that glowed and pulsated blue from its center, protecting the contents of the cave. I asked the crystal if it was okay for me to go in and the words, 'you are permitted,' came into my head.

"It smelled musty. The whole cave glowed from crystals. It was magnificent." Katrina's eyes twinkled. "Huge, pulsating crystals of all shapes and colors lined the dark, jagged walls. I seem to remember that the crystals talked to me of ancient secrets, though none that I can remember right now. There were two colossal generator crystals that stood seven or eight feet tall that alternately emanated a blue and purple glow. And there were clusters, three and four feet in diameter, with individual points six inches in diameter, shooting out two and three feet in all directions. I'm telling you, Roxy, it was awesome."

On another journey-while-in-trance, Katrina found herself riding, rodeo style, on the back of a six-foot tall spider on the planet Venus. She explained to David and Roxy, as Athena had told her, that Venus is Earth's sister planet. The inhabitants of Venus are ethereal, which is why man's space cameras never see them. On Venus, humanoids and spiders switch sizes and the spiders eat the humanoids. Katrina's original home, when she first came out of God, was Venus. She experienced several lifetimes of being eaten by the spiders. Now Katrina's Guides-of-Light, who orchestrated her journeys, were using this excursion on the planet Venus as an opportunity for Katrina to work through her residual fear.

"It's hot and red up there," Katrina began, "and the people all live underground, where the spiders can't get them. The only time they go out is to get food and they usually only go out in groups."

"What do the spiders look like?" Roxy asked.

"Ugly and hairy!" A scowl appeared on Katrina's face. "They're about six feet tall and look most like daddy long legs, I guess."

"Did you freak out?" David chuckled, amused at Katrina's skittishness.

"Only for a second. Then I realized that the only way through the ordeal was to get centered, without fear. The spider feeds off the fear. Fear wasn't the way to go. How long was I gone?"

"About twenty minutes," David said.

"Athena told me that I rode the spider for the equivalent of nine Earth hours."

"They twisted time on you again, huh? Are you exhausted?" Roxy asked.

"Yes," she sighed.

"Did the spider know you were there?" David asked.

"Yes. He tried to buck me off the whole time." Katrina shuttered at the remembrance. "I think I'll go rest for awhile."

Her journeys ranged from confrontational to recreational to educational to rejuvenational. On one such journey she went to a healing center.

"It was a peaceful midnight blue everywhere," she began. "The building was an open-air structure, with tall Greek pillars all around the outer edge. There was a second-story circular open-air structure shooting out of the roof, with a dome ceiling. Inside the main structure there was a pink and pale yellow ball of light that pulsated from the center of the building and emanated a warm, inviting, calm feeling. The rock the healing center rested on wasn't much bigger than the building itself. And it all floated in mid-heaven.

"There were purple and yellow flowers everywhere, with a kinda mossy grass growing on jagged rocks. There were pools of blue, sparkly water. The air was thick with a sweet soothing smell. There were olive-like trees growing out of the rock, and a deep blue background of stars. There were these waterfalls that had dots of light flowing over the edge of the rock, disappearing into nothingness. Magical glitter of all colors danced around everything. And the moon lit everything up. Cool, huh?"

"Why were you there?" David asked.

"To heal. I was laid on a table inside the structure where the pink and yellow glow came from. The table looked like a cold hard slab of rock that floated but it was satiny and warm. Master Zoozer appeared out of nowhere and began to do a healing on me. He moved his hands over my body, healing my energy field until I felt deeply rested and peaceful. The next thing I knew, I was back here in my body."

"How do you feel now?" David gently touched her shoulder.

"Better! The strain is gone." Katrina smiled back.

The recreational trips were whimsical. It was the Fourth of July. Katrina knew there was a spaceship hovering above so she decided to journey up and check out the view.

"There is a big screen in the control room similar to the screen on the *Enterprise* in the "Star Trek" series. They had the fireworks up close on the screen. It was like being one foot away from the top of the spray of colors. It was *so* cool," Katrina said, her eyes gleaming.

It was amazing that just a few weeks earlier Katrina had been asleep to the spirit world. She had never heard of the Guides, never had a hint of psychic abilities, had never channeled.

David and Roxy had been devoted to spiritual studies for years; still, they had only experienced one spirit guide, Evangeline, through channeling years ago. Katrina was an open pipeline to the beyond, a spiritual prodigy.

Out of their living room window, palm trees soaked up the rays of the bright early morning sun. Greens and blues reflected from the mirror that hung over the old couch. David, home from the night shift, kissed Roxy goodnight, and went to bed. Within moments, his snoring could be heard in the distance. A light breeze caressed Katrina's and Roxy's faces and arms as they sat in the living room finishing up their morning meditation.

"Athena wants to talk to you, Roxy," Katrina said.

"Great!"

Katrina, sitting on the couch in a lotus position, prepared herself to channel Athena by resting her hands, palms up, on her thighs, and closing her eyes. She breathed deeply several times, as if going into a deep meditation. A moment passed. Her head dropped. Another moment passed. Her head began to lift. Her back became board straight. Her thumbs and middle finger pinched together so tight they turned red and yellow. Facial muscles melted into a serenity never before seen on Katrina.

"Greetings," came forth the whisper.

"Is this Athena?" Roxy asked.

"It is I."

Katrina talked softly, but Athena could hardly be heard. Roxy had to lean forward to catch Athena's words.

"Welcome. I have come this day to suggest that you and Katrina do an exercise. We wish to test your ability, Dear Lady, in discerning, by feel, ethereal entities in the room with you. This one Katrina will confirm if you are correct. Do you wish to participate?"

"Sure. I've been sensing things for years. It'll be interesting to see if I'm right."

"The time has come for you to trust this gift. It will be most useful in the near future," Athena said.

"Why? What do you mean?"

"It shall unfold soon. I bid you farewell. *Adonai*." Athena left Katrina's body.

"Did you hear what we're supposed to do?" Roxy asked Katrina when she had fully returned.

"No. Well, yes ... I mean, I left but the Guides told me while I was gone. Well, are you ready?" Katrina was perky.

Roxy agreed and within seconds she felt a presence enter the room and stand by the chair across from her.

"Is this Commander Vesta?" Roxy asked.

"That's right!" Katrina cried.

"The energy has shifted ... a different presence. Hmmm ... Arena?" Roxy said, not fully confident.

"Yup," Katrina confirmed.

"Switched again ... could that be Ashtar?"

"Right on!" Katrina encouraged.

"Oh, I'd know this energy anywhere. Athena?"

"Exactly," Katrina confirmed, using her keen third-eye vision. "How do you do that, Roxy?"

"I don't know," Roxy shrugged. "I can just feel it. It seems so clear to me. Wow, this is exciting!" The anxiety of a few minutes ago melted away as confidence took its place.

That day Roxy recognized eight Guides but failed to detect one. When the process was complete, the Guides told Roxy through Katrina that she had an eighty-three percent accuracy rate.

Up to now, the channeling sessions had been a private affair. From Roxy's point of view, she was prepared and had a chance to make sure her "act was together" when the guides were present.

Then it happened.

Katrina and Roxy were in line at the cash register in a crowded fabric store. A brightly-colored bolt of fabric caught Roxy's attention. "Katrina, what do you think of this one?"

"I am not Katrina! I am Tenaiia. Have I fooled you?"

A thunderbolt shot down Roxy's spine. Her eyes grew wide and her stomach did flip flops. "Y-y-yes!" she stammered. There had been no discernible difference in Katrina.

"Good! It is my job to be undetectable. I must be able to come and go unnoticed. Have I succeeded?"

"Uh-huh!" Roxy said as the ramifications of what was transpiring began to settle in.

With that, Tenaiia disappeared.

Roxy's foibles were exposed to their core. Katrina was like an open conduit to "the other side." There was no control over when the ethereal Guides would come through Katrina. There was no place to hide. Roxy was thrust into an acute awareness of Katrina's energy. Was it Katrina or Tenaiia? Excited and frightened, her insecurities rushed to the surface like a teenager on her first date.

"Do you realize you just channeled in the store?" a stunned Roxy asked Katrina as they drove home.

"Yeah. I'm not in control of it, you know. Kinda weird, isn't it?"

"Do you know who Tenaiia is? The one you just channeled?"

"Athena told me that Tenaiia is the soul we all chose to guide us in our mission together."

"Mission? What mission? Together?"

"Don't know. No one's talkin' yet."

Tenaiia, a light, bouncy, happy-go-lucky young soul came often—multiple times daily—and began to oversee, or manage, Roxy's, Katrina's, and David's lives. She had a reputation on the ethereal plane, as Athena told them later, of catapulting others through tough lessons.

Her first task was to unite Katrina and David. David worked nights so he wasn't around much when Katrina channeled. But Tenaiia prevailed. She suggested that Katrina and David meditate together. They retreated to Katrina's bedroom each morning before he went to bed.

On the fourth day, Katrina emerged grinning and eyes aglow. "David just channeled!"

"What?" Roxy gasped. "I mean, really? I wish I could have been there. Who was it, David?"

"I don't know … I don't feel so good," David said.

"Do you know, Katrina?"

"I don't know yet." Katrina was giddy with excitement. "But I could clearly see him in David's body."

"Will you do it again for me?" Roxy pleaded.

"No," David said, shaking his head, disoriented and in shock. "I can't. I mean, I don't think I can do it again. I'm exhausted. I'm going to bed."

"Did you know he was going to channel?" Roxy asked Katrina.

"No. It surprised us both. Wait! Athena's telling me something telepathically. She says that David was destined to channel; it was written in his prebirth contract. If we three came together, then his ability to channel would unfold."

Roxy had never heard Katrina sing to herself before. She didn't understand Katrina's joy, or the new bond emerging between Katrina and David.

The next day David and Katrina meditated again. Another effort was made to channel. They progressed daily for six days. David's process, unlike the graceful transformation Katrina had experienced, reflected a lifelong issue involving feelings of incompetence that permeated all areas of his life, except for his lovemaking. Channeling was no exception. He had to overcome this feeling that he "wasn't doing it right." He had to surrender to the process and trust that it would move forward.

He was to be a conscious channel, another major obstacle. Unlike Katrina, a trance channel whose consciousness left her body entirely, David's consciousness remained present while channeling. He and the Guide shared his body in those moments. Sometimes with a conscious channel, it's difficult to discern who's speaking—the Guide or the channel. David's initiation process was difficult and challenging.

Katrina's ability to "see" the entity come into David's body helped bolster his confidence. When Roxy watched them on day seven, she could feel the soothing presence of the entity inside David.

Katrina and Roxy were transfixed on the edge of the couch. David, rigid with strain, endeavored to channel. The Guide strove to channel through David with immense patience. With great mastery and persistence, this ethereal Master nudged the process forward.

"How do you feel?" Katrina asked David.

"Fine," he lied. His eyes were closed, his back as stiff as a post. His anxiety was so thick it was hard for him to breathe.

"Just breathe and relax," Katrina coached.

"I know! I know!" David snapped.

He went silent. Then the Guide inside him moved his mouth, trying to speak. Still no words were forthcoming. Repeatedly David's mouth opened, producing only scratchy sounds. The vocal cords were tight from David's tension. Several attempts were made. Roxy feared the Guide would abandon him. Twenty minutes into the strained process, the Guide opened David's mouth once more. David's face, red from the exertion, forced out a rigid, "I .... "

Katrina and Roxy looked at each other, eyes wide in excitement. They squirmed on the couch. A breakthrough! Actual communication!

The mouth opened again. David's neck was taut with exertion. Fatigue filled the air. David reeked of perspiration, his head moving forward in an all out effort to get the next word out. "Am .... "

Katrina and Roxy pulled with all their psychic force to help the Guide break through. At last, David's entire upper body, red and unbending, leaned forward and the entity was able to say, "... Leviticus!"

Master Leviticus had, indeed, arrived.

Once Leviticus had broken through, progress was swift. Within weeks, David was proficient at channeling. Unlike Katrina, who channeled many entities, Leviticus was the only ethereal Guide-of-Light David would ever channel.

Who Are Lightworkers?

People who know that
Our intuition knows what is best
And have begun to listen.

—Jack Clarke

CAVE OF CRYSTALS

KATRINA ON A SPIDER

HEALING CENTER

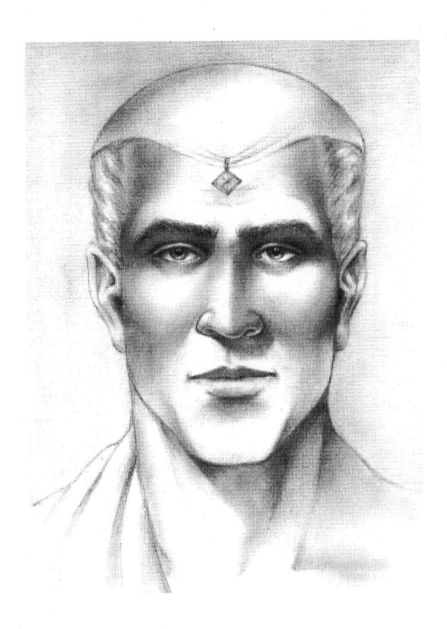

MASTER LEVITICUS

TENAIIA

3

The Directive

The night was dark and still. Katrina had been asleep for hours. To David and Roxy it felt like the whole world was asleep. David felt like talking on his night off and Roxy obliged.

Leviticus saw this as the perfect opportunity to break new ground and begin preparing Roxy for their future.

"Leviticus would like to talk to you," David announced.

"At this hour of the night?"

"I don't think time is an issue for him, Roxy," David chuckled.

"No, I don't suppose it is. Sure, I'd love to talk to Leviticus."

David closed his eyes and centered his energy. His hands rested, palms up, on the arms of the chair, his thumbs lightly touching his middle fingers. His head dropped. Roxy was eager. Leviticus was her favorite entity to talk with, though she had no idea why.

After ten seconds, a soothing energy came over Roxy, filling the living room. David's head began to lift. Leviticus opened David's eyes and looked at Roxy. "Hello, Dear One," he began.

"Is this Leviticus?"

"Indeed, it is I," Leviticus smiled, eyes effervescent.

"How are you?" Roxy asked, great love in her voice.

"I am fine, Dear One. Are you enjoying your early morning talk?"

"Yeah, it's kind of fun. You know, like the old days when David and I used to sit up and talk, or make love 'til four A.M. Then off to work we'd go at eight. Those were the days." Roxy stared off into the distance.

"Indeed. The good old days."

"Yeah, I guess they were. David said you wanted to talk to me. What's up?"

"Indeed I do, Dear One," Leviticus said. "David loves you very much."

"I know that."

"I want you to know that David has no knowledge of what I'm about to say."

"Okay."

"Very well. I should like to hear your thoughts about sharing David."

"Sharing? How?" Knots formed in her solar plexus.

"Sharing him with another woman."

Fear hit like a fast-ticking bomb. "You mean, let David make love to another woman?"

Leviticus nodded.

"No! I'm not interested. Why do you ask? Is there someone David wants to make love to?"

"No, Dear One," Leviticus assured her. "As I stated, I am not here on behalf of David. And he is certainly not having such thoughts. He has been loyal to you for some time, has he not?"

"Yes. Then why are you asking?" Fear rang in her voice.

"Well," Leviticus went on, "I should like to hear your views on it."

Stunned, her body filled with tension. Am I really talking to Leviticus? Roxy silently wondered. Perhaps it's really David? The trouble was, she could *feel* by the energy that it was Leviticus. Her mind raced. There was no answer. She wasn't so sure she wanted one. She just wanted out of the conversation.

"How would you feel about sharing David?" Leviticus persisted.

"No part of me even wants to think about it, much less do it. It stirs in me memories of David's need to date others after his divorce from Jan so he wouldn't feel trapped. I hated it. You know, he told me three times that he loved me in our first two months together."

"Yes."

"Then I had to wait three and a half years before he said it again, and all the while he dated others. It was awful."

"I know." Leviticus smiled gently.

"I feel sick."

"Yes, Dear One, I know. You must always remember that you will be fine. I must depart now. I only ask that you ponder these thoughts." Leviticus smiled. "In Love and Light."

After Leviticus left, David asked "Did I hear that correctly? You're suppose to share me?"

"Yes. Were you having those thoughts before tonight?"

"Of course not! I don't think I influenced what Leviticus was saying. I haven't had thoughts of other women in years."

"Well, I was skeptical at first, but I could feel that Leviticus was in you. He said that he wasn't speaking on your behalf. God, I don't like this one bit. It makes me crazy."

"Wanna make love, hon?"

David took Roxy by the hand and led her to their bedroom.

After making love, Roxy fell into a fitful sleep, the conversation echoing through every corridor of her dreams.

Restless, Roxy got up early, put on wrinkled clothes, and wandered into the dining room. Unsettled, she sat at Katrina's dented wooden table in the dining room, still pondering Leviticus' words. What frightened her the most was that some inner part of her knew that Leviticus was preparing her for something.

"Are you okay, Roxy? You don't look so well."

Startled, Roxy gasped, "Oh! Hi, Katrina. You startled me. I didn't even see you there. Yeah, I'm fine. Long night with David, and Leviticus wanted to talk at three."

"About what?"

"Stuff,' she said. "Yeah, David and I made love in the wee hours of the morning."

Katrina's face remained unchanged but her vibes rolled over Roxy like a hundred-foot tidal wave churning her solar plexus. Confusion, combined with the onslaught of Katrina's vibes, catapulted Roxy into a frightened quandary.

"I've got to go," Katrina declared.

"But your breakfast … aren't you gonna eat it?"

"Go ahead. I'm not hungry anymore." And out the door Katrina went.

That afternoon, Roxy took a call from a friend who offered to take her on a journey north to Mt. Shasta. Roxy accepted.

Several months earlier David and Roxy had been to a psychic who had told them of a vision she saw of the Plumbs living on Mt. Shasta. The Guides, unknown to them at the time, had placed that vision in the psychic. The vision persisted in their thoughts. David, an adventurous sort, was up for anything that forwarded their spiritual path, even if it meant quitting his job and moving. Roxy felt the magnetic pull from the mountain. Though it mystified her, she could not resist it.

Mt. Shasta is a powerful contact point between the physical and spiritual planes. The strange spherical or "lenticular" clouds that form and vanish around the volcanic summit are said to be spacecraft for the ethereal extraterrestrial forces. The community at the base of the mountain contains a high ratio of psychics and Lightworkers. It felt like a potent place to dramatically forward their spiritual growth, the number one priority for David and Roxy.

"David, the energy up here is incredible," Roxy panted over the phone from the mall in Mt. Shasta City. "We've just got to move up here. I just know it's the right thing to do."

"Okay, okay! You've enrolled me, Roxy. We'll move. Let's talk about it when you get home," David said.

David had just completed his state insurance licensing exams for the state of California. "Why don't I work for an insurance company in Mt. Shasta?" he suggested after Roxy had returned home. "You could write me a résumé and we'll mail them to all the companies."

Two weeks after they sent the résumés, David was offered a job. He was due to start in 1987, two and a half months away. It felt like a good omen, but they would be leaving Katrina and the valuable channeling behind.

The directive for Katrina, David and Roxy hung in the air from some unknown origin. Elusive yet effective, it was instrumental in nudging them past their resistance. It was hard to even put a finger on it. It was as though their Higher Selves filled the air with thoughts of going forward on their confrontational paths. In a quandary, each fought separate internal opposing forces. No one realized at the time that there could be no turning back.

The sexual tension was thick. Katrina's frustrated sexual longing permeated the walls of their apartment like a cat in heat locked indoors. What the Plumbs didn't realize was that the source of her burning desire was David. Her energy was beckoning and his hormones were responding.

Blaming Katrina for transmitting those kind of vibes, or David for crumbling to temptation, was not appropriate. It wasn't anyone's fault—it was their prebirth contracts revealed in perfect timing. This was what the three of them had agreed to do.

It was written in detailed script. David, Katrina, and Roxy had constructed the scripts before they were born. Of course, they weren't

David, Katrina, or Roxy then. They were in the form of their Higher Selves. These contracts ensured that each was presented with specific lessons, gained mastery in particular areas, and accomplished certain tasks. They'd asked the Guides, which they'd chosen at the same time the scripts were constructed, to make sure they all found their way to this path, even though, in this moment, none of them remembered any of it.

But that's what hung in the air. Katrina's hormones were awakened by the Guides-of-Light, even though her Earth rules would never permit her to make love to a married man. David was responding as he should, even though it confused him, and his loyalty was with his wife. And Roxy was supposed to say "yes," even though it paralyzed her with fear.

This is what they all had agreed to. This was the path their Higher Selves had chosen before they were born. It was their very purpose at this point in each of their lives.

One evening, after making love, David said, "This seems really strange to me, Roxy." He paused a moment. "But I feel like I'm supposed to make love to Katrina."

The ecstasy of the moment disappeared as fear consumed Roxy. "What do you mean?" She was sure she'd misheard his words.

"It just keeps coming up for me, over and over again: 'It's okay to make love to Katrina.' I don't understand it. It's not like I'm unhappy with our relationship or our love life, hon, but that phrase just keeps running through my mind like a broken record: 'It's okay to make love …' "

"Okay, okay, I get the point!" But before she could say no, "okay" had already slipped past her lips. She couldn't believe her own ears.

David was relieved. He'd been haunted all week, fighting the constant and compelling urge to tell Roxy. He didn't want to hurt her but he couldn't shake the phrase running through his head. Nothing like this had ever happened to him before. He didn't like it, either.

"Only once!" Roxy added. "Just this time. That's our agreement, right?"

"Right, just once." David nodded.

Roxy reasoned that she and David were soon moving to Mt. Shasta alone, but it did no good. Apprehension filled her core. It was as though her life was being propelled into troubled waters by an unseen force. There was no turning back now. Their destinies were sealed.

David chose a day when Roxy was out on errands for three hours and Katrina was home from school.

"Roxy and I talked and she said it would be okay with her if we made love today. That is, if you want to, of course," David said.

"Excuse me?" Katrina's eyes were wide. "I don't make love to married men!"

"I know," David cooed, "but isn't there some part of you that wants to?"

"Sorry it's been so obvious, but it's certainly not your problem."

"I know, I know," David said. "I don't want to seem assuming, either, but it sure seems like you've been in the mood and I'm offering, though I don't fully understand why. But you know, Roxy and I have been aware of it and it just seems like this is the right thing to do."

"Are you *sure* it's okay with Roxy?"

"Yes, I'm sure. She gave us the afternoon. She's not due back till four."

Though Roxy had urged David to do some things while she was gone, he spent the whole time making love to Katrina.

Soon thereafter, Roxy's fingers swelled. She took off her wedding ring and rubbed her fingers, trying to bring the swelling down. Each time she took it off, it was even harder to push the ring back on. Her finger felt suffocated. Roxy took the ring off and left it off. For four years she had been the model of patience with David, waiting for him in order to earn that wedding ring. She was in no mood to take it off— ever.

"Why don't you have it re-sized?" David asked.

"Because I keep thinking the swelling will go down."

But the swelling never went away.

Who Are Lightworkers?

People guided by a Power higher than,
Yet part of,
Themselves.

—Jack Clarke

4

Moving In Tune
With The Guides

It was the end of October and Katrina's junior college days would be through in six weeks. She had already chosen, and been accepted, at a local college to obtain her B.A. in Education. Then Athena had a chat with her, away from the apartment. Katrina's Light body was on one of her journeys-while-in-trance out in the universe on a star called Arianne.

"Katrina, do you understand the attraction, the yearning, you feel for this one, David?" Athena began.

"No. It's terribly confusing to me," Katrina replied. "I can't shake him out of my system. I thought making love to him would make it go away, but it didn't. That only made it worse. He's a happily married man. I'm not one for breaking up marriages."

"There are higher laws and forces at work here, Katrina. At this time it is not so easily understood. I am here to suggest that you consider moving to Mt. Shasta with the Plumbs."

"What? Move *with* them? I don't understand. What are you suggesting?"

"There are reasons why you feel this way, Katrina, reasons you will soon understand. For now, I am here to encourage you to move with them. It is your destiny; it is their destiny."

"It would be far easier for me to stay here and go to school. I'll forget David after a while," Katrina persisted.

"My dear, you shall not so easily forget him. Is there not a part of you which greatly desires going with them—with him?"

"I feel a mixture of things, Athena: scared of my feelings, consumed with feelings for David like I've never felt before, and I feel like I'm betraying Roxy."

"Look here, Katrina." Athena pointed to a screen that appeared out of nowhere. It was the size of a big-screen television but flat. It floated in mid-air. "I wish to show you a scene from your future, with your Higher Self."

Katrina was captivated. She watched as her Higher Self, Arianne, come into focus. She was magnificent, with translucent shimmering purplish wings that stretched from her feet to just above her head. Her body was tall, slender, and draped in a flowing iridescent pink robe. She had a beautiful gem-studded tiara atop long blond hair that cascaded down to her belted waist. A serene, gentle demeanor graced her loving face and fine features. The glow surrounding her pulsated.

Then Katrina saw a likeness of herself appear on the screen and somehow merge with her Higher Self. The whole scene left her in awe and wonderment at the possibility through this connection.

Next, David appeared performing CPR on Katrina, face red with strain. The wonderment transformed into horrifying turmoil. Then Roxy became visible, hovering around Katrina's body. David's and Roxy's faces were filled with anxiety. Katrina realized they were protecting her, keeping her alive. The screen faded to black.

Before Katrina could ask the multitude of questions zooming around in her mind, her Light body was on its way back to her body in their San Diego apartment. Athena's words were echoes fading in the distance: "It is your destiny, Katrina. It is the destiny of the Plumbs."

Back in her body, Katrina was frantic. Her mind reeled.

"Are you okay, Katrina?" Roxy asked.

"Fine," she lied, jumping off the couch. She grabbed her school books and flew out the door without even saying good-bye.

Katrina made herself scarce for a week as her internal battle raged on. She avoided the Plumbs. An awkward, thick tension permeated their home.

On Saturday Katrina had a strange, euphoric demeanor when she announced to Roxy, "I'm thinking about moving with you guys. You know, to Mt. Shasta."

"What?"

"It was Athena's suggestion. What do you think?"

"Well, it would be cool to have the channeling move with us, but where would you go to school?" Katrina and David's lovemaking flooded back into Roxy's thoughts, gripping her heart.

"That is a bit of a problem. The closest school is three to four hours away."

"Three to four hours both ways! Are you nuts? Why bother?" Roxy grew edgy.

"The driving doesn't bother me," Katrina said. "Three hours each way is easy. What I mean is, is it okay with you? Me moving with you? Like, we'd all live together?"

"This was Athena's idea?" Roxy demanded.

"Yeah. I haven't made a final decision yet. I need to talk to David first anyway."

That smacked of something Roxy didn't like either.

Pressure built up in their house as Katrina struggled over the decision. Roxy braved the question only once. "Have you decided whether you're going to be moving with us or not Katrina?"

"No." Katrina snapped, leaving the room.

As was true of David's chameleon-like personality, it was fine with him either way. She could move with them or not; he simply didn't care. Katrina didn't like his indifference. While she was consumed by thoughts of David, he seemed oblivious.

On day seven, Athena channeled through Katrina and asked David and Roxy to leave the house for three hours. While they were gone, Katrina was visited by Lady Commander Athena, Master Merlin, Commander Ashtar, and Aria. Once they were all "seated" in "invisible chairs" the large, flat screen appeared out of nowhere to float in the living room.

"If you do not go with David and Roxy," Merlin began, "*this* is the alternate reality you have chosen, as stated in your contract."

The screen lit up with an image of Katrina teaching a classroom of children. Her left ring finger was noticeably bare. She looked forlorn and lifeless, as though trudging through the motions of life. She was a good teacher, yet something was missing. Happiness, fulfillment were absent.

Katrina remembered the vision of herself and her Higher Self. There had been a remarkable magic about that future.

"You are a stubborn one, my daughter," Aria sparkled. "This higher path is fraught with strain and challenge, yet the path brings boundless joy, fulfillment, and accomplishment. Do not let your fears stop you. Follow your highest calling. Follow your heart."

His words made Katrina wiggle in her chair.

"Do not fear; we will guide your way Katrina/Arianne," were Ashtar's only words.

Katrina wondered what that meant.

Athena remained quiet, allowing Katrina space to process the internal battle.

Katrina remembered feeling the hurricane-strength battle of the first vision. She yearned for David, but David was not a part of the second vision. Oh God! What am I getting into? she wondered.

Seeing her waver, Athena pointed out, "You will not find the happiness you desire down the second path, Katrina. It is not written in your contract."

"Okay, okay, okay!" Katrina declared. "I'll move with David and Roxy."

Merlin, Ashtar, Aria, and Athena simultaneously bowed their heads and acknowledged her choice. Katrina felt her decision was sealed in stone.

That settled, the room emptied as if it had all been a dream, but residual feelings left no doubt in Katrina's mind that the conversations had occurred and that her decision was irrevocable. She knew that she must move with David and Roxy.

Tenaiia came into Katrina's body just as David and Roxy returned. She was beaming as she declared, "Katrina has decided to move to Mt. Shasta."

"Great!" David replied.

"What made her finally decide?" Roxy asked tersely.

"She had visitors while you were gone. They helped her see the wisest direction for all concerned."

After that conversation, the topic was never brought up again and the nauseating, thick tension never left their space. Concerned for Katrina and their eroding relationship, Roxy asked her one day, "Are you okay? Something buggin' you? Wanna talk?"

"No. Look, I gotta go."

"But I thought you didn't have to leave for another hour?"

"Schedule change." And Katrina was out the door.

As the moving day descended upon them, Katrina became tenser. The closeness she and Roxy had enjoyed during Katrina's spiritual unfolding evaporated.

"David has finished loading the truck," Roxy said to Katrina as she walked into the bare apartment. "And we're right on schedule. We'll be ready to leave by six."

They planned to drive all night, unload, and return the truck in a twenty-four-hour period because of their shoe-string budget.

"Did you check everywhere, Roxy?" David asked.

"Sure. Twice."

She followed David into their bedroom to see if he'd find anything. When they returned, Katrina was nowhere to be found. Her bedroom was empty and she wasn't by the truck. Several eerie minutes passed before Katrina reappeared, pack of cigarettes in hand, her vibrant green eyes wild with fright. With trembling hands she lit a cigarette. Her body shook from head to toe. Roxy watched her red hair and her enormous hour-glass figure reverberate with apprehension.

"I'll take one." David said, moving toward Katrina.

"Oh David! You haven't smoked in two years. And you, Katrina, for over a year. Do you have to start again?" Roxy moaned.

"Just this once," David snapped.

Katrina inhaled, eyes evasive. When they had finished their cigarettes, David said, "Let's go, shall we?"

"I'm ready," Roxy said, getting into the car.

"Fine," Katrina mumbled, getting in the car with Roxy. David drove the truck.

Ominous feelings swirled through the car. Roxy didn't trust Katrina and David alone. By daybreak, the feeling of impending doom was so intense that Roxy fidgeted as they found themselves just outside Redding, heading up the skirt of Mt. Shasta.

Shasta-Trinity National Forest was breathtaking. From desert-dry to profuse green in the blink of an eye, it was home to tall, lush pines, clean fresh air, sprawling Shasta Trinity Lake, and jagged red walls of rock and clay. The lake was especially gorgeous against the backdrop of craggy green forest, red coastline, and deep blue sky.

Interstate 5, carved out of the rough border of the mountain, weaved around curve after sharp curve and provided panoramic views of spiked overhanging cliffs and the lake receding in the distance. The vibrant colors dazzled their eyes.

"This is some view you'll be driving through to and from school," Roxy said.

"Yeah. When it's light out," Katrina grumbled. "I figure I'll be driving in the dark most of the time."

"Good point," Roxy said, dropping the subject. After driving all night, she didn't need an extra stroll on eggshells or to dance around Katrina's moods.

They rounded one more curve and there was all 14,162 feet of the snow-capped majestic lady—Mt. Shasta. This particular morning the show was spectacular. Clouds that resembled a stack of perfectly formed pancakes defied the wind that swept surrounding clouds away. There were six layers of flawlessly-shaped oval clouds, one atop the other, in perfect formation. That was great.

In sixty seconds the clouds evaporated into thin air. In a matter of minutes, another magically appeared, shaped totally different. This one was longer than the last and just one layer thick. It stayed for five minutes and then it, too, disappeared, to be replaced by another, a round one three layers thick.

"Look," Katrina said, pointing to a sign.

"Mt. Shasta, Next Right," Roxy sighed. It was New Year's Eve, in the morning.

A foot of snow had fallen through the night and everything was crisp and new. The three-bedroom log cabin Roxy and Katrina had rented on a previous trip was securely nestled at the end of a ninety-yard long driveway. There were no neighbors within fifty yards. They were surrounded by a forest of tall aspen and Douglas fir, pockets of lodgepole here and there, and a creek that ran behind the house. It had been vacant for two months and the log walls were frozen to their core.

"I'll get a fire going," David offered. From afar Katrina and Roxy heard him say, "Oh no!"

"What's wrong David?" they said in unison, heading to the garage.

"The wood's wet," David sighed, shaking his head.

"What do you mean?" Roxy asked.

"Wet wood burns slowly, coolly. No BTUs."

"BTUs?"

"Yeah, Roxy. British Thermal Units. The amount of heat a fire puts out. Wet wood is useless. That's why you buy seasoned wood, wood that has sat around for a year to dry out," he said, exasperated.

"But we don't have any more money to buy seasoned wood!" Roxy argued. "Shit! That's why I got the wood so cheap, isn't it?"

"Yep. You got it and now we're stuck with it. Those guys knew they had you, Roxy. Well, there's one thing we can do. We'll place logs around the main fire to dry them some. Warming this house is going to take days. We'll just dress in layers and use hot showers to warm up."

Moments after the logs hit the kindling, they sizzled like a juicy steak on a grill. Moisture popped and danced under the heat of the flames. The firewood smoked and whistled, producing very little heat.

While they stared at the bleak fire, Katrina was shown another vision. This time the large flat screen was brought to her outside of her trance state.

She saw an image of her and David making love. It was blissful, peaceful. As they lay together in harmony, a menacing presence came into view. Hovering overhead, the dark one began shooting lightning bolts into Katrina's now contorted body. David flew into action, yet there was nothing he could do. By now Roxy was looking on anxiously. Then the screen went black.

Katrina bolted from the living room and collapsed in the corner of her new bedroom.

Roxy followed. "Katrina, are you all right? What's wrong? Can I help?" Roxy felt responsible for her. She touched Katrina's arm trying to get a response—any response—but there was none. Katrina stared vacantly without moving a muscle, paralyzed from what she'd seen. Lost and feeling useless, Roxy left. There was still a truck to unload and return.

Twenty minutes later, Katrina joined the unloading party as though nothing strange had transpired. Scenes similar to this one would repeat themselves often over the months to come.

Two hours later, the truck coughed up its last box. David and Roxy headed out to return the truck and buy take-out food.

Showers were next on the agenda. Roxy went first. As the steaming water rushed over her aching, tired body, that same mysterious tension she'd felt through the night returned, tightening every muscle. She didn't trust Katrina and David alone. Even now her mind raced as she wondered what they were up to. She tried to dismiss the feelings as silliness but her doubts persisted like a swarm of hungry mosquitoes. She hurried through her shower so she could check out her suspicions but she found nothing amiss.

Katrina's shower followed, then David's. As they ate, they discussed sleeping arrangements for the night.

"It can't be anymore than twenty or thirty degrees in here," David said. "Why don't we share our queen-sized bed in front of the fire?"

Roxy's uneasiness screamed inside of her; nevertheless, it was the only logical solution. Everyone agreed and proceeded to make the bed.

"Where do you want to sleep?" Roxy asked Katrina.

"Where do you want me?"

"On that side." Roxy pointed to the other side of the bed. "Is that okay?"

"Yeah, sure. Whatever."

"David, what about you?"

"I don't care. Put me where you want me."

Roxy's turmoil persisted. Should she put David in the middle next to Katrina, or scrunch in the middle herself? Roxy's claustrophobia won out. She opted for the outer edge of the bed.

Shadows danced on the walls and against the black windows. Gloom hung in the brisk air. Sleep was elusive. Three bodies lying close together were unsuccessful at alleviating the chill.

As Roxy drifted into a troubled sleep, she rubbed the indentation on her swollen ring finger. She still couldn't wear her wedding ring.

Who Are Lightworkers?

People who know that it is through change
From the old to the new
That we grow.

—Jack Clarke

MASTER MERLIN

COMMANDER ASHTAR

LENTICULAR CLOUD OVER MT. SHASTA

5

Caretakers?

David snored all night and Roxy got little sleep. Katrina drifted in and out of consciousness. In her lucid moments she noticed that her hand encased David's penis, despite the fact that she continued removing it each time she found it there.

At daybreak the towering wall of boxes reminded everyone of the task at hand.

"Sweetie, let's get up and start unpacking," Roxy nudged David.

"It's too early!" he whined. "Let's rest a little longer."

"That's the problem," Roxy climbed out, "it's too uncomfortable to rest."

Throughout the night the fire had little effect on the chill factor. Roxy dashed back to their bedroom to secure a frosted pink turtle neck pullover, a red cotton sweater, and thick white sweat pants. Shivering, she moved boxes, hoping the movement would help keep her warm. Then, out of the corner of her consciousness, apprehension crept back in. "David, come on and help me!" she called, walking down the short hallway to the living room.

"It's too cold," he insisted. "I want to stay warm a little longer."

"The great hunter wants to stay warm? What's going on?"

"Nothing. Just give me a few minutes," David snapped.

Bewildered, Roxy headed back to their bedroom. She finished unpacking a box and found a glass bowl safely snuggled between undies and socks. She headed to the kitchen where her consciousness was pulled toward strange breathing sounds in the living room. Her heart jumped. Her throat went tight and her breathing quickened. She cocked her head, straining her ear towards the living room. Erotic breathing! Hushed, erotic breathing. Her mind raced and her heart pounded out of her chest. She gasped for air.

A force pulled Roxy into the living room. She had to see, although she was petrified. Without a sound, she crept toward the living room until she reached the entrance. Peeking around the corner, her worst fears came to life. There they were, entwined in their own world.

The force continued pulling Roxy into the living room until she found herself sitting on Katrina's upright box springs. Her voice was paralyzed and her jaw hung open. She shook her head, insisting the images leave but they wouldn't.

An eternity passed before they finished. For David and Katrina, the three minutes felt like seconds.

"What the HELL is going on?" Roxy demanded.

David flipped over. "What?" His eyes were wide with bewilderment.

Katrina, startled, yanked the sheet over herself.

Roxy glared at David and said again, "What the HELL is going on?"

"I thought you said it was okay?"

"I said it was okay *just once!* We agreed to *just once!*" Roxy turned to Katrina. "What the hell is going on?"

"I thought if it was okay with David, then it must be okay with you."

"Well it's NOT okay with me!"

It was several minutes before instinct took over and Roxy began to move. She felt animated, driven by some force to insure that the task at hand got done. Her body unpacked boxes, as though following a well-rehearsed ritual, while her mind grappled with disbelief, shock and alarm.

The scene replayed itself in Roxy's mind hundreds of times, as though trying to warn her of some yet-elusive future. Tears trickled down her face, betraying her wound. She was oblivious to her cold, white fingers. Her breath froze the instant it hit the air.

A psychic chill imbued with shock, betrayal and guilt, filled the air. Few words were spoken. Late in the afternoon Katrina said, "The Troops want to talk to you guys when you're ready."

"The Troops" was a term they'd adopted for their Guides-of-Light who channeled through Katrina or David.

Katrina and Roxy continued unpacking while David painted both bedrooms. By then it was dark and everyone was tired and hungry.

The fire crackled and sputtered as they settled in front of it. Katrina's body needed to be warm and relaxed, energy flowing with ease, a requirement for successful channeling. David wrapped her in a red and black wool blanket and rubbed her arms, back, shoulders, feet and hands. Jealousy stirred in Roxy.

Finally Katrina announced that she was ready to channel. David sat next to Roxy. Katrina closed her eyes, shifting her body to and fro as she became centered. Moments passed before Tenaiia, bubbly and alert, opened Katrina's eyes and spoke.

"Hello," she began with a smile. "There are several in line who wish to deliver a message to you. This will not be a session where questions will be answered," she said. "Are you ready?"

They nodded and looked at one another, apprehensive. Tenaiia closed Katrina's eyes and made way for the next Guide to come through. Lady Commander Athena, with her wispy quiet voice, spoke first. "*Adonai* and greetings. It is my greatest pleasure at this hour to thank you in advance for taking care of this one Katrina."

Katrina's head dropped and Athena was gone, replaced by the formal, brisk personality of Commander Ashtar. "Greetings. I am Commander Ashtar. You have agreed to take care of this one Katrina. Know that we are relying on you to fulfill your agreement. I must depart; there are others in line waiting to speak."

Katrina's eyes closed, her rigid back curved over, and the energy shifted again. Her back crept upright, her body adjusted to and fro, and jovial Aria opened Katrina's eyes and smiled. "I, too, wish to thank you for taking care of my beloved daughter. Know that you are up to the task."

Then came the soft and gentle Joshua. "We all wish to thank you for this important work that you will do, taking care of Katrina."

Commander Vesta was next. In a formal yet feminine tone, she delivered the same message, followed by Katrina's ethereal mother, who said, "You do not know me, for we have not previously met. I am Katrina's ethereal mother. I love her very much. I, too, wish to thank you for being such competent caretakers on her behalf."

Nine Guides came and went, all with the same message. No one offered any clarity: No one addressed Katrina and David's early morning transgression.

By the end of the channeling, Roxy was crying, gasping for air. Her entire body was in knots. The messages had triggered an overwhelming panic, a fear that came from an instinctual knowing in her subconscious. Her resistance was all consuming. She wailed for several minutes.

Katrina returned to her body while Roxy was still overpowered by emotions. "What's wrong?" Katrina asked, disturbed by Roxy's state.

"I don't know," David said, shrugging his shoulders.

But Katrina already knew. She understood Roxy's misgivings because she had her own. She had been shown images of their future on the screen. She understood the ramifications but she didn't like them. Nor did she like the idea of needing caretakers. She'd been independent all of her life and she was in no mood to change now, contract or not. Prebirth contracts do not guarantee an absence of resistance to the plan.

David was unaffected by the idea of taking care of Katrina, whatever that meant. It was okay with him either way. He rolled with the punches and went with the flow.

"Shall we go to bed?" David asked, trying to pull Roxy out of shock.

"Okay," she whispered. She became more alert. "Yeah, okay, but where?"

"Well, the bedrooms still reek of fumes. "Why don't we sleep in the living room again?"

"No," she said. "I'd rather sleep in the bedroom."

Katrina needed to go to the campus and select classes for the semester due to begin in two days. Prompted by the previous evening's caretaking messages, David and Roxy felt duty-bound but no rules or boundaries had been given. What did "taking care" of Katrina mean?

David's approach took one form while Roxy, whose emotional body quaked, took quite another. David and Roxy were required to make joint decisions since they were both designated caretakers.

"Maybe one of us should go with Katrina today to help her adjust to the long drive," David suggested.

"I guess someone should go," Roxy said. The thought of being alone with Katrina all day made her nauseous. She didn't trust them alone either. "You go," she said.

David was blind to the inner turmoil bubbling to the surface in Roxy, and in Katrina.

They left by nine that morning. Katrina was grateful for the company, even though the previous morning's adventure had caused such a strain between her and David that most of the long day was shrouded in a miserable cloud of silence. Neither one quite knew how to bridge the gap.

Finishing the unpacking, Roxy's mind twirled around David and Katrina's affair. She decided she wasn't making love to her husband enough. Like a crazed, driven woman, she proceeded to make love to

David that night, the next morning, that evening, and twice a day thereafter.

Her crazed behavior was predictable, had been planned for. Included in their prebirth contracts was a tool called "thoughtforms," designed to keep all three on track through just such reactions. Thoughtforms work by surrounding a person with energy containing specific thoughts, which then "ping" into their minds.

For Roxy, each time she and David made love during that two-week stretch, she was haunted by recurring thoughts such as *open marriage. Taking care of Katrina. Is Katrina okay? Katrina and David ... sharing.* Whether Katrina was at home or three hours away at school, thoughts of her were constantly on Roxy's mind. Katrina added to the mix with her constant yearnings for David that traveled through the psychic airwaves.

But the root cause was the thoughtform the Guides had placed in their home, a safeguard to ensure that The Trinity would take root and blossom. The Trinity was part of the ethereal contract the three of them had made. They had agreed to become aligned on all levels, to combine their energies thoroughly so that the work of anchoring The Melding in Katrina/Arianne could be fulfilled. But Roxy was tormented.

So was Katrina. She craved David, wanted him all to herself. Her hormones were activated through visions she was shown of their lovemaking. Thoughts pulsed through her head such as, *David is yours, too. Share David with Roxy. You three are in this together. Find peace in their lovemaking.* Moreover, there was a stress-induced distance between her and David that exacerbated her pain.

David was unsuspecting. The torment in both women eluded him.

From January 1, 1987 onward, whenever Roxy and David made love, thoughts of Katrina were always present. Though Roxy resisted progressing with The Trinity, the thoughts persisted, nudging her ever forward.

Normal physical necessities became luxuries in this Mt. Shasta saga. One day David was reveling in a hot, soothing shower when the water went frigid. Their fate was sealed: they didn't have the eight hundred dollars to get the propane tank filled. There was barely enough to pay bills and buy essential, non-soothing food. The repercussions were chilly and long term. While their emotional bodies were being activated, their energy was being forcibly funneled into handling the basics. Their ability to resist change was being systematically disabled.

Who Are Lightworkers?

They are people who
Deliberately
Decide to learn and grow.

—Jack Clarke

6

Choosing Growth

Roxy didn't know whether the trepidation of not knowing what was next was worse than embracing the portent of the messages and signs and getting on with it. Haunted, she worked up the nerve to ask Leviticus, who did not waste the opportunity.

Before leaving San Diego, some of the more ragged furniture had been sold and replaced with fresher, garage sale furnishings. Their log cabin living room was outfitted with two cushioned and comfortable, faded mauve straight-back chairs and a newer chair with a large circular bamboo frame with a fluffy, dark-blue, floral cushion anchored in the middle. Though the chair rocked, that probably wasn't the original intent behind the design.

The three living room chairs crowded in a semi-circle in front of the fireplace, the warmest spot in the house during the long cold winters.

Snuggled against the corner wall was a sectional on wheels, separated by a square coffee table decorated with Katrina's fish tank. The couch doubled as a guest bed, though guests rarely came.

The fireplace had an efficient, if ugly, black insert. In moments of self-indulgence, they would reduce its effectiveness by opening the front doors to enjoy the flames.

"Why don't you join us, Katrina?" Roxy asked.

"Are you sure?"

"Yeah. Better than my having to repeat it later."

David settled in his chair and allowed Leviticus to come through, a challenge with all the strain in the air.

"Hello, Dear One. It has been a rough period, has it not?" Leviticus said.

"Yes," Roxy replied.

"I understand you have a question for me."

"Yes, I guess I do." She gathered up her courage. "What's going on? You know, all these thoughts in my head ... and this caretaking stuff. What does it all mean?"

"Very well. Do you remember your lifetime in Salem?"

"Some," Roxy said. "Years ago I spontaneously remembered being drowned for being a witch."

"Precisely. Well, during that lifetime, Dear One, you and David were very much in love. In fact, you were due to be married. Then David was called away to war. It was an unfortunate time. You missed David deeply, so deeply that you felt a need to fill the void his absence created. You sought out another—you had an affair. When David returned from the war, he found out. He loved you very much and this news shattered him. He was unable to forgive you and felt he could not marry you. This, in turn, crushed you, Dear One."

"How did he find out?"

"Your sister told him."

"My sister?"

"Yes. You had a sister," Leviticus said. "David ended up marrying your sister."

"Do you know who my sister was?" Roxy asked.

"Yes. It was Katrina."

"*Katrina!*"

"Yes," Leviticus went on. "It was a difficult life for all three of you. David did not love Katrina as he had loved you. This hurt Katrina greatly, for she loved David as you had, with all her heart. You were able to make amends with Katrina and David, and you all remained friends, yet the hurt inside of you never healed. You never married. All of you were miserable in different ways. You died young. In a weak moment under interrogation, Katrina confessed to the authorities about your psychic nature. This qualified you, at that time, as being a witch. This confession caused the authorities to hunt you down and drown you."

Torrents of hurt, betrayal, and jealousy flooded into Roxy. That lifetime, with all its pain, was here now, alive in the present. It smacked of all the hurt she had felt during the first three and a half years of her and David's current relationship.

"What about all the pain I felt in this lifetime when David slept with other women?"

"The pain, Dear One, was equal to the pain which David felt in that lifetime from your affair."

"You mean that was my karma?"

"Yes," Leviticus replied, enormous love in his eyes.

Roxy slumped over in her chair. The pain, the realization, were debilitating. Those three and a half years of David's dating had been a living hell for her. Realizing the amount of pain she had caused David was shocking; it hurt her feelings. She'd hurt David, the man she loved so much. Both sides of this karmic lesson were unbearable.

"So what does all of this have to do with *this* lifetime?" Roxy asked.

"Salem was the lifetime that set you all up, prepared you for this lifetime," Leviticus explained. "You shared David then in one sense, and you are to share David now in a fuller sense."

Warning alarms went off. "Share! What do you mean, share?"

"Dear One, you are to share your husband, in all aspects, with this one Katrina."

"And why should I do that?" Roxy glared at Katrina.

"Because, Dear One, that is what you have agreed to do. It is written in each of your prebirth contracts. This is the destiny you chose before you were born so that you could each help humanity in your own way. It is what your soul wishes you to do."

"All right!" Roxy snapped out of her reverie. Directing her glance at Katrina, "If that's what I agreed to do, then fine, you have my permission to make love with David." But this permission was not granted from Roxy's heart. Katrina remained silent.

"It is time for me to allow this one his body back," Leviticus said. "This conversation has been a great strain on him. In Love and Light, I bid you farewell."

David's head dropped. A moment passed. David brought his hands to his face as he lifted his head and rubbed his eyes, trying to massage the fog out. He opened his eyes to find a frantic Roxy breathing laboriously.

"Do you remember what Leviticus had to say?" Roxy asked.

"No, not really. What?"

"I'm sure Katrina would love to tell you," Roxy huffed, bolting from the room.

Her mind churned faster than it ever had. A marriage where she shared David with Katrina? "I can't do it," she mumbled. The emotional ramifications were staggering. Never would she have guessed it. Never!

The problem wasn't that Leviticus had suggested they embrace an open marriage but that Roxy's inner knowing had concurred. Roxy had a strong inner knowing that had always guided her. In the past she had rejected other ideas she knew weren't right for her. She had never been prone to following anyone.

The same psychic who'd shown her the vision of David and Roxy living in Mt. Shasta told her that one of Roxy's contracted spiritual gifts was partial, rather than total, amnesia. The psychic had explained that when the amniotic fluid breaks, enzymes are activated to induce amnesia in infants. This causes a gradual memory loss over the first two years of life. They forget who they are, where they're from, why they're here. In some souls' prebirth contracts, it is stated that there is not to be a full amnesia.

In Roxy's case, she was left with twenty-five percent of her ethereal memory intact. The psychic said this explained how Roxy knew so much about the ethereal plane without having seen any movies or read any science fiction or spiritual/metaphysical books. Leviticus later confirmed this.

Over the years, Roxy had come to realize that this gift was what guided her. She would get a strong inner knowing that something was right or wrong. Most people have similar feelings and inner knowledge but the difference with Roxy was that hers headed her off the beaten path in bold directions.

For instance, Roxy chose to change her last name when she was twenty-three, long before she got married. She realized that the numerology and vibration of her surname were no longer right for her. Against tremendous family opposition, in her heart she knew it was the right thing to do. Years later there is still a wound of misunderstanding in her family in the wake of that decision. Nevertheless, she was sure she made the right choice.

With that knowing in place, Roxy was certain that Leviticus had spoken the truth. Her feeble mortal mind was so shattered she couldn't think straight. She couldn't bear to see their faces. She desperately tried to forget everything she had just heard. She pleaded with the feeling in her to melt away, to leave her alone. The terrible sickness in her gut, the fear of facing the emotions inside of her, was there to stay; it was her monster to face. Roxy hid for hours, petrified that David and Katrina were already making love.

Thoughts of making love to David electrified Katrina, and the connection with her Higher Self captivated her. She was consumed with David and the thought of sharing him wrenched her heart.

David was the glue designed to hold Katrina, Roxy and himself together. It was his job to flow where needed with Katrina or Roxy. He didn't pursue; rather, he was simply available. Tenaiia, guiding David's way, based her strategies on their prebirth contracts.

After a neurotic week, Tenaiia, channeling through Katrina, asked Roxy, "Are you truly ready for them to make love, Roxy?"

"Well, no, but it's what I'm supposed to do, right?"

"Yes, but there is a right way to do this. You must give them your blessing from your heart." Tenaiia paused. "Can you do that?"

"No, I guess I can't."

"Take the time, Roxy. Find it in your heart," Tenaiia cautioned. "Your Trinity depends on it."

"But how?" Roxy asked as Tenaiia left Katrina's body.

As soon as Katrina was present, Roxy made a new announcement. "I'm retracting my permission for you guys to make love."

"Fine," Katrina snapped, disappointment etched in her face. She didn't like being controlled, and her raging desires were difficult to contain.

Roxy's and Katrina's Higher Selves intended to bring in raw jealousy and place their lower selves in rigorous circumstances whereby they had to mature the pain, the emotion. The Trinity forced the lesson to the surface. But Roxy got lost. At the onset, the task seemed too big.

Roxy sat down in the only chair that rocked and stared into the flames, looking for answers and strength. She found none. Each time she embraced the idea of blessing David and Katrina's lovemaking, she became nauseated with jealousy. Wounded, she retreated further from them.

She rocked and stared for most of February. Katrina and David brought her ambrosia, a warm mixture of milk and honey to help heal the heart's emotional wounds. Each time Roxy tried to find a blessing for them, the pain in her heart dazed her and she recoiled further into herself. She lost her will to live. She was focused on the pain, not on the end result.

Tenaiia joined her at the fireplace one afternoon after she had channeled through Katrina. She had a plan. She picked up the poker and began playing with the fire, moving the burning logs to and fro. "Do you see, Roxy," Tenaiia began, "how this lone flame goes out quickly when there are no other flames nearby for support?"

"Yes."

Tenaiia continued to move the embers around until she had two flames by each other. "These two feed each other. Do you see?"

"Yes," Roxy replied, thinking, so what?

Again Tenaiia moved the embers until she had three flames in a triangle licking at each other. "Do you see the strength of these three flames?"

"Yes." The voltage in Roxy crept upward. She began to notice what Tenaiia was referring to as they stared at the fire. The greatest strength was in the three flames together. Unattended, they lasted the longest.

"As you can see with the fire, the single flame dies." Tenaiia pressed the point further. "The pair flickers longer but with three flames together, they support each other indefinitely. There is great power and strength in three. This is the power and strength of The Trinity. It is what you embark on here with Katrina and David, the power of three. You must find the desire in your heart to be aligned with them. Do you understand? The focus is not on the pain but on the Light at the end of the tunnel, on the power of three, the point past the pain where you realize your dreams. It's where you realize the power of three, the power of The Trinity, the power of what you three aligned together can accomplish."

Vague aliveness crept through Roxy.

"It is a great gift, this Trinity," Tenaiia said softly. "It is an opportunity for you three to help much of humanity. Is that what you want Roxy? To help humanity?"

"Yes, it is." Roxy perked up. "I have always wanted to make a difference in this world, but this is so big." Then Roxy remembered Leviticus' words: "The power of one is one. The power of an aligned two is twenty. The power of an aligned three is sixty."

She and David were aligned. They were capable of accomplishing anything together. Now, with three aligned on all levels, the possibilities stretched into infinity. She began to comprehend the vision of The Trinity. She was captivated. Roxy moved her focus from the pain by shifting it to the Light at the end of the tunnel, the potential end result. Roxy captured her inner resolve.

Tenaiia was relieved. "There are only six Melded Trinities on Earth at any given time. It's a rare opportunity."

Roxy found her will to live and a willingness to do what she had to do. She took the challenge. She was later told that her resistance to follow her path had been so great that it had brought death knocking at her door.

Once the log jam broke, Roxy remembered how to transform such issues. She began by imagining David and Katrina making love over and over again, focusing on achieving alignment instead of pain. The process crawled forward. Each time Roxy imagined them together, the sting evaporated further.

During this period, her thoughts drifted back to a conversation she'd had with Master Zoozer on the trip she'd taken to Mt. Shasta when he had spoken through another trance channel. The conversation had taken place in Panther Meadows, on the side of Mt. Shasta.

"We are seeking several individuals," Master Zoozer had begun, "whom we intend to place in key positions designed for high impact to help raise the consciousness of humanity. These positions will, of course, require a rigorous training period, with much adversity, which you will need to overcome and master. It will require a full commitment."

"Can I be a part of this?" Roxy had asked, blind yet driven.

"The choice is yours, Dear Lady."

Zoozer's words echoed now in Roxy's mind: "You must choose to meet the challenges that lie before you. You must successfully pass the training."

"Okay, I'm choosing." Roxy declared to herself as she imagined David and Katrina together one more time.

Truth That Sets Us Free.

Many are called but few are chosen.
More accurately, few choose to yield to and be guided by,
The paths and truths,
That are Intuited, Inspired, and Guided.

—Keith Amber

7

Three Become One

Tenaiia was the soul that Katrina, David, and Roxy chose during their prebirth negotiations to assist in the birthing of their Trinity. They knew that, left to their own devices, they'd probably resist pushing themselves in the areas needed for their success. Tenaiia thrived on catapulting others. Sometimes her strategies to get "the three" aligned left Katrina and Roxy wounded and angry, with David wedged in the middle. They hated to admit it, but Tenaiia almost always advanced their objective.

"Naturally," Tenaiia pointed out two weeks after Roxy's conversion, "you need to develop the bond between Katrina and David, and between Katrina and you." She smiled at Roxy. "Your Trinity is lopsided."

Everyone knew what "bonding" meant for Katrina and David but Roxy wasn't ready. Bonding for Katrina and Roxy was emotional and that proved to be a challenging chore. They had to fight resentment and jealousy and find love for one another. It wasn't easy.

It was a Friday evening and Katrina had a lab at school the next day to attend. Saturday would provide the prime bonding opportunity since Katrina drove three hours each way but only needed to be at school for two hours.

"Roxy shall accompany Katrina to school tomorrow," Tenaiia announced, "to bring more balance to your Trinity."

Tenaiia's plan jolted Roxy, who'd seen Katrina's day away as a perfect chance to spend some time alone with David. Their quality time had dwindled since David spent more time helping Katrina get through old surfacing wounds. He held and rocked her, rubbed her head to calm her, and dried her tears as she released mountains of repressed pain over her father's death.

Tenaiia drove a hard bargain. "If you stay home, Roxy, then David must go to work. If you go, then David can stay home and have a day of play."

Katrina and Roxy left David standing in the garage smiling at seven-thirty the next morning. Awkwardness filled Katrina's cramped little white Volkswagen Rabbit. Neither of them was quite sure where to begin.

"This is really strange for me, Roxy," Katrina finally said, half way to school. "You know, making love to David. I mean, I can't deny it—I really want to. How much I want to even bugs me. But the idea of a married man, and worse, with his wife around ... Athena keeps encouraging me. She says it'll help you."

"*Help* me?"

"The other day when I was channeling," Katrina said, "Athena took me on a journey and showed me another one of those screens. This time there was an image of you. Remember how I told you that the screen emanates essence and feelings?"

"Yes."

"Well, the essence coming out of your soul was strength. You have an enormous amount of strength. Then they showed me mine. In all my existence as a soul, I'll never come close to having the amount of strength that you have. It doesn't matter what I do, that kind of strength will never be available to me. But it's available to you. Athena said it's written in your soul. It really bummed me out, Roxy. I wish I had that kind of strength."

"I sure don't feel that strong."

"That's just it, Roxy. You have to be forced before you'll tap it. See? That was Athena's point. The Trinity is designed to force you to access your strength. Overcoming jealousy will force you to tap your strength. Athena says I'm doing you a favor by making love to David. Go figure, huh?"

A lump hit Roxy's throat.

"You know, I really feel a strong bond with David," Katrina said.

"I know. I can feel it."

"This is all pretty weird, you know?"

"I know." Roxy sighed, feeling trapped.

They arrived in Davis at the University of California, and Katrina drove straight to the lab building. "Here," she tossed Roxy the keys, "be back in two hours." And then she was gone.

Two hours alone, Roxy thought. Why not make good use of the time?

She drove until she found a safe place to scream. She settled down and began replaying the internal tape. There they were, in Roxy's mind, making love.

Roxy screamed her jealousy out, declaring over and over again, "I bless David and Katrina's lovemaking! I am bigger than this jealousy!" Her screams, filled with intent, lasted for fifteen minutes. When she was spent, a resolve emerged: She was ready.

There will be no retracting my blessing this time, Roxy thought. I am opening a door that will permanently and irrevocably alter all of our lives. She took a deep breath and tried to sigh her fear out.

Tenaiia, in Katrina's body, drove them home. Tenaiia was the only ethereal Being that channeled through Katrina who had total mastery over Katrina's entire body.

"Hello," Tenaiia said.

"Is Apollo around?" Roxy asked.

Apollo was the code name David and Roxy used whenever they wanted to talk to any of The Troops through Katrina, without Katrina listening. Once Katrina went into trance and the Guide began speaking through her, by simply saying "Apollo," David or Roxy could send Katrina's personal consciousness to some faraway place in the universe where she could not overhear the conversation. In this way, they could talk to the Guides about Katrina, or their own process, without activating Katrina.

"I'm ready to give David and Katrina my blessing," Roxy said, resolve mixed with fear.

"You have many who are here to help you," Tenaiia said, referring to the non-physical helpers assigned to assist their process. "Yes, it is unanimously agreed upon by The Troops. It is time for you to take the next step in your Trinity."

The fire crackled and waves of heat washed over their faces. There was a quiet, expectant feeling in the air. Roxy spoke before she gave herself any chance to change her mind. "I give you guys my blessing. You can make love tonight if you want."

Katrina's face lit up. David's eyes glimmered. With the announcement made, Tenaiia channeled through Katrina.

"Congratulations, Roxy," Tenaiia began. "It is felt by The Troops that it would be wise to have David and Katrina sleep together for the night."

Roxy stiffened.

She tossed and turned all night, her thoughts running wild, but no sounds came from Katrina's room. For four consecutive nights, David and Katrina slept together. Tension filled the log cabin.

On the morning after the fourth night, Tenaiia set dynamite in motion. She placed the thought into Katrina's mind to turn and hug David. At the same time, she placed the thought into Roxy's mind to go past Katrina's room and retrieve the Reflections card deck, similar to a Tarot deck, out of the meditation room at the end of the hall.

Roxy stole a glance as she passed Katrina's room. There they were, hugging. Roxy flew into her bedroom and collapsed into a fetal position on the bed, screaming, crying, and writhing in pain. Katrina grabbed her clothes and ran to Roxy, David right behind her. Katrina snuggled up to hug Roxy and David touched Roxy's feet.

That glance catalyzed all the pain Roxy had felt over David's other sexual encounters during their first years together. Faces, voices, and instances flashed in her mind, along with the pain she had repressed. David's touch triggered a continual flow of consciousness. The purging lasted an hour, until Roxy was spent.

"You know, Roxy," Katrina said gently, "that hug you saw was the only touching we did over the whole four nights. Really."

Roxy stared in disbelief. "How'd I manage to catch that? Perhaps it's time to talk to Tenaiia."

"That was dynamite," Tenaiia said after coming into Katrina's body. "I used dynamite to get things moving."

"Dynamite?" Roxy said, reeling.

"Yes, Roxy. You needed to have this release before it was appropriate for Katrina and David to go forward with their lovemaking."

"I heard this voice suggesting that I go get the Reflections cards," Roxy said.

"I hope so," Tenaiia said. "I said it loud enough!"

"And you said it just as they were hugging?"

"Bingo!"

Roxy shuddered. Thoughts of escape flooded her mind but there was nowhere to go. "Why haven't they made love yet?"

"You haven't really been ready," Tenaiia said.

"Yes, but that didn't stop them. What did?"

"They were prevented."

"Prevented? How? Why?"

"The Troops surrounded them in a thoughtform of desire," Tenaiia explained. "Then I instructed them that it was their karmic debt to you *not* to make love. This was their karma for violating their agreement with you the first morning they made love in Mt. Shasta. Their debt to you is now paid in full."

"You mean that they had a thoughtform magnifying their desires but they were told *not* to make love?"

"That is correct."

"That must have been really hard."

"Yes, it was."

On day five of this grueling process, Roxy said, "I'm exhausted. I need some rest. Maybe you guys can make love tomorrow night?" A moment passed and Katrina said, "Tenaiia wants to talk to you, Roxy."

"On a scale of one to ten, Roxy," Tenaiia said, "with ten being the most, how weary is your emotional body?"

"Seven," Roxy answered.

"How tired is your physical body?"

"Eight."

"Very well. How ready are you for them to make love?"

"Three."

Then, true to Tenaiia's confrontational style, she said, "I believe that you are ready to handle this tonight. Tonight they shall make love."

They played cards and laughed that evening. There was a curious mixture of strain and strength in the air. Roxy found the strength from somewhere to encourage Katrina to go forward, blessing intact. Roxy felt good but apprehensive. Pandora was about to be set free.

The hour descended upon the house. Neither Katrina nor David wanted to make the first move. Roxy offered an opening. "I'm going to bed. How about you guys?"

"Yeah, I guess I'm ready," Katrina said, smiling at David.

"Okay." David stood up. "Let's go." He took Katrina's hand.

Katrina and David went into Katrina's room and Roxy went to David's and her room. All the doors remained open.

It was quiet at first, then the sounds of pleasure intensified. Katrina was in ecstasy to be finally back with David. Their chemistry was electrifying. David's every move sent her into a deeper state of bliss and David moaned in delight with Katrina's every kiss.

Lying in bed, Roxy was frozen. She heard every moan, groan, and shriek of pleasure. Over the past week, she had worked herself into such a state of desire to break through, that while they made love she found herself experiencing unconditional love and joy for them. It was calm, peaceful, love-filled. Roxy was aligned with them from afar, experiencing joy over their lovemaking. She was happy—free of jealousy and control issues—in an aligned Trinity.

Roxy maintained that enlightened space for fifteen glorious minutes. Then it faded. They were taking too long. Katrina was too excited, too satisfied.

When the noises stopped, Roxy crept in to share a poem with them. Katrina, glassy-eyed, was curled up next to David, her head snuggled on his shoulder. David was radiant.

Sitting on the edge of the bed Roxy said, "I wrote a poem while you made love. Can I read it to you?"

"Sure," David said.

"Breakthrough begins,
Their lovemaking wins.
Aligning our love,
Three become one."

"How'd you like it?" Roxy asked.

Katrina replied "You wrote that? Wow!"

"Yeah. It just came through. For a brief time I was really happy for you two."

Roxy wished that David would magically offer to go to bed with her, leaving Katrina behind, but he didn't.

On the edge of sleep all night, Roxy listened to see if they would make love again.

Who Are Lightworkers?

They are people who recognize
LOVE
Doesn't have to have conditions attached.

—Jack Clarke

8

The Dark One Begins

"Tenaiia suggested that for a while David and I should get your permission before we make love. I gotta admit that I don't like it much, though I understand your need for it," Katrina said.

Roxy sighed. "That ought to help some. I'm crazy all the time with this."

"I love you, Roxy," David said, touching her arm. "You must know that. We're trying to make this as painless as possible on everyone."

"I know. I'm not sure if it's better to know when you're going to make love or not. Anyway, I'll try not to explode at every request and I'll try not to psychically molest you while you're in the middle."

For months, however, Roxy was not successful.

New sleeping arrangements were also in order. Tenaiia suggested a roving-bed routine, using the sleeping arrangements to push Roxy's selfish limits.

"Roxy, where do you wish to sleep tonight?" or "What sleeping arrangements do you think would be wisest tonight?" Tenaiia would ask, leaving Roxy cornered.

By now there was never a way for everyone to win. Katrina hated sleeping alone and sleeping with Roxy wasn't much better; she preferred David. With David she felt safe, protected, and loved. Her nights alone were excruciating. Her yearnings for David left her thrashing in the depths of profound loneliness. Sleep was slow in coming.

Roxy didn't like sleeping with Katrina either, even though it was productive for bonding. When Roxy slept with David, she felt guilty. When Katrina slept with David, despite their agreement, Roxy didn't trust them. Her nights were high-strung and restless.

David didn't care. Alone was fine, with Roxy was great, with Katrina was great. He followed Tenaiia's lead. He cemented The Trinity together. It wasn't part of his lessons to care.

Then their roving-bed routine was jarred.

David and Roxy were alone in their bed fondling each other when Katrina came in and sat down. Her eyes closed as she said, "I have come to inform you that Katrina wept all night long and now she must attend school without sleep."

"Who are you?" Roxy inquired.

"I am Arianne, Katrina's Higher Self."

"Why did Katrina weep all night?" Roxy asked.

"Because she is desperately lonely. She would not tell you this herself. That is why I have come to inform you."

"What does this mean?" Roxy was baffled. How could Katrina have such intense feelings for David? "What are you suggesting we do?"

"It is not my position to suggest," Arianne explained. "I am merely here to point out a problem, as Katrina would not do this on her own."

"That's easy," David piped up. "We'll trade our queen-size bed for a king-size and we'll all sleep together!"

Roxy's desire vanished.

With that suggestion, Arianne left Katrina's body and Katrina rushed off to school.

Taking care of Katrina took on a broader meaning. The old marriage of the Plumbs was slipping away and The Trinity was taking its place. Katrina and Roxy agreed to the new sleeping arrangements, though it had its pros and cons. Neither of them got David alone often but they got to share him in the middle.

As The Trinity evolved, so did their caretaking duties. The Guides opened the next door, allowing the battle between them and their dark adversary to begin.

Katrina channelled several Guides in what had become a normal fashion. She sat, relaxed and peaceful, as one Guide after another came through, altering Katrina's body language, quality of voice and syntax. Each Guide brought an individual personality to the session. David and Roxy could usually tell who came to speak through Katrina before the Guide even spoke. Between Guides, Katrina's face was neutral—calm and peaceful—until the dark one began. Caretaking Katrina began to expand into territory a mortal mind could never imagine.

Athena, with her soft voice and gentle manner, had just left Katrina's body and David and Roxy waited for Commander Ashtar to make an appearance. Suddenly Katrina's eyes shot open and the usual radiance was replaced by a malevolent glare. Her face became hard and a chill filled the air.

Startled, they called for Tenaiia. The eyes closed and the face became soft. Tenaiia came into Katrina' body, opened her eyes and said, "Yes?"

"Is this Tenaiia?"

"Yes."

"What's going on? Who was that in Katrina's body?" David asked.

"He is one of the dark forces," Tenaiia said, unruffled.

"*Dark forces?*" they echoed in unison.

"Yes," Tenaiia said, baffled by their surprise.

"Why is he coming into Katrina?" David asked.

"Because that is what you agreed to. He is here to prevent you from accomplishing your mission," Tenaiia reminded them.

"Excuse me?" Roxy said.

"He is a dark one. He is here to see to it that you do not succeed. Do you not remember?"

"No, I don't remember." Roxy paused to arrange her thoughts. "What are we supposed to do about it?"

"That is for you to figure out," she said and left Katrina's body.

David's and Roxy's eyes grew wide. Their attempts to get the dark one out of Katrina's body were feeble at best. No one solution worked for long. That would be the signature of this process to the bitter end. They played catch-up as the dark one advanced.

Their first approach was to call Katrina while a dark one was in her. This worked a time or two and either Katrina or a Guide-of-Light replaced the dark one. When that failed, they had to slap her face or make a loud noise to shock the dark one out. They quivered when they noticed that each time the dark one came in, he gained in strength and ability to manipulate Katrina's body.

Days later David and Roxy were meditating in their meditation room when Katrina's towering naked body filled the doorway. The wicked gleam in Katrina's eyes made it clear the dark one had come to visit. He delivered an evil sneer for a long moment and then laughed as he shut and locked the door from the hallway.

"Katrina!" David yelled.

David and Roxy glanced at each other, mouths agape. "Katrina!" Roxy yelled. There was no response.

"Katrina!" David screamed, but there was only dead silence.

David climbed out the window, came around the house and in through the front door, and unlocked the meditation room door. He found Katrina back in bed, sound sleep. Was this an omen of things to come? What else did the dark one have up his sleeve?

Roxy's selfish side was afraid to give up the dwindling time she and David shared. "David, let's meditate outside the house," she suggested.

"I don't know if that's a good idea, Roxy."

"Why not? The dark one won't be able to bother us."

"Well, I don't like it." He thought a moment. "We'll try it once."

While they were gone, the dark one came into Katrina's body, took her to the kitchen cupboard, opened the jar of valerian root, and ate three or four ounces of the extremely bitter-tasting natural tranquilizer. Normally used for making tea, a small amount induces relaxation. The dark one's intent was to cause an overdose.

What else would their non-physical adversary try? Suicide? Broken body parts? Self-inflicted wounds? The probabilities became staggering. David and Roxy realized that they could not leave Katrina alone. It was Tenaiia's job, while they worked or while Katrina was at school, to protect her from the dark one from the ethereal plane. Otherwise the responsibility fell squarely on David's and Roxy's shoulders.

The dark one's intensity increased. How to keep him from remaining in Katrina's body? They tore into their memories to find solutions. Every solution worked a mere time or two before he got past them. While in Katrina's body, he continued to gain strength.

Roxy's next attempt was to use the Father, Mother, God Prayer of Protection: "Father, Mother, God, I ask that Katrina, David, myself, our house and our property be cleared and cleansed within the universal White Christ Light, the green healing Light, and the purple transmuting Flame. Within God's will and for our highest good, I ask that any and all negativity be completely sealed in its own Light, encapsulated within the Ultraviolet Light, and cut off and removed from us. Impersonally, with neither love nor hate, I return all negativity to its source of emanation, decreeing that it never again be allowed to reestablish itself within us or anyone else in any form. I now ask that we be placed within a triple capsule of the universal White Christ Light of protection, and for this blessing, I give thanks."

Days later Katrina was in bed, not feeling well. Roxy sat on the edge of the bed. Leviticus, in David's body, sat in a chair near the bed. The dark one, now in Katrina's body, glared at Roxy. Intimidated, she telepathically beckoned, "Lord Archangel Michael, please help us with the dark one."

Lord Archangel Michael arrived within seconds, his bold steadfast presence in the corner of the room. He surrounded Katrina's body with a calm, loving, peaceful energy, a natural shield against the dark ones.

Roxy collapsed into safety. The dark one in Katrina's body began to weaken, causing Katrina's face to soften and her eyelids to droop. After a minute or so, her body went limp.

Another small battle won.

Then Lord Michael was gone. He was permitted to help just one more time. Then they had to find another solution.

On the next visit from the dark one, Roxy invoked the assistance of The Great White Brotherhood by saying, "I invoke the symbol," while visualizing a white plus sign inside and connected to a white circle against a magenta background. David had visualized this symbol over the hotel on his shift as security guard when they lived in San Diego. Crime had evaporated but only on his shift, thanks to the protective help of The Great White Brotherhood.

But The Great White Brotherhood's assistance only lasted a couple of days. This would not be the case for most people, but that's how it was written in their contracts. Part of the lessons in their contracts was to learn the ways of the dark ones. Their Higher Selves wanted them to learn how the dark ones interfered with people's lives and how to prevent this from occurring.

By now, David and Roxy wandered through the days, lost and confused. The evidence was mounting; they were not going to be "saved" from going through these vexatious experiences.

A couple of days later Katrina was sitting up in their king-size bed, still not feeling well. Her eyes closed, a second passed, and when they reopened, the dark one glared at David and Roxy, challenging their abilities to thwart him. Their bag of tricks depleted, they had no idea which way to turn. Exasperated and lost, Leviticus channeled through David to help show Roxy the way.

"Hello, Dear One," Leviticus said.

"Is this Leviticus of the Light?" This was their new, rigorous discipline of asking each Guide if they were of the Light.

"Indeed it is I," Leviticus assured her. "I am pleased to hear you ask, Dear One."

"Doesn't it bother you guys to be repeatedly asked that same question?" Roxy tried to get on solid footing in this troublesome arena of discernment.

"Indeed, it does not," Leviticus said. "We much prefer being asked. You see, the problem is that many channels are not truly channeling who they say they are. For some channels, they are consciously deceiving their audience. For others, they are simply unaware of the potential problem and are not versed in discernment. In either case, the responsibility falls on the person who is listening to the channel. They must ask, 'are you of the Light?' Beings of Light will happily respond. The dark ones can mislead you, but according to universal law, they cannot lie outright. In this, the age of discernment, it is vital that *all* individuals learn to ask, to discern from their heart and never blindly follow anyone."

"You have no business here, Leviticus. You have no right to interfere!" declared a harsh guttural voice from Katrina's body.

Roxy's eyes widened and jaw dropped. They know each other! He can talk!

Undaunted, Leviticus said, "Indeed, I do. I have a right to show them the way. Then they must do the rest."

The truth had been spoken. The dark one fell silent.

Leviticus, a teacher at heart, wanted to show Roxy by example the path that lay before them. Love began to emanate out of every cell of Leviticus/David's body. He was showing them how to love everything God created as God does, as the God in everyone is capable of doing. Love heals, transforms, and glows and Leviticus glowed from head to toe. The room filled with love-filled flickering energy, touching every microscopic molecule. Tension and fear were powerless and melted into bliss and heavenly rapture. Roxy experienced Leviticus' deep unconditional love for her, and for All That Is.

Without effort, Leviticus continued beaming the glorious high-vibration energy outward. With each breath, the knots in Roxy's body melted into sublime peace and serenity. With each breath, the dark one grew more uncomfortable, twitching to and fro. The translucent gentle energy intensified until Roxy's eyelids drooped in tranquillity, her skin breathing in love. Harmony tingled throughout.

Moments into this eternal experience, Leviticus focused on the eyes of the dark one. The essence of Love is Light and positive emotions; the essence of the dark is hate, fear, and negative emotions. The dark cannot withstand the vibration of Light and Love. The dark one began to writhe in pain, overtaken by weakness fading from Katrina's body. She went limp.

Tenaiia came into Katrina's body next. "Well done, Leviticus!"

"Indeed," Leviticus replied, turning to Roxy. "Now, Dear One, do you see what you must do?"

It was the most daunting task Roxy had ever faced. She knew what she must do. But how to do it? All she knew was that it had to be done. Katrina's life depended on it.

Who Are Lightworkers?

Anyone who Loves
Without
Limits or prerequisites.

—Jack Clarke

ARCHANGEL MICHAEL

9

The Melding

The deep clean, bright snow in their Mt. Shasta front yard melted in trickles. The sun's rays streamed between the tall Douglas firs, reflected off the snow and then bounced through the large window, making the living room seasonally bright despite the dark-colored log cabin walls. The air was brisk as David, Katrina, and Roxy sat before the fire.

"What's this all about, anyway?" Roxy asked David and Katrina.

"What do you mean?" Katrina asked.

"What are we doing all of this for? The Trinity, the dark ones constantly around ... why? What for?"

"We're supposed to take care of Katrina," David said.

"Yeah, but why?" Roxy was lost.

"Maybe Tenaiia has some answers, Roxy. Do you want to talk to her?" Katrina offered.

Tenaiia entered Katrina's body and began to speak. "You have a question for me, Roxy?"

"Yes. Why are we doing all of this? What's the point?"

"The point is that you are helping Katrina to become Melded."

"Melded? What's that?"

"An extremely rare spiritual gift." There are only six people who are spiritually Melded on Earth at any given time."

"Only six out of all the billions of people on earth? Why only six?"

"Because a Melded person anchors so much Light that any more than six Melded people at any given time would throw off the balance of Light and dark on planet Earth. You see, the process of the dark moving into the Light on Earth must be done organically, one person at a time. Each Melded person anchors massive amounts of Light—equivalent to thousands of Lightworkers—and can affect the enlightenment of millions. Too many of these unique people would make it an unfair battle."

"The Light of thousands in one person? How can that be?"

"Yes, the Light of thousands in one. How? Because they have the Light of their Higher Selves walking the Earth. Humans are not able to contain that much Light within their physical beings at this time on Earth. There is too much denseness and the gap between the vibration of Earth and all that Light is too great; the pressure would be unbearable. When one is Melded, he or she is in a sort of permanent warp where *all* of the Light of the Higher Self is physically here on Earth. The Melded connection offers some protection because the Higher and lower selves sort of equalize each other. They are likened to a tractor-beam between heaven and Earth or, more accurately, a tractor-beam between the ethereal plane and the physical plane."

"What do you mean by Melded?"

"Hmmm ... let me see," Tenaiia pondered. "Very well. This is somewhat complicated. You shall stop me if you do not understand?"

They nodded their agreement.

"Very well. Generally speaking, an individual is connected to his or her Higher Self by a silver cord. Also, the lower and Higher selves share the eighth chakra. For the lower self, it is the chakra which hovers about one foot above the top of the head or the crown chakra. For the Higher Self, it is the chakra that remains suspended just below the feet. However, with the six individuals who were chosen to be Melded on Earth at this time, the Higher and lower selves' seven main chakras overlap and combine, or join. In essence, the Higher and lower selves become one, with no veils separating them. If you had inner vision, you'd see the Higher Self permanently merged with the lower self, at least for the duration of the Melded lifetime. On the ethereal plane, we call it 'being Melded.' The Higher Self melds with the lower self, who melds with the Higher Self. Do you understand?"

"So it's like having a Higher Self in a physical body?" Roxy said.

"Bingo! A Melded Higher Self does not have to go through the filters of the lower self. Universal knowledge does not get distorted by the veils and filters present in all human beings. Also, all the universal knowledge available to souls, or Higher Selves, remains easily available to the Melded lower/Higher Self. The six Melded Ones become an invaluable resource to those seeking enlightenment and higher wisdom. The six people who are chosen for this rare destiny of being Melded on Earth accept the responsibility and burden which this fate bears."

"How do they get chosen?" Roxy asked.

"Souls apply for such positions."

"Why, if it's such a burden?"

"Because of the mastery a soul gains in embracing such a challenging lifetime or mission," Tenaiia explained. "And because it provides such a tremendous opportunity to serve God and humanity. Very well, where was I? Ah, yes. Each Melded person has a particular field they are equipped to radically affect. The result is a dramatic increase of Light or enlightenment in a particular field that can positively affect the masses. In essence, these Melded Selves are to bring fourth-dimensional technology to humanity's current more limited third-dimensional systems."

David and Roxy knew from past metaphysical schooling that "filters" are belief systems—limits, rules, and conditioning—that result from the circumstance of youth. These filters come from what is taught by parents, teachers, religious figures, and other authority figures. Such filters can distort pure, incoming information.

This distortion occurs through most channels, telepaths, and psychics to some degree or another. It is an enormous task for the dedicated spiritual student to clear the distortions, an even bigger task to remain clear. This clarity is accomplished through intense work on spiritual growth by re-examining filters, positions, and judgments, and abandoning or transforming them. Few people ever accomplish pure clarity; even fewer maintain it.

"How is this different from channeling?" David asked.

"With a channel, almost always the entity goes through the physical body and so must go through the filters. With The Melding, the Higher Self becomes one with, or melds, with the lower self. The Higher Self bypasses the filters after one is Melded, although the fewer filters to be bypassed the better. The physical and ethereal aspects become one. The Melded person coexists on the physical and ethereal planes."

Tenaiia paused to let David and Roxy digest the information. David tried to imagine what it would be like for an ethereal spirit to be physical and at the same time for the physical person to be aware of their ethereal life.

Tenaiia continued. "You must understand that this is a very difficult job for both the physical and ethereal aspects of the soul or person. There is no line or veil between the two worlds. Both selves live in both dimensions at all times."

"Why be Melded if it's so difficult?" David asked.

"Because the Melded connection is necessary for the mission of Katrina/Arianne to be successful."

"What is the mission?"

"Katrina/Arianne must bring the fourth-dimensional ethereal teaching skills to Earth. They must transform the school system for the incoming new generations. For the children to lead the planet forward, they must be supported in remembering who they are and what they've come to do. Their intuition and inner knowing must be fostered. Can you imagine what it would be like if children were encouraged to develop telepathy and third-eye vision? Schools need to have a system that insures that the children remain awake, en masse. There must be teachers and teaching methods to empower and maintain the awakening. All learning styles—intuitive, kinesthetic, and intellectual—must be equally honored.

"Initially, Katrina/Arianne will merely appear to be ahead of her time, with fellow teachers following her lead because her unusual techniques work so well. Over time, Katrina/Arianne will begin teaching the teachers. The enormity of this mission requires a direct access to fourth-dimensional teaching skills. This can only be guaranteed through a Melded connection by someone who is grounded on Earth with full access to fourth-dimensional clarity, techniques and wisdom. Arianne is a master teacher. This is why she was chosen for this mission. The Melding, in effect, allows Arianne to personally teach on Earth while in ethereal form."

"That is a huge responsibility," Roxy said, stunned.

"Yes," Tenaiia replied. "You three have come to Earth to do selfless missions, to confront your deepest fears and transform your emotions in the interest of accomplishing a bigger objective. You are here to profoundly help humanity. It is what each of you agreed to do before you were born. It is written in your prebirth contracts; it is your highest destiny. You are infinitely capable."

"Okay," Roxy sighed. "What does The Trinity have to do with The Melding?"

"It is in The Trinity that you will find your greatest strength. And it will take the power of all three of you, aligned, to be successful against the dark ones."

David and Roxy shot questioning looks at each other.

"And Katrina will need help in staying grounded so that she can anchor the enormous amount of Light which naturally comes through a Melded person. She is certainly not able to do this alone. She will require both of you to caretake her. The ungrounded nature of a Melded person leads to forgetfulness around eating, remembering to wear clothes properly, waking at the appropriate hour—in short, all the grounded activities most people take for granted. So much of Katrina will be ... ah ... how do you say? ... 'a space case.' As she becomes more Melded with the ethereal level, it will become increasingly difficult for her to do grounded things for herself. It will take effort from both of you to maintain her physical needs. The most intense assistance, of course, will be required during the initial stages, where the primary focus will be on keeping Katrina alive. It will take both of you to accomplish this."

They perked up. "What do you mean?" David asked.

"The dark ones have a right, according to God's universal laws, to attempt to prevent The Melding connection from successfully anchoring. This is because The Melding produces a powerful human tool of Light, which is capable of threatening the existing control the dark ones now enjoy on Earth. It is your job, David and Roxy, to see to it that the dark ones are not successful at killing Katrina, and that Katrina accomplishes her mission."

"Our job?" they chimed together.

"Yes. Katrina's job is to trust you, to place her very life in your hands. Your jobs are to keep her protected and alive."

"Alive!" they both said, shocked.

"Yes, alive!" Tenaiia said. "You do not think that the dark ones wish for Katrina to be successful do you? To anchor all that Light here on Earth? I think not."

Prior to this conversation, nothing like this had ever occurred to David or Roxy. New, scary ground was being tread upon.

While David and Roxy talked to Tenaiia, Katrina traveled in her Light body. When she returned from her journey-while-in-trance, she had even more information, vital pieces of the puzzle that helped their current dilemma make more sense.

"I found out who the dark one is that you guys have been dealing with," Katrina said.

"Well, who is it?" Roxy asked.

"Get this—he's my ethereal half-brother! You remember, our Higher Selves have siblings and parents just like we do on Earth."

"Yeah?" Roxy said. "Continue."

"Well, he's my half-brother."

"Brother?" Roxy asked.

"Yeah, great, huh? Anyway, his name is Zeeq."

"Zeeq." Roxy pressed the name into her head.

"Anyhow, we ...."

"'We' who?" Roxy wanted clarity.

"You, David, and I made a deal with him as part of our prebirth contracts. See, we needed to go into contract with the dark ones one way or another. You know, as a part of this Melding thing."

"Tell me again why that is," David said.

"Because the dark ones have a right to try to prevent us from being successful," Katrina continued, "they're going to try to stop us. So Arianne, my Higher Self, asked Zeeq if he would be the one to go into contract with us. The deal is that Arianne has been trying to get Zeeq into the Light for a long, long time so she saw this as a perfect opportunity to try again. By the way, Zeeq has also been trying to get Arianne into the dark."

"Who's winning so far?" David asked.

"Neither one is budging. Anyway, they both agreed to put it all on the line, to make it like a once-and-for-all deal with this Melding thing. Here's the catch, guys: the only way Zeeq would agree was if the odds were in his favor so the three of us gave him a seventy percent chance in our overall contract to win, which, by the way, is way out of balance."

"Seventy percent! Were we nuts?" Roxy asked.

"Athena told me that we three figured that together we could do anything. I was also told that these odds were so out of balance that we had to get them approved by Sananda."

"What did Sananda say?"

"He trusted the combination of the three of us together. He said that if we felt confident in our ability to win, then he, too, felt confident. Zeeq simply wouldn't agree under any other terms. I guess he really doesn't want to come into the Light."

"So let me get this straight," David said. "If he wins, you go to the dark, and if we win, he comes to the Light?"

"Yep. If he wins, I physically die and Arianne goes to his castle on the ethereal plane. If we win, his soul moves more into the Light. Some bargain, huh?"

"Shit! What have we gotten ourselves into?" Roxy said.

None of them had ever been challenged in matters of life and death and their reactions spanned the gamut. Roxy was overwhelmed and insecure. Katrina was calm and centered but burdened. David catapulted from stunned to nervous cockiness.

"What made us do this?" was the only question Roxy could muster.

"Arianne is desperate to get Zeeq into the Light," Katrina said. "He's our half-brother. She really loves him."

"Damn!" David said.

"So what's our strategy?" Roxy asked.

"Love. The dark cannot get past love."

"Love. Amid all our strain and rampant emotions. Great! Just great! Anything else?" Roxy asked.

"Oh, yeah," Katrina said. "They also told me that what I'm supposed to do is to completely trust both of you with my life, that if I don't trust you and have total faith in your ability to protect me, you might fail."

David and Roxy exchanged glances.

Katrina took a deep breath. "But if I have complete trust and faith in your abilities, that will empower you to succeed to keep me alive. Fun, huh?"

Truth That Sets Us Free.

Earth was designed for Soul Growth.
There is no greater treasure,
One can attain on Earth,
Than Growth for one's Soul.

—Keith Amber

JESUS/SANANDA

On June 1, 1961, Sananda appeared in visible, tangible form, and allowed the above photograph to be taken. He then gave permission for it to be used in association with the work of A.S.S.K. which sends out the transcripts given by him to Sister Thedra. Copies of both are available by writing to:

The Association of Sananda and Sanat Kumara
2675 West Highway 89-A, #454, Sedona, AZ 86336

10

The Adversaries

David and Roxy wandered beneath the tall Douglas firs on their five acres while Katrina was away at school. Their feet chilled as their shoes absorbed the melting snow of May. Still, it was a refreshing change from the constant battles they had to fight with the dark whenever Katrina was present. Roxy figured that it was time to find out who their adversaries were and what their best defenses were.

She asked David if he would channel Leviticus so she could get some answers. Leviticus was able to operate David's body as well a David himself. In fact, aside from the energy present, the distinct syntax, and the fact that Leviticus knew things that David didn't, it was impossible to tell them apart.

"Hello, Dear One," Leviticus said as they continued their walk.

"Is this Leviticus of the Light?"

"Indeed."

"Well, the dark ones have certainly accelerated. What a mess!" Roxy said.

"Indeed. They are making their presence known, are they not?" Leviticus chuckled.

"I guess! And I get this eerie feeling that we haven't seen the worst of it," Roxy said.

"Indeed, you have not." Leviticus noticed the fear in his faithful student. He knew as much as anyone how capable Roxy was. He loved her as much as he had ever loved any of his students, though he realized that Roxy could not remember their history or their bond at this time.

"So," Roxy proceeded, "I know what they want—Katrina dead. And I know we're directly battling Zeeq but I'd like to understand more of who the dark ones are. Are they what people call Satan? And what motivates them? Where do they come from?"

"Very well," Leviticus said. "Dark souls come from God. And yes, this is who people refer to as Satan, although when they are referring to Satan they are usually referring to one entity. In actuality there are many and they come with many names, but the essence remains the same between those called the dark ones and the one called Satan."

"And they come from God? I thought only Light came from God."

"*Balance* comes from God, Dear one," Leviticus said. "The balance of dark and Light. We are all of God, and the dark ones are no exception. Dark souls come from God, just as you do; but unlike you, who are anchored in the Light, they are anchored in the dark. All souls in their journey back to God, whether they began anchored in the Light or dark, will choose lifetimes in both the dark and the Light. It is what God desires, that we learn from *all* that He has created."

"Do humans ever have a dark Higher Self?" Roxy asked.

"Indeed they do! Let's see, what would be a good example? An organized crime boss would be a good example. Another example would be a world leader, one seeking power despite the cost in lives. Can you think of any?"

Roxy thought as they climbed the slippery, wet hill beneath the lodgepole pines. The pungent smell of the mossy earth scented the air. "Got one. How about a drug lord?"

"Very good. Let us now turn the tables. Whom do you think would be souls containing mostly Light?" Leviticus probed.

"Jesus/Sananda?"

"Indeed."

"Buddha?"

"Yes."

"How about Ghandi or Mother Teresa?"

"Precisely!" Leviticus exclaimed. "Mostly, Dear One, there are humans with souls who are either part Light and part dark, or varying degrees of gray. Some of these souls are more anchored in the Light, others in the dark. And *all* humans are here on Earth to transform the various parts of their souls.

"Terra, which is Earth's ethereal name, the name she will be called after her transition into the fourth dimension, offered to serve God by allowing humanity to experience a season in the dark while living on her. The season is turning, yet the dark ones in control on Terra do not wish to turn Terra over to the Light. It is Earth's destiny, after all, and her greatest desire, to move back into the Light and into her next Golden Age. This, Dear One, is the great battle at hand. And you are in a microcosm of just that battle."

"Katrina, anchoring massive amounts of Light with The Melding, and Zeeq, who's on the dark side, is trying to stop her?' Roxy asked.

"Precisely."

"Okay then, what's our defense?"

"Focus on transforming the dark holes in your aura into Light. As you do that, you will not only be anchoring more Light on Terra, but you will also make it far more difficult for the dark ones to sabotage you."

"What are dark holes?"

"Negative patterns create dark holes in your aura," Leviticus said. "These negative patterns are the very lessons each person comes to Earth to transform. Lessons can include transforming negative emotions such as anger, hate, jealousy. Also blame, control issues, arrogance, egocentric focus, greed, power hunger, or dependency/guru types of relationships. These are all dark patterns that produce holes in the aura so the dark ones can easily come through."

As they talked, they wound their way back to their front yard. Leviticus suggested that they sit on the cast iron yard furniture and luxuriate in the sun to finish their talk. Roxy felt a chill from the metal chair through her thin sweat pants.

"You see, Dear One," Leviticus said, "both humans and non-physical souls who are focused and anchored in the dark want to keep Terra—and humanity—lodged in the dark. That way they will remain in control. To this end, they will go to extreme lengths to burrow into people's auras and thoughts, to magnify and perpetuate their dark sides. They do this by magnifying negative feelings, fueling arguments, and generally working to keep negative patterns such as low self-worth, fear, or egocentric focuses alive."

"Why do they want to do that?"

"Because the dark ones wish to remain in control on Earth and in order to do that, they must keep the Light from growing in humans and, therefore, on Terra."

"What's the solution?"

"Humans must wake up, Dear One, and become aware of outside forces influencing them. Awareness is a huge step towards prevention. Secondly, you must focus on transforming your own dark sides so the dark ones can no longer affect you. Awareness, intent, and personal transformation—these are your primary tools," Leviticus emphasized.

Roxy grappled with this information and the ramifications as it applied to their predicament. They had a powerful opportunity to help humanity and Earth. A powerful adversary was intent on stopping them, at any cost. To their adversary, Roxy realized, Katrina's life was a major threat.

Who Are Lightworkers?

They are people who search for strength from
The Universe
By going inside themselves.

—Jack Clarke

11

The Stakes Go Up

Katrina shared a small sum of money with David and Roxy from a limited trust fund set up by her father to help her through college. She had been told on a journey-while-in-trance that this sharing was a part of the bargain. It wasn't enough, however. It was inadequate to buy food and David had not yet sold any insurance. It was time for Roxy to begin contributing. Since there was no demand for résumés in Mt. Shasta, Roxy fell back on her old reliable skill of housecleaning. Over a period of two months she secured jobs that kept her busy five days a week.

Housecleaning became Roxy's friend. It gave her a legal break from the heavy caretaking burdens of home. It was something she did well and felt good about, and it helped her process her emotions more quickly, which became invaluable.

Emotions exist in the body and auric field in the form of energy, which is either in motion dispersing outward, or stalled and stagnant. When the intent is to transform the emotion, energy flows. When the intent is to hold on to negative emotions, such as not forgiving or refusing to include love with the negative emotion, energy comes to a standstill. Stalled emotional energy, over the long haul, causes physical "dis-ease."

With an intense desire to transform, Roxy chose to think of Katrina and David making love repeatedly during work, while choosing not to feel jealous. It was a lie but with her intent in place the lie, over time, became the truth. The physical movement of her work was grounding and it also promoted energy circulation.

As Roxy's energy flowed, her emotions flowed. With each passage of the image there was less of a sting to it. She would give them a tiny bit more space. Still the jealousy did not magically transform overnight.

Katrina's catharsis continued, and with it came occasional nights when Katrina and David spent a night alone together. On one such night, Katrina was so grateful for David's loving support she thanked him by kissing and massaging him into bliss. Then they lay together in peace.

"Look, David. Can you see it?" Katrina asked, pointing off into the darkest corner of her bedroom.

"See what?"

"Over there. See? The light is getting brighter, more pronounced."

A moment passed. "I *can* see it!" David said, fascinated.

A glimmering green glow intensified for their viewing pleasure. Growing in intensity, the beautiful sparkling lime green sphere grew brighter, illuminating the dark corner. An oval about four feet tall and three feet wide, it floated in space. Green and white pinpoints of light like Christmas tree lights, pulsated and danced to and fro. The energy inside the sphere undulated with a life of its own. No physical form manifested, only a soul essence. The color reflected Katrina's most recent focus of green for healing. The magical display lasted fifteen minutes, with continual waves of profound love emanating forth from Arianne, Katrina's Higher Self.

The next morning, Katrina bubbled as she told Roxy about Arianne's appearance. She was also compelled to be honest about her gift to David.

"Why didn't you come and get me to see Arianne?" Roxy demanded.

"I don't know. It never occurred to me." Katrina replied.

"You broke our lovemaking agreement!" Roxy snapped.

"It's not like we made love!" Katrina yelled back. "I just gave him pleasure," she said, stomping off. These episodes weren't good for bonding.

Their lives became a series of twists and turns. Either Katrina, Roxy, or both were hurt, getting activated, or not getting their needs met. And Zeeq's attacks escalated.

"Her heart stopped again!" David screamed to Roxy. She ran from the kitchen into the bedroom where she found David, flushed and sweating, performing CPR. Zeeq had come into Katrina's body and stopped her heart once again. This was Zeeq's new attack on The Melding, and on Katrina's life.

They had nine minutes and no more. Tenaiia had warned them of possible permanent brain damage after nine minutes of CPR. Frantic,

David continued pushing on Katrina's chest four times, then blowing into her mouth. Then Roxy took a shift, while David watched the clock. Seven minutes ... eight ... eight and a half—and whoosh!—Katrina breathed on her own. The strain left Katrina's caretakers breathless and taut.

"Another close call!" Roxy panted. David and Roxy attempted to regain self-composure. A minute passed ... two ... three ... four.

"It's stopped again!" David shrieked, resuming CPR.

"It's ten forty-six, " Roxy noted. "Ten forty-seven ... ten forty-eight ... ten forty-nine ... ten fifty ... ten fifty-one .... "

"Come on, Katrina! Get back in your body! KATRINA!" David screamed.

"Ten fifty-two ... ten fifty-three ... KATRINA! COME BACK!" Roxy cried, out-willing Zeeq's intense desire, his need, for her to die.

Katrina jerked back into her body.

This continued four grueling hours. They were all bone-exhausted. Katrina's chest was bruised, but she was alive. Zeeq used this frightening, wearisome, life-threatening strategy every night for six brutal weeks.

His next tactic brought with it a different kind of death potential.

David, Katrina, and Roxy, after a long search, found a card game called "Spades" that they all enjoyed. It required bidding on tricks and clever strategy, skills that needed honing these days. They played most evenings for one or two hours until bedtime, snaring fragments of pleasure.

To add to the frolic, Tenaiia popped in and out of Katrina's body, as she had long since become accustomed to doing, playing Katrina's hand with her. Tenaiia's style, opposite Katrina's, was gutsy and bold. Tenaiia would bid high, then leave Katrina to play the hand. Even Katrina had to admit that she won more often than she expected to.

It was ten o'clock and time for bed. Katrina climbed in on David's right. Roxy was on his left. In an instant Katrina's eyes closed and she began mumbling, "Two ... three ... four ...."

"I don't like this," David declared. "Something doesn't feel right."

"Seven ... eight ... nine ...." Katrina mumbled in a trance.

"Tenaiia!" David called, "what's going on?"

"Indeed, David, you are wise to be concerned," Tenaiia said upon entering Katrina's body.

"Is this Tenaiia of the Light?" Roxy checked.

"Yes, it is I."

"What's going on?" David's plea was urgent.

"Zeeq has placed a bomb in Katrina's mind. If she says either one or ten aloud, the bomb will detonate and Katrina will die."

"Excuse me?" Roxy cried. "Did you say 'die'?"

"Zeeq does mean to win," Tenaiia answered.

"But isn't the bomb ethereal?" David asked. "How can it physically kill her?"

"Ah, I see your point," Tenaiia said. "You see, the bomb will affect her Light body. Hmmm, let me see. Yes, let us liken this to an amputee who can feel his missing limb. What he is actually feeling is his Light body. Similarly, if this bomb is detonated, it explodes first in her Light body, then instantaneously seeps through to her physical body, causing permanent brain damage and certain death."

"And the trigger words are one and ten?" David asked.

"Precisely," Tenaiia said, glad to see David prepared for battle. "You must keep her from saying one or ten aloud. Now I must go. Good luck." Tenaiia's smile faded from Katrina's face and Katrina, in a Zeeq-induced trance, continued mumbling, " ... six ... five ... four ... three ...."

Desperate, David interjected, "Three! Four! Three! Four!"

" ... three ... four ..." Katrina followed, then continued with, "five ... six ... seven ... eight ...."

David interrupted, "Eight, seven! Eight, seven!"

Katrina followed. "Eight ... seven," then continued down, " ... six ... five ... four ... three ...."

"Three, four! Three, four!" David inserted.

Then Roxy took a shift. Each passage lasted twenty-five to thirty seconds. The process continued for four exhausting hours until Katrina went quiet. The attack ended at its usual hour of two in the morning. During Katrina's school year, they got four hours of sleep.

It took David and Roxy a week to figure out that the card game, with its residual numbers floating inside of Katrina's mind, was the feed-in for this evil strategy. Then, as wise caretakers, they put an end to playing cards. Katrina suggested "Yahtzee." After one night of the same results, they put an end to that, too, and all numbers games.

Katrina, who thrived on having fun, went into an angry frump. She wasn't used to being told what she could do, and she didn't like it. Although she was the one mumbling the numbers, she never remembered any of it. To Katrina, David and Roxy were not saving her life, they were taking her fun away.

When the numbers bomb was ineffectual, Zeeq switched to his next scheme. Katrina's eyes would close before her head hit the pillow, her body writhing and screaming in great pain. Confused, David called for Tenaiia.

"You called?" Tenaiia asked.

"Is this Tenaiia of the Light?"

"Yes, it is I," Tenaiia confirmed.

"Why is Katrina screaming? What's Zeeq doing now?" David asked.

"He is projecting horrifying images onto her third-eye screen." Tenaiia shuddered. "They are really quite ghastly. I do not know where he comes up with such trash. They upset Katrina greatly."

"How do we stop them, or him?" Roxy asked.

"This is for you to figure out. I must depart." And then Tenaiia was gone.

Katrina began squirming on the bed. Her face was contorted and she moaned as though in pain.

"She wasn't seeing them before we went to bed, David. Let's wake her up," Roxy suggested.

"Katrina, wake up," David said, shaking her.

"What! What do you want?" Katrina yelled. "What's wrong? Stop shaking me! What's the problem? What time is it? Don't you realize I need to get up in five hours for school?"

"Don't you remember the images on your inner screen?" David asked.

"Images?" Katrina shook her head. "I need to get some sleep."

"Sorry."

Before her head hit the pillow, her eyes closed and the writhing and moaning continued. She seemed tortured and David and Roxy felt compelled to help her, to wake her up again. They knew of no other way to protect her, to stop the projection.

Katrina grew angrier at each waking. When they woke her, Zeeq would erase the memory of her horrific scenes so she had no idea what her caretakers were talking about. Asleep, she was tormented. Awake, she was angry at losing sleep.

The game continued for hours and days, until Zeeq tired of it. At this point, each attempt Roxy made to melt Zeeq away with love failed.

Zeeq knew his opponents well. His next strategy pushed Roxy's buttons to intolerable emotional levels. Katrina was oblivious to it all. It was as though Zeeq took over her body and Katrina's consciousness was thrust to some far-away place. Zeeq by now had mastered looking like Katrina. David and Roxy could no longer tell them apart.

Again, Katrina's eyes closed before her head hit the pillow. She began provocatively gyrating, her whole body sending a desperate invitation as she moaned in her most sensuous voice, "David, make love to me ... David, make love to me ... Oh David, take me into your arms!" over and over and over again. Roxy squirmed towards insanity. Was she supposed to send them off to make love? Was it Katrina? Was it Zeeq?

A part of Roxy wanted to say, "David, why don't you and Katrina go to her bedroom and make love and then come back in here to sleep for the night?" It would have broken the spell but Roxy was incapable of saying it and Zeeq knew it.

This strategy worked on Katrina because she craved David. The dark can only magnify that which is already inside an individual and Zeeq had plenty to work with. If all they had felt was pure, balanced love, there wouldn't have been any negative actions the dark one could have used against them.

Somehow David was on to this strategy; he knew it was Zeeq. Despite all of Katrina's or Zeeq's pulling on him, David remained balanced and clear.

"Wake up, Katrina," David said, rubbing her arm and forehead.

"Where am I?" she said, looking confused. "I don't belong here. I need to go to my own bed." She lifted the covers to get out of bed.

Zeeq knew that Roxy would want to let Katrina go but somehow Roxy was able to encourage Katrina to stay.

"No, Katrina, you belong here," David said. "We love you. Lie back and relax. It's okay. That's it." David tucked Katrina back into bed, aware of how much he loved her.

This strategy entertained Zeeq for a week. He watched Roxy fidget. Each night it began at ten o'clock, and lasted until two in the morning. Roxy beamed unconditional love into Zeeq to melt him away but her emotions were still too much in the way.

During the day, Zeeq's attacks took on a different form. One Saturday afternoon Roxy heard the familiar sound of the front door creaking open but not closing. That's strange, she thought. Suspicious, she scurried to the bathroom to check on Katrina, who was supposed to be taking a bath. Sure enough, Zeeq had Katrina, nude, running down the drive.

"David!" Roxy shrieked.

David, outside chopping wood, lifted his head to see Katrina on the run down the drive, unclothed and glimmering wet. He dropped the ax and ran.

Mid-stride, David threw his arms around Katrina and drew them both to a halt. He managed to do this before the neighbor's house came into view. Zeeq fought David with a vengeance but Katrina's cells remembered David's touch and their natural chemistry was re-ignited. Love spread through her body and Zeeq, who was rendered weak and useless, faded from the scene. Katrina's body, leaning against David's, regained its own consciousness and strength.

"How'd I get here?" Katrina asked, baffled. Then she looked down and realized that she had been taken for another naked jaunt. "Great! Just great!" she said, shaking her head in disgust. "I'm fine, David." She wiggled free and headed back to the house to finish her bath.

"Guess you'd better watch her more closely, Roxy," David suggested.

"Got it."

Zeeq frequently took Katrina wandering, often nude, into the woods or down the road toward their neighbors, summer or winter.

Roxy and David remained on constant vigil.

Truth That Sets Us Free.

Indulgences . . . Comfort Zones
Can ruin whomever they own.

—Keith Amber

12

Transforming The Core

"You have an addiction to sex, Katrina," Athena said to Katrina's Light body on one of Katrina's journeys-while-in-trance. Tenaiia was in Katrina's physical body, speaking to Roxy.

On top of everything else, this was the last thing Katrina wanted to hear, though some part of her had been aware for some time that there was a problem. She could never seem to get enough sex. When she was satiated, it never lasted very long. She had confided in David that she thought she was a nymphomaniac. The idea made her shudder. Now someone was addressing the issue, someone she trusted.

"This is understandable, child," Athena continued, "for it is a result of a gift that you have been given."

"Gift! It doesn't feel like much of a gift. It's more like a plague!"

"You have chosen a heavy 'work' life that carries with it much stress, one that will give you little time to play. You will be burdened with great responsibility. For this reason, Arianne felt it necessary, and wise, for you to have a potent release valve. You have been given the gift of sexuality. This gift will help you to balance difficulty with pleasure. For you, the sexual experience takes you through bliss to other worlds, other dimensions."

Katrina knew this was true. She'd experienced it as often as she could. However, there was a flip side. "It drives me nuts. The need never goes away."

"Yes, gifts such as this one cannot be ignored," Athena agreed. "It was understood that in your early years this gift would cause you problems without a steady partner. This has caused your imbalance, your addiction. We do not scold you here, child. It is merely time for you to approach the problem and balance the addiction. For your Trinity to succeed, this must be addressed."

"What are you suggesting, Athena?"

"That you refrain from making love with David for a period, until you are able to turn the problem around. You must find balance from within."

Katrina knew that Athena was right. She was relieved to tackle the issue but the very nature of this obstacle made it difficult to "go without." It was even worse now; the few times she and David had made love together caused her to fall in love even deeper. She couldn't help herself. Married or not, Trinity or not, all Katrina knew was that David already lived inside of her. Although she didn't understand any of it, thoughts of him consumed her every waking moment.

"Katrina has the gift of sexuality," Tenaiia told Roxy that same sunny afternoon while in Katrina's body. "Without a steady, natural sexual outlet during her teenage years, she became obsessive and addictive. It is time for her to find a sexual balance. It is time for her to turn this addiction around. She will not have any more sex until she has accomplished this task."

Roxy sighed in relief. "The *gift* of sexuality?" she asked.

"Yes," Tenaiia said. "For others without this gift, sex is like crossing the ocean in a small sail-boat. For Katrina, it's crossing in a luxury cruise liner. Also, Katrina, like David, heals through sex. You do not. You are not connected to sex in any of the ways that Katrina and David are."

Roxy saw the writing on the wall. David and she would dwindle to the occasional session, while Katrina's and David's sexuality—with Roxy's blessing—would flourish. She shuddered. Later that day, after David returned home, she asked if she could talk to Leviticus.

"Greetings, Dear One."

"Is this Leviticus of the Light?"

"Indeed it is I," Leviticus said. "Shall we go for a walk? It's a lovely day!"

It was a warm seventy degrees. Most of the snow was gone, except in the deep shade of the Douglas firs and high up in the glacial region of the mountain. A warm breeze caressed their faces as they talked. Puffy clouds drifted by and an oval, lenticular cloud surrounded the mountaintop. It was curved like a roller coaster track.

Despite the wind that moved the puffy clouds, the lenticular cloud remained, unaltered in its position, for their entire hour walk. They monitored it at every break in the tall pines. It had a magnificent energy about it, as though it was alive.

Leviticus held Roxy's hand on occasion in order to balance her energies. "Very well," he said, "What was it that you wished to speak with me about?"

"My emotions; they are driving me nuts. Frankly, they're driving everyone nuts!"

"Indeed, they are. It is time, is it not? Very well, what do you wish to know?"

"Everything! How do I get through them?"

"Ah! yes. Very well, let us begin with the emotional body. You act, Dear One, as if you *are* your emotions."

"Well, that's how it *feels*," Roxy whined.

"Indeed, yet it is not so. You see, you have an emotional body just like you have a physical body. You also have an auric body, a spiritual body, and a mental body. You already know that you are not your physical body and in the same way, you are also not your emotional body."

"I had no idea it was separate. It feels so *me*," Roxy said, shaking her head.

"Indeed! Yet it is not," Leviticus said. "Your emotional body is merely a lesson that your soul must, at some time, embrace en route back to the Godhead. You see, you haven't always had an emotional body. When you complete the lessons of the emotional body, you can then choose whether or not you wish to have emotions ever again. There are many lessons that souls must embrace before rejoining God. The emotional body is one. Service is another. Mastership of self is yet another. Do you understand, Dear One?"

"You mean emotions are not an automatic part of the human existence?"

"That is correct."

"We aren't stuck with them forever? There's a way through them or something?"

"Indeed, there is a way through them."

Roxy was hooked. "How do I get through them?"

"I thought you'd never ask. To mature the emotional body, Dear One, you must include unconditional love with *all* emotions."

"Are you serious? That's impossible! I mean, unconditional love with anger, jealousy, hate? Is that even possible?"

"Indeed, it is possible and it has been done by many before you, Dear One. Commander Ashtar, for example, is complete with his emotional body. He has chosen to have a band of compassion. He feels that this enables him to better complete this mission. David also has a band of compassion and very limited emotions. He is mostly complete with all the lessons of his emotional body. Have you not noticed that it takes a great deal to get him riled?"

"I thought he was repressing his emotions."

"Sometimes that is so; people do repress their emotions. Sometimes, however, they either do not have an emotional body, or they are complete with these lessons and have matured all their emotions into unconditional love. It isn't all so black and white, Dear One. Have you not noticed the occasional child who appears mature and wise at a young age? Or the old person who still has many tantrums and emotional explosions?"

Roxy thought for a minute. "Yes, I see what you mean."

"The mature child," Leviticus explained, "is mostly finished with his emotional body. He is mature at a young age because he brought with him mature emotions. The emotional adult is still in the early lesson of the emotional body, which is why the emotions are still so out of control. Another example is a family with four children. All the children are essentially raised the same, yet all have various emotional states. One is always angry, one is mature, one is sad, and one is happy, happy, happy. Do you see? They are all in different stages of their emotional bodies and all have a different focus."

"I see," Roxy said, fascinated. "How many lifetimes did it take David to reach this point in his emotional body lessons?"

"Twenty-seven. Mind you, it takes different amounts of time for each soul. Some take hundreds of lifetimes, while others do it in far less."

"How many have I done?"

"You are in your fourteenth."

"How close am I to being finished with the emotional body lessons?"

"You are about half way through. However, your intent in this lifetime was to mostly complete it. This is partly why you chose this Trinity, to give yourself a vehicle to get through your emotional body."

"Rather daunting, don't you think, Leviticus?"

"Perhaps, but very do-able, Dear One. You are infinitely capable of the task at hand. It would be wise for you to remember that."

"Okay, I'll try. Where is Katrina in her emotional-body lessons?"

"Though she has had several lifetimes on Earth, this is only the second lifetime where she's had an emotional body with her."

"Second?"

"Indeed. This is all quite new for her. She is quite activated, is she not?" Leviticus smiled.

"I'll say. No wonder she's a walking time bomb. God, what a mess," Roxy said. "Okay, tell me again: How do I get through my emotions?"

"With pure, unconditional love, Dear One. You must choose to experience all of your negative emotions simultaneously with love."

"With love?" Roxy wondered how to do that. Jealousy and love, anger and love, forgiveness with love.

"Indeed," Leviticus said, listening to her thoughts. "When you include love with negative emotions, the negative emotions begin to melt into love. Remember, we all have God within us. God *is* love. Indeed, we are all capable of experiencing love at all moments, as God does. Try it, Dear One, and you shall see!"

Love ... jealousy. Love ... God! Roxy sighed loudly.

As Leviticus continued listening to her thoughts, he added, "Do not let your ego get in your way, Dear One. Your ego will want to be right; it will not want you to include love. Beware of your ego," he warned and then was gone.

Roxy pondered the ramifications of this information for days. It all fell back to choice. To progress, she had to *choose* to include love with the pain, with the jealousy, with the hurt. It was frightening. Yet that was exactly what her Higher Self wanted her to do—mature *their* emotions.

A few days later Leviticus reminded Roxy that her soul, while in mastership training, had completed the section on subconscious programming.

"Would you help me to remember what I know about subconscious programming?"

"Indeed. You begin and I shall add as necessary."

Roxy wrote and then said aloud, "I *accept* Katrina and David's lovemaking."

"How does that feel inside, Dear One, when you repeat it aloud?" Leviticus asked.

"I accept Katrina and David's lovemaking. Tension, tightness in my solar plexus."

"Very well. How does this feel? "I *bless* Katrina and David in their lovemaking."

Roxy repeated, "I bless Katrina and David in their lovemaking. Oh, that has a real punch."

"Very well, Dear One. That is the feeling that says you are transforming the core of the matter inside of you. Do you see?"

"Yes, I see. God, this stuff's really confrontive!"

"Indeed. And it works! You shall see."

After further work, Roxy came up with the first of many sets of subconscious programming. It went like this:

I am joyful with Katrina and David's lovemaking.

I bless Katrina and David's lovemaking.

I am releasing all jealousy around Katrina and David's lovemaking.

I release all jealousy.

I am peaceful.

I release my need to be in control.

I am no longer controlling others.

I am living in the flow.

I am unconditional love.

I am loved.

I am whole.

I am an aspect of the Universal Power Source.

I am love. I am all. I am one. I am God.

Very little of this was Roxy's immediate truth but it was the truth she desired to become. The process of repeating one's desired truth empowers it into reality, from the inside out. While those using traditional affirmations tend to pull, will, or desire God or the universe to bring them something or someone from outside themselves, subconscious programming works internally and demands that the soul transform negative unwanted patterns. Subconscious programming is self-transformation, not begging, forcing, or willing.

Roxy evolved her subconscious programming weekly over a period of a year. When the intensity of the sick feeling in the solar plexus lessened, she would turn up the heat, using a more powerful phrase to keep the punch alive.

As she transformed, she went from, "I Bless David and Katrina in their lovemaking," to "I enjoy David and Katrina making love," to "I am lovingly giving Katrina and David time to make love."

With a lot of hard work, progress was made. With progress, came increased self-worth.

Roxy's formula was to repeat each line three times, doing the whole set six to nine times per day. She included Bach Flower Remedies, homeopathic flower tinctures to promote emotional release and transformation.

It was Leviticus who suggested that Roxy add the last four lines to help empower her self-worth and experience that she is one with All That Is, as everyone is.

During these times of upheaval, it was comforting for Roxy to remember that God was within her, guiding her. Often, as she recited her programming, she remembered why she had chosen such a difficult path. It empowered her to mature her emotional body, so that she could be instrumental in providing Earth with a Melded Being. Through their mission, Katrina/Arianne could then make a tremendous difference in transforming the educational system. These were the thoughts that fueled Roxy forward despite the pain.

Who Are Lightworkers?

People who know that freedom
Comes from within,
Regardless of their circumstances.

—Jack Clarke

13

To Serve With Love

Both women were in the front yard enjoying the summer sun when Tenaiia came through Katrina to talk with Roxy.

"How many times did David make love to Katrina last month?" Tenaiia asked.

"Six times."

"Do you think this is what a Trinity is all about? Tally keeping?"

"No," Roxy said, "but I'm stuck, and scared to let go. I'm afraid that if I let go, they'll be making love all the time. I don't feel I can handle that."

"I understand, Roxy," Tenaiia said, "yet, you are here to serve. Do you know what that means in this Trinity?"

"No, I guess I don't know. Service is kind of foreign to me."

"Service is what *all* souls eventually aspire to be at-one with. Serving God, in all of its many aspects, is the true path to enlightenment. That is, to serve with love and joy. It is your job, for example, to ensure that Katrina's needs get met first."

Ensuring that others got their needs met first scared Roxy to death. She didn't trust that God was taking good care of her. This mistrust originated in Roxy's Higher Self. The circumstances of Roxy's soul's youth left her with the feeling that her needs were not being met. From that the selfish pattern of "I want my needs met *first*" emerged. Roxy was here to change that pattern in herself and in her Higher Self.

For Roxy to do this, she would have to adjust her perspective, which would in turn adjust her Higher Self's perspective. Her Higher Self needed to notice that her needs were met during her youth, though it hadn't fit her picture. The way she was raised had its purpose and was designed for her learning. Roxy and her Higher Self had to learn together to trust God. The Trinity was the perfect catalyst.

"Let us look together at how you can serve in The Trinity, through caretaking," Tenaiia said. "Can you give me any examples?"

"Prevent Katrina/Arianne from Zeeq-manipulated jaunts?" Roxy offered.

"Yes, that's a good example. What else?"

"Keep her fed four or five times a day when she's home, diplomatically, of course. She's constantly fighting us, and she forgets all the time."

Katrina flirted with the fringes of anorexia because she wanted to be thinner. Without sufficient grounding food, she could not keep *all* of herself firmly anchored on Earth. Being grounded was vital in maintaining the Melded connection.

"What else?" Tenaiia asked.

"Keeping the house and the clothes clean."

"What else?"

"Sexuality," Roxy regurgitated. "Caretaking Katrina/Arianne means ensuring that *all* her needs be met."

"Very good, Roxy. There's one more. Do you know what it is?"

Roxy thought about it. "No, I don't. What is it?"

"Very well, Roxy. The last on your list of services is that it's your job to break through Trinity issues first. This will help you to tap your inner reserve of strength. Once you have broken through, then Katrina will break through the same issue in about a three-week lag time. This is a great gift you give to Katrina and yourself. Breaking ground is always the most difficult. This is the only way that you will access your own hidden strength."

Back to that damn inner reservoir that lies just beyond pain, Roxy thought. My least favorite. "So how do I change my selfish pattern?"

"By choosing two, four, ten, a hundred times a day, the new unselfish direction. These patterns change because you no longer give them energy, no longer follow their lead because you choose an unselfish path instead. Do you understand?"

"Yes." But she didn't like it. As David's and her relationship diminished, it was her job to peacefully allow David and Katrina more time alone. Then, in three weeks, Katrina would break through and allow David and Roxy time alone.

Roxy was scared. She didn't trust Katrina but she forced herself to forge ahead, finding that inner reservoir. Now her programming included being in service and including love with all emotions.

Tenaiia delivered the next blow. "Katrina has been working with Athena out in the universe on her journeys-while-in-trance and has made significant progress in transforming her addiction to sex."

"How far has she gotten?"

"She is sixty percent complete."

"Wow! That's great!" Roxy lied. "Soon she'll be ready to make love again!"

"I believe she is ready now—today!"

The vacation was over; there was progress. The punch in Roxy was less potent.

"Are you excited?" Roxy asked Katrina later that day.

"Yes," Katrina admitted. "I really miss him. But I'm also nervous."

"Why?"

"Because the Guides will be testing me. If I fail, or if I don't continue transforming my addiction, then sex will be taken away again."

They made love that night. Katrina *had* changed. She pulled less on David. She was passing her test.

Roxy trusted Katrina more, was less activated. The Trinity inched forward.

Who Are Lightworkers?

They are people seeing problems
As lessons,
Perhaps in a long series of lives and lessons.

—Jack Clarke

14

Ethereal Emotions

With summer vacation came a quickening of The Melding connection between Katrina and Arianne. In the initial stages, Arianne's ethereal consciousness had to spend time on Earth not influenced by Katrina.

To anchor The Melding union, which would be complete before Katrina went back to school in the fall, Katrina had to remember her ethereal roots. Most of that was accomplished on her journeys-while-in-trance. More difficult was the flip side of the process: Arianne had to develop as a human while in her ethereal awareness. It was fascinating and enlightening. Over the summer all the veils that separated Katrina's physical world from Arianne's ethereal world melted and dissolved.

For Arianne to be versed in the human existence, she had to come into Katrina, remove Katrina's training as a mortal, and be trained herself. Basics such as how to eat, dress, and drive all had to be relearned. It was amazing to realize that Higher Selves send down aspects of themselves to experience a life on Earth yet they have no clue of how to survive themselves. That's what infancy is all about: learning the ways of Earth.

As a Melded Being, Arianne had to be versed and competent in the human reality and Katrina had to be versed and competent in being ethereal because they lived in both dimensions simultaneously.

The closest analogy would be someone on his deathbed. One moment he is talking to a person at his bedside who is comforting him and the next moment he is speaking to unseen spirits or dead loved ones who beckon him forward into the other world. The dying person is a conduit between the two worlds, the physical and the ethereal. Just like the dying person, Katrina would be aware of her physical surroundings while concurrently aware of her ethereal surroundings. And Arianne would experience a human existence without the veils designed to separate the two worlds.

Unlike the trance-like state of a dying person, Katrina would be fully conscious. The focus would not be so much about non-physical loved ones on the other side, but rather the ability to tap invaluable universal knowledge pertinent to her completing her mission, information that was available to Arianne at every breath.

Until now, The Melding consisted of Arianne speaking through Katrina while Katrina was lying down, her eyes closed. This was an odd channeling position that only Arianne used. It was actually less of a channeling and more a bleeding through of consciousness. This would change over the summer months as Arianne got stronger on the physical plane and learned how to manipulate Katrina's body with greater ease, the way Tenaiia was versed in doing.

As The Melding continued its anchoring process, Arianne was available more often and the conversations were enlightening from a myriad of directions. For instance, she had great difficulty speaking English because her favorite incarnation was lived in France so her language of choice was French. She never learned English, only her incarnation, or lower self, had. Initially, Arianne spoke only French to the Plumbs until she learned English, which she did on the ethereal plane.

This struck Roxy as curious. All the Divine Guides who spoke through Katrina or David spoke English. Roxy took it for granted that all Guides did. Then she thought about it and realized that ethereal Beings probably didn't even speak. Master Merlin later told her that they use telepathy, or thought transference. This shed more light on what life is like on the ethereal plane, where most of Earth's inhabitant's Higher Selves live.

"We are attempting, in this lifetime," Arianne began one afternoon, "to complete the entire lesson of our emotional body."

"But Leviticus said this is only your second lifetime working on your emotional body. Is that even possible?" Roxy asked.

"It is possible. However, it will be extremely difficult, though we have certain advantages that make it possible."

"Advantages?"

"You see," Arianne said, "Katrina has an ability, through the Melded connection, to see the perfection of any situation quickly. She does not stay stuck in the emotions for long."

Roxy had observed Katrina's capacity to experience the pain of the emotions and see the underlying truth in the same moment. Her emotions dissipated quickly and she again found love.

"But she's always so jealous! She's worse than me!"

"That is because I am funneling all of Katrina's emotions through jealousy," Arianne said.

"But why? Why jealousy?"

"Because that is an easy access point," Arianne said. "There are many opportunities for her to experience jealousy, are there not? In that way, she works through the emotions more frequently; therefore, faster."

"I'll say! God, no wonder she's completely activated *all* the time. What a mess." Roxy paused. "What's it like for you to feel emotions on the ethereal plane?"

"It is extremely painful," Arianne said. "You see, pain does not move in an ethereal body as it does in the physical body. It is much more painful, like a searing pain. In the physical body, there are nerves and nerve endings, which were prepared specifically for the emotional pain to move through. Emotional pain disseminates outward, toward the nerve endings, until it loses its intensity and is no longer painful. You see, Roxy, the physical body is designed for the lessons of the emotional body. In part, that is what God made the physical existence for—to go through the lessons of the emotional body. It's surely the easiest place in the universe to do them. Yet so many resist because it's painful. I assure you that it's far more painful to do it in the ethereal body."

"So when you're fully Melded, will you also feel emotions as Katrina does?"

"Yes. Katrina will feel the emotions through her nerves and I will feel them as a searing pain because the veils that normally shield me from the pain will be removed."

"Then why do those lessons in this Melded lifetime if it's so painful?" Roxy asked.

"Because we have a great advantage. I remind you that with the ethereal perspective always available to Katrina, she can process through the emotions quickly, finding truth easily. You see, when you find the underlying truth below the emotional upset, the emotion loses its activation.

"For instance, say you are angry at Katrina for wanting to make love to David. Then you realize that this is another opportunity for you to gain in your strength, so it's actually a gift. When enough of you realizes, and can accept it as the gift it is, it becomes difficult to remain angry any longer. So for us, in one sense, it's more difficult because of the pain in my ethereal body but in another sense, it's much easier because Katrina processes the emotions rapidly."

"Yes, I see."

One night while David hugged Roxy, he got an erection. He turned to snuggle Katrina but she fired off emotionally and bolted out of bed. She got dressed and headed for the garage. David followed.

"It really activates me," Katrina said, "when you hug her and get an erection. It makes me nuts. My jealousy goes crazy thinking that you want to make love to her. Maybe that's what you should do, go make love to Roxy."

"I wasn't being sexual, Katrina," David insisted. "It was an involuntary response. I think the Guides did it just to push you through your jealousy. Please come back to bed. I love you, and it's very late."

"Are you sure you don't want to make love to her?" Katrina persisted.

"I don't want to make love to Roxy, I just want to get some sleep. I love you," David assured her, stroking her arm.

"I love you, too."

"Can we go get some sleep now?" David took her by the hand and led her back to bed.

Truth That Sets Us Free.

To Get Through an Obstacle,
Become one with it.

—Keith Amber

15

Mastering Thoughts

The women wanted to know and David was stuck in the middle. From Roxy came, "What did you and Katrina do while I was gone?"

Katrina said, "Did you enjoy your time with Roxy after I left for school?"

The questions were loaded. David's answers were simple and consistent. "I don't know. I don't remember."

Beneath the surface, Roxy had brewed over David's claims for years, until Tenaiia brought the question to the surface.

"I understand you have a question for me, Roxy." Tenaiia asked after coming into Katrina's body.

Roxy thought for a moment, then the nagging question zinged into her consciousness. "Yes, I do. I'm tired of David's always saying 'I don't know,' or 'I don't remember.' Is it really true?"

"Yes. David has the gift of forgetfulness."

"Gift of what?" Roxy asked.

"Of forgetfulness. David's soul has a photographic memory. Unfortunately, his soul developed an arrogance over this ability. For that reason, his Higher Self chose to incarnate with the gift of forgetfulness, to humble his arrogance. This is also a vital gift in preserving The Trinity. Do you think life here would be easier for either you or Katrina if David remembered everything?"

Good point. The less information David offered the two women, the less ammunition they had to obsess with or argue over.

David sighed in relief at hearing the answer. He'd wondered for a long time if something were wrong with him, the way he forgot things all the time, though of late he found it to be a useful condition. Leviticus telepathically interrupted David's thoughts. "May I come through to speak with Roxy ?"

"Sure," David telepathically responded and Leviticus entered David's body.

"Hello, Dear One." Leviticus was bright and cheery.

"Is this Leviticus of the Light?"

"Indeed, it is I."

"To what do I owe this great pleasure?" Roxy smiled.

"Tenaiia and I wish to make a suggestion to you," Leviticus said. "It is felt by The Troops that you are ready for the next step in your process."

"Next step?"

"Yes. Do not worry, Dear One, it is not all that bad! You see, it is felt that it is time for you to learn how to master that vast and skilled mind of yours."

"What do you mean?"

"Do you not think it would be wise for you to begin to screen your thoughts?"

"What do you mean?"

"You must think before you speak. You must choose what you shall allow yourself to say, to control what comes out of your mouth rather than having your words control those around you."

"Time to let go of the reactive verbal barrage? Is that what I'm hearing?" Roxy blushed.

"Indeed," Leviticus smiled. "Begin to take a moment to notice your thoughts before they are said. See if they are what you really want to say."

"Are they aligned with your intent?" Tenaiia added.

"This technique used properly," Leviticus assured Roxy, "will begin to starve out your emotional body."

"Un-fed," Tenaiia added, "the emotional body withers, dies, and is replaced by unconditional love. Fed, the emotional body flourishes forevermore."

"Have you not voiced the negative emotions enough?" Leviticus asked. "Is it not time to evolve your emotions onward? Is that not what you desire, Dear One? Again I remind you, evolving the emotional body falls back on choice. You must choose the direction that you allow your emotions to go. Will you control them, or will they control you? This will also give Zeeq less ammunition to work with. Is that not what you also seek to accomplish?"

"Yes. I got it," Roxy said. "Notice my thoughts before they're said. Decide if I really want to say them. Control myself rather than use my reactions to control others." She breathed heavily. "Okay, I'll do my best. Time for mastery, is it? Time to thwart Zeeq by giving him less to work with?"

"Indeed, Dear One," Leviticus said. "You shall see, you will feel better about yourself as you walk this path. I must depart. In Love and Light." He placed his hands, palms touching, at his chest and bowed his head in namasté, honoring the God presence in all of creation, and was gone.

This, too, was added to Roxy's internal programming.

Truth That Sets Us Free

Perseverance is one of the necessary keys to success.
It builds character,
The Soul's building blocks.

—Keith Amber

16

Souls From God

Master Merlin channeled through Katrina to speak to Roxy and David, a rare event in itself. Merlin, a busy soul, made himself available only when it came time for nudging their lives in specific directions. He left the question and answer sessions to Tenaiia, Leviticus, and Athena. However, in a good mood, Master Merlin offered to answer a question or two before he got down to business.

"How are souls born out of God on the ethereal plane?" Roxy asked.

"On the ethereal plane," Master Merlin said, "it is quite different from how humans procreate on Earth. The two ethereal bodies of the parents-to-be do not 'connect' as physical bodies do; rather, it's more like a prayer. Once two souls decide to request the birth of a soul from God, they sit facing one another and meditate together, sending the request by prayer to God: 'If it be the will of God, may a soul come forth from God to bless us.' If God chooses to send a new soul, the soul is usually likened to both parents, since like attracts like."

"Do the souls come out young or old? Are they raised by their parents?" Roxy was fascinated.

"Similar to Earth, they emerge from the Godhead in their infancy. On Earth, it is the infancy of one incarnation of a Higher Self's many incarnations. On the ethereal plane, it is the infancy of the soul itself. It is valuable to note that Earth is merely a denser mirror reflection of the ethereal plane and much of what exists on the physical plane also exists on the ethereal plane, in a more refined form, or higher vibratory rate. As such, there are family units on the ethereal plane, although quite often young souls are raised predominantly by one of their parents.

"Souls can be 'born' out of God onto any plane. Some souls never experience the physical plane or the ethereal plane, and on up. You see, there are no rules in this area. The Great Radiant One chooses. Wherever the soul out of God lands first is its home base for the first phase of its existence. Then the soul can choose incarnations on other planes, in other worlds and with other souls. As the soul evolves, its home base continues to raise to the higher planes until it ultimately merges back into the Godhead. Of course, this takes millions of Earth years to accomplish. There is much in God's grand universe to experience.

"Getting back to business, I must ask you now, Dear Lady, to depart our company. I have instructions for the ears of this one only," Master Merlin said, nodding in David's direction.

Roxy's curiosity skyrocketed but there was no point in pushing Merlin; it never worked and only made him irritable.

"When Roxy's soul was young," Master Merlin began once he and David were alone, "a mere ethereal child, her father called upon Leviticus, a master teacher, to teach her the ways of her soul. She and Leviticus immediately resonated. Their bond was potent, even though she was far younger than Leviticus. You see, Roxy's soul, like Leviticus', was talented and a quick study. And like Leviticus, she had a propensity to boldly go where few others ventured. As student and teacher, and as friends, their essences were similar, familiar. Over time, their love became eternal and their respect for one another immense. Whether they are together or apart, their bond and love flourishes."

David wondered why Master Merlin was telling him all this, although it sure made some things fall into place. Like why Roxy always craved talking to Leviticus, and the feeling of profound love that remained inside of him after Leviticus left. In all the years that he had loved Roxy, he had never felt as intense a love for her as Leviticus did. That puzzled him, though he'd let it go.

Master Merlin pulled David from his reverie. "I speak to you of this today because Roxy will soon be thrust into a process which will require you to allow her to move through it very much on her own. Katrina has similarly been coached. I must depart."

"How will I know?" David asked before Master Merlin departed.

"You will know." Katrina's eyes closed and Master Merlin was gone.

Four days later, Roxy and Leviticus, who was channeling through David's body, were walking through a dense patch of majestic Douglas firs. Spongy moss flourished under foot and colorful lichen clung to the south side of rocks and trees. They wandered into a small clearing where they found wild delicate pink and white Mt. Shasta lilies in bloom. The sun's backdrop was a vibrant blue, and birds chirped in harmony. In the distance, peacocks screeched.

"How old is my soul?" Roxy asked.

"Thirty-four million Earth years."

"Wow, that's old."

"In fact, it is quite young, Dear One," Leviticus corrected.

"Well, how old is David's Higher Self?"

"He is forty-six million Earth years old."

"And Katrina?"

"Seventy-eight million Earth years old."

Just as Roxy was about to ask about how spaceships were made, Leviticus interrupted her. "Dear one," Leviticus began, an unusual sternness in his manner, "you are here, in this Trinity, where circumstances involve the life and death of Katrina, are you not?"

"Yes."

"Do you not think that it would be wise for you to focus your insatiable curiosity on matters related to your process?"

Roxy rolled her eyes. "Yes, I suppose."

"I will no longer answer any more questions unless they pertain to your process, or that of Katrina or David. You must learn how to control your curiosity. Teach it to be the great asset that it can be, not the out-of-control child that it is."

She tried but her mind went blank. The time Roxy spent with Leviticus was such a joy that it was impossible to discipline herself. Living with her process so many hours of the day, she craved her time with Leviticus, wanted it to be fun, light-hearted, enchanting. It was her escape.

For three days Roxy attempted to ask the right questions. "How am I doing in my process? What more can I do? How is Katrina doing?" Roxy was going nuts.

Then the inevitable occurred.

"If you ask one more inappropriate question, Dear One," Leviticus warned, "I will be forced to withdraw, answering no more questions until you change this pattern."

The thought frightened her. Yet the inescapable came to pass. On the fourth day, she failed.

"I will return when you have gained sufficient control of this pattern," were Leviticus' final words as David's body left the room.

Roxy doubled over in pain as a wave of shock rolled through her body. Trembling, she rocked herself on the blue tropical couch as she cried. The pain was debilitating, inconceivable.

Katrina walked into the living room. "What's wrong?"

"Leviticus left," Roxy said between gasping sobs. "He won't come back till I transform my addiction to asking questions."

Katrina understood about being forced into a corner like that. Still, Katrina was in a near state of engulfment herself. Besides, the Guides had coached her as they had David. She abruptly turned and left, leaving Roxy to get through this on her own. The catharsis ensued for several minutes. Then Roxy picked herself up and forged ahead.

Roxy now had to deal with transforming this pattern on top of her other lessons. In her time away from Leviticus, Roxy saw her out-of-control curiosity. She also realized that their relationship was, in part, based on her unhealthy dependency on him. It was also time for that to change.

Roxy's approach was to remember the importance, the value, of each lifetime in a soul's evolution. A physical life may seem long, but it is a mere pinpoint in a soul's existence. Roxy reminded herself that she was here to learn her lessons and to do her process. Knowledge about the universe was not forwarding her where it really mattered: keeping Katrina alive.

And she remembered that when she died, she had to answer to God, her Guides, and to her Higher Self about what she had accomplished while on Earth. What remained undone would have to be addressed in another lifetime. There was never an escape.

As for the dependency, Roxy realized that, in the absence of Leviticus, a new independent strength began to surface. She found herself more capable, less dependent. She was surviving without him. Her inner strength began to flourish and an independent maturity emerged.

Leviticus had been gone for a month when Roxy braved the question, "Can I talk with Leviticus for a few minutes?"

David paused. "Yes, he'll speak with you."

Cathedral bells rang for joy. Though Roxy would be tested and monitored to ensure that she continued progressing forward in these lessons, her friend was back. And just in time for the "hate process" to begin.

Who Are Lightworkers?

They are people who feel they can change the world
By changing themselves,
Not by trying to change others.

—Jack Clarke

17

Unconditional Love

They sat on the front cement steps outside the living room door, soaking up the warm June sun. A gentle breeze caressed their faces, reminding them that summer had snuck past winter. Roxy had already asked Tenaiia about Apollo (the code word), so Katrina's consciousness had been flung to some faraway place where she couldn't hear the conversation.

"Katrina is driving me nuts lately," Roxy began. "I can hardly be around her. I don't know what to do about it."

"The problem, Roxy, is that you have a backlog of unexpressed emotions dating back to your childhood. Also, you have never learned how to safely, and wisely, express those emotions," Tenaiia counseled.

"I suppose you're right. My mother wasn't too much into experiencing emotions besides anger. The pain scared her," Roxy agreed.

"It is time for you to work through your old emotions, your old hate, Roxy. That is what is feeding your current feelings towards Katrina."

Roxy was skeptical; the idea frightened her. Was it safe to be honest about how she felt toward Katrina? Was it safe to dredge up all those old feelings? What would Zeeq do with more hate and other negative emotions rumbling about? And what of her progress of including love? Would she lose the ground she'd covered?

"The problem is, Roxy," Tenaiia said, eavesdropping on Roxy's thoughts, "that you can only go so far on the path of love with repressed hate and other negative emotions buried underneath. It is time to address your unresolved emotions."

Unresolved emotions, Roxy thought. That nasty slew prudently tucked away in the back corner of her inner feeling world in a box labeled DANGER! DO NOT ENTER.

"But how can I caretake Katrina if I have all those negative emotions surfacing? Surely that will give Zeeq unlimited fuel for his antics."

"I assure you, Roxy, it is safe," Tenaiia said. "You have a window of time right now when you are permitted to take some space from watching over Katrina to do your hate. When David is not present, I shall watch over her. Use your time wisely, Roxy. Go and heal those old emotions. Get them out of your system. It is time!"

A wave of trust flooded over Roxy. The Guides-of-Light, who can catalyze with precision—always in alignment with people's prebirth contracts—melted the walls of Roxy's inner box. She noticed as she slipped out of Katrina's sight just how much she hated her caretaking duties. The barrage had begun.

The Trinity issues were a miniscule portion of the feelings that needed to be freed. Roxy possessed a truckload from her childhood. Lost, and still holding residual judgment over the idea of regurgitating these old emotions, Roxy asked her friend Leviticus for help. Leviticus held the flashlight as Roxy wandered through the dark corridors of her repressed emotional world. Together they exposed the old feelings and wounds, adding understanding to the mix. To do this, Roxy had to embrace the perfection of each experience and see the lesson, the purpose, in it for her. Once she saw the perfection, or the value of the experience, it was difficult to remain attached to the residual negative emotions. Then she was able, with love and forgiveness, to transform her old feelings, wounds and hate into Love and Light.

This all produced a terrible sick feeling in the house. For four weeks Roxy could taste hatred's vile, rotten taste. Katrina and David squirmed over the hate permeating every corner of their home; it took its toll on everyone. Katrina was sure Roxy hated her forever. As Roxy vented at David about Katrina, David was thrust into the middle. He defended Katrina. He couldn't support Roxy as he had in the past. Their lives were evolving.

"This process sure doesn't feel very good," Roxy said to Leviticus who had come into David's body. "It feels like the negative emotions are so destructive."

"It depends on what you do with them, Dear One. It's important to remember that emotions are not good or bad. In fact, Light and dark are not good or bad, they simply are. God loves all. God has no judgment that the dark ones are bad. The dark is here to help teach the Light, albeit through adversity. It is how you deal with dark emotions that is important, not that you have them. You see, Dear One, you have dark inside of you. Your jealousy, control issues, and hate are all a part of your soul, the part of your soul which is dark. I understand that it is your intention to grow beyond these dark emotions. This intention is what keeps you firmly anchored in the Light. So, as you experience the negative emotion with the intent to love, you remain anchored in the Light and the emotion slowly transforms into love. It melts; it does not remain in the dark."

"So because my intent is to transform the negative emotion and not stay stuck in it, or positioned, then it will eventually melt into love? I have to *want* to go into that direction, to transform it into love."

"Exactly," Leviticus smiled.

"But it irks me to even think of myself as being like Zeeq." Roxy shuddered.

"Zeeq is not bad, he is simply doing his truth, the same as you are. And as Zeeq does his truth, you get presented with a myriad of lessons and opportunities from which to grow and learn. Zeeq is doing the best he knows how to do, albeit dark. His soul, at this junction of his overall existence, is committed to, and anchored in, the dark. There is nothing wrong with that. We all go through our dark lifetimes and periods in our soul. We all choose to have at least some lifetimes focused predominately in our dark areas. We do this so we can fully experience all that the Creator has given to us to experience. We must also balance the karma and learn lessons by living these lifetimes.

"Earth is a giant schoolground serving humanity, which has been anchored in the dark now for centuries. Zeeq and his emissaries have controlled Mother Terra for their turn. It is now time for Terra to be back in the Light. The dark ones do not want to give up their control. This is the great torque, confusion, and battle at hand. Just look at the world; conditions are escalating daily."

"I had a dark past life of my own," Roxy remembered. "I was a gladiator in Rome, one of the best gladiators of my time. Tortured and killed many Christians. Not too proud of that. Humbling."

"Indeed you were, Dear One," Leviticus smiled. "We have all had a lifetime—or several—like that. It may seem unpleasant, yet we must remember that we all go through such lessons on the way back to God." Leviticus paused. "You see, Dear One, as individuals like yourself choose to experience your hate with the intent to move through it, release it, and heal it, then you help yourself, those around you, and humanity in general."

"Humanity? How so?"

"As you anchor more Light in you, you then can anchor love and Light more fully on Terra. The Light helps everyone. It is like each individual becomes a dot of Light which, added to the others who are becoming enlightened, keeps multiplying, expanding, and overlapping till all of humanity becomes one huge combined force of Light.

"The more dark in your soul that you are able to transform into Light, the more Light which you then anchor on Terra. Intent is the key, Dear One. Those who hate, blame, make excuses, or hold anger with no intent to heal, continue to anchor dark on Terra through the dark emotions of deception and hate in themselves. This is true of all of the negative emotions. What is your intent while you are experiencing the emotion? To hold onto the emotion or to heal and transform the emotion? After all, eventually each soul must experience all emotions. One must fully embrace each emotion, feel it, and marry it with love"

Roxy became proficient in seeing the lessons, their perfection, forgiving, releasing, immersing further, deeper into love. She learned not to judge any emotions and to embrace them all in love.

During the process, David bonded further with Katrina. Katrina trusted Roxy less for weeks and against Roxy's preference, David and Roxy's relationship faded further. Caretaking responsibilities were edging out their relationship.

Now, amid all the hurt, she was able to embrace Katrina—and Zeeq—with love.

Who Are Lightworkers?

Those that know that
The season has come
To make FORGIVENESS Universal.

—Jack Clarke

18

Power of Love Over Dark

David was exhausted from caretaking by himself when Roxy pitched in again. The pressure had been building all month long with Katrina on summer break. Though she had volunteered as a teacher's aide in the elementary school in Mt. Shasta, she was still home every day from noon onward so, naturally, Zeeq was present more. With more time on her hands, Katrina wanted to spend extra time with David.

That's when the phone calls began.

It was a hot Thursday afternoon and Roxy was at one of her jobs, on her hands and knees. Her face was hot and red and sweat dripped onto the wet floor. Her back and knees ached as she scrubbed the wax off the kitchen floor. Then the phone rang at one o'clock. Roxy knew who it was; the request had already reached her through the psychic airwaves.

"Roxy, the phone's for you," Roxy heard from the living room.

Weary and apprehensive, Roxy took the phone. "Hello?"

"Hi," came David's voice.

"Hi. What's up?" The tension rose in her body.

"Katrina wants to make love," David said.

"I see," Roxy answered, not wanting to arouse the suspicions of her employer. "Well, yes," Roxy forced the words out, "I suppose that would be fine."

"When do you expect to get home?" David pushed.

"I'll be home by two," Roxy lied.

As she continued scrubbing the floor she could not keep her mind from wandering to their lovemaking, another strain-filled opportunity to work through her jealousy. At two o'clock, her mind was again set free and the anxiety lifted as she continued scrubbing the floor.

Struggles were abundant but there were also little successes. Isolated days popped up where the three managed to all be in love together. Each time this happened, the experience rendered Zeeq incapable of penetrating any of their auras to cause disruption.

"Let's go for a walk, Roxy," Katrina suggested. "David, wanna come?"

"Sure," David smiled.

"Where to?" Roxy giggled.

"How about the meadow? It's all abloom," Katrina glowed.

Clad in summer shorts and T-shirts, they all headed, barefoot, out the front door. The peacocks greeted them by strutting their bright blue-green plumage. The beautiful Shasta lilies were vibrant with their pretty pink spots. Birds chattered and the pungent scent of the Billy goat permeated the air.

Katrina grabbed Roxy's hand, then David's, and ran across the grass over to the meadow. Yellow daisies were everywhere, floating atop the tall, lush-green grass.

Katrina grabbed two choice strands of grass and handed one each to Roxy and David to chew on. The taste was fresh and green, the blade rough and scratchy. No one ever mowed the meadow, leaving it for the neighbors' geese, goats, and peacocks to frolic and graze in. Katrina giggled as she pointed out a caterpillar.

Roxy noticed Obsidian, the stray cat who'd adopted them, cavorting and chasing through the grass.

Katrina paused to gently hug David, then turned and invited Roxy to join them. Their energy was bubbly and calm, until Katrina started to tickle David. All three hit the ground, giggling. David squirmed to get free.

"If only we could keep this mood, this space forever," Roxy wished.

"Really!" Katrina added. "Like, is there some magic potion in a bottle we could drink to make all those nasty emotions go away forever? Maybe we should ask Merlin if he would help us."

"Oh! That it were so easy," Roxy giggled.

"It could be this easy all the time," David laughed.

"Go to hell, David!" the smiling women snickered back.

Three hours with no sign of Zeeq was extraordinary. That, they discovered, was the power of love over the dark.

Another minor success occurred a few days later.

Roxy geared up for the weekend. She was determined to maintain a keen awareness of her thoughts, to restrain herself from making typical jealous comments. As Roxy prepared dinner the phrase, "I hate myself," plunked into her mind. Confused, she asked David if he would channel Leviticus for her.

"Greetings, Dear One," Leviticus cheerfully began.

"Is this Leviticus of the Light?"

"Indeed it is I. And what can I do for you on this Friday eve?"

"I just noticed a thought in my head that isn't my truth. I heard 'I hate myself.' You know that's not how I'm feeling right now," Roxy said.

"Well done, Dear One! You have caught Zeeq in the act. He placed this thought in your subconscious mind to thwart your progress. Your keen awareness allowed you to catch this implanted comment designed to sabotage your progress. He wishes to perpetuate the weekend arguments and prevent the three of you from becoming aligned. You have rendered his strategy useless."

"Are you suggesting that Zeeq has done this before?" Roxy's stomach turned.

"Indeed I am! The dark often use this kind of strategy on unsuspecting people to keep them stuck in negative patterns. The dark will place self-negating comments in unaware minds and the individuals think they are hearing their own thoughts. At times they are, and at times they are not. Discernment is crucial. Comments such as, 'I'm no good,' or 'I'm too fat,' or 'I'm not lovable,' or 'I'm not smart enough.' It is difficult to find one's own self-worth when one is so focused on negative thoughts, is it not?"

"I see your point."

The ramifications of Zeeq's implanted thoughts disturbed Roxy. She wondered how to warn others.

Truth That Sets Us Free

God is interested in growth, not punishment.
You can't change who you were or what you did in the past.
But you can learn from the past
And change who you are and what you do today.

—Keith Amber

19

Arianne

With Katrina's summer school finished, it was time to complete the transformation of transforming Katrina into a mature Melded Katrina/Arianne. During this final transition, David and Roxy enjoyed Arianne's presence in pure, unfiltered form because Katrina's consciousness was elsewhere. Arianne had to learn for herself how to act, survive, and fit into a physical culture. The experience was like teaching a brilliant adult child the ways of the world, dressing, eating and proper manners for starters.

Katrina, David, and Roxy decided to indulge in having breakfast out. Their typical out-in-the-world-strain was intense over who would sit with whom in the booth. Katrina was frustrated that she had to hide her "marriage" with David. Roxy was frustrated because she had to choose between self-indulgence—sitting with David—or The Trinity alignment, sitting with Katrina. This time she sat with Katrina.

Omelets ordered, Roxy noticed that Katrina was looking at her spoon, turning it round and round as if inspecting it for the first time.

"What's wrong?" Roxy asked.

"I do not know what this is, or what it's for," she said, still looking at the spoon.

"Is this Arianne of the Light?" Roxy guessed.

"Yes. Were you expecting someone else?"

"Uh ... no. What are you doing here?"

"I am learning how to eat! Is it not time for food?"

"Yes, soon."

"Very well. What is this for?" Arianne still looked at her spoon.

"Ah, yes. This is a spoon. Here, I'll show you. Hold it like this," Roxy said, showing her. "Then you put food on the spoon and put the food into your mouth."

"Why do you not use your fingers?"

Good question. "It's bad manners," Roxy tried. All David did was shake his head and shrug his shoulders.

"What is this 'bad manners'?" Arianne persisted.

"Manners. Um ... well, manners are how other people expect you to act, especially in public. It's how to be socially acceptable. Adults use manners." Even as Roxy said it, her answer seemed empty. Something that she'd accepted all of her life now seemed useless. Why not eat with your fingers? But Arianne was not here to change these rules; she was here to learn them.

"I see. Very well, show me this again. Yes, I see. Very well. Now, where is the food? This body is *very* hungry."

"Hungry? I thought Katrina said that she wasn't very hungry!" Roxy said.

"Katrina has not entirely told you the truth! She wishes to get thinner so she suppresses her hunger. It is not good for her to do this. Where is the food? This stomach is *very* hungry!"

"Soon. It'll be here soon!" Roxy appeased her. "How is The Melding coming?"

"It is progressing on schedule. It will be complete soon," Arianne answered.

"Do you like being Melded?" Roxy asked.

"I do not like it or dislike it. It just IS. We shall endeavor to do the best job that we can."

"What's it like being one of only six Melded Beings on Earth?"

"It is a great responsibility, a heavy burden, and a remarkable opportunity. We are simply focused on the task at hand."

"Does transforming the educational system seem enormous to you?"

"For Katrina alone it would be insurmountable. As part of a Melded team, Katrina will have vast resources and knowledge from the universe at her disposal, making the job quite manageable. The future does not disturb me. We simply address each day as it comes."

"Couldn't Katrina do this mission by being psychic rather than going through all this to become Melded?"

"It would be too difficult, even if she were a very gifted psychic. Tapping such vast resources at all moments throughout her career would be much too great a strain. And it is unlikely that she could remain clear enough at all times. It is only through a Melded connection that she would be able to maintain crystal clarity while easily accessing the information and techniques she'll need to be successful."

The omelets arrived.

"What is this?" Arianne asked, pointing at the warm, yellow pile in front of her.

"It's an omelet. It's made of eggs."

"Very well." Arianne picked up her spoon.

"Here, Arianne, use your fork. Hold it like this." Roxy instructed her in the art of cutting a piece of omelet free, then stabbing it with the fork and shoving it into her mouth.

"Mmmm, tasty." Arianne gobbled until every morsel was consumed. Then she rubbed her stomach like a child, delight written across her face.

David paid the check while Arianne and Roxy went to the car. Enroute home, Katrina returned to her body, moaning, "Why am I so full?"

"Arianne came in and ate for you. She said you were starving!"

"I see!" Katrina was outraged. She needed the weight, and food, to ground herself. The immense Light and higher vibration that came with The Melding connection produced a spacey, or dizzy, feeling. If a Melded person is going to be of any value, a clear, crisp mind is needed. That was why Katrina had been given such a large body, to make grounding easier. But in a society where thinness is worshipped, Katrina fervently fought her destiny. Against wisdom she attempted to starve weight off continually. Tenaiia, Arianne, David, and Roxy struggled to sustain her eating. The battle raged forever.

As Roxy watched over Katrina a few days later, they soaked up the sunshine. "Look Katrina! The horses are looking up at the top of Mt. Shasta."

"They're listening to the music from the cathedral that rests atop the crest."

"Cathedral? Music?"

"Yeah. There's the Hall of Masters, ethereal, of course," Katrina said, "and they usually play music. It's a celestial type of music, like the sounds I can always hear when I'm on my journeys-while-in-trance. You know, the universal sounds that heal. Anyway, there are always some Masters gathering for one reason or another in the Great Hall. It's really beautiful—tall spires reaching into the sky and walls that you can kind of see through, like translucent walls of color in deep shades of purple and rose. Kind of looks like big stained glass windows that emanate color from the inside out."

"I guess you've been in there before?"

"Yeah, and so have you, David, too. You go in your dream state and probably don't remember."

Roxy kept watching the horses, whose fixed attention was on the cathedral, until she noticed Katrina pick up a rock and look at it with the awe and wonderment of a child.

"What are you doing, Katrina?"

"I am Arianne," she replied, turning the gray, jagged rock around in her hand. "This spirit has a delightful essence. And look! A blue sky. Where I come from there is a purple sky. And the sun. Isn't it magnificent?"

Arianne put the rock down gently so as not to damage it and walked over to the grass. "Isn't this wonderful? Such a healing green. May I taste you?" she asked the tall blade of grass. Arianne pulled it carefully from Mother Earth, broke the root off, and put it in her mouth. Her eyes lit up like a Christmas tree. "So earthy!" she exclaimed. "Look!" she said, pointing to a squirrel and walking toward it.

"That's a squirrel," Roxy instructed. Arianne had such a peaceful reverence that the squirrel allowed Arianne to pet it. "You are a wise soul, my little friend," she said. "Thank you for treating us to your antics of play." The squirrel scurried off, gathering a pine cone on the way.

"What is the smell in the air?" Arianne inquired.

"That's the billy goat. Pretty rude isn't it?" Roxy said, scrunching her nose.

"It is not rude," Arianne corrected, "it is natural. Can we go for a walk? These legs require exercise. Katrina does not exercise this body sufficiently."

"Sure. Let's go this way."

Roxy was captivated. They didn't walk far before Arianne stopped to inspect the tree bark. "What is this?"

"That's lichen; it's like a fungus, a plant that grows on the tree."

"Can you hear the tree breathe?" Arianne asked Roxy. "Its energy is so soothing." She hugged it then looked up and saw a robin take flight. "God's creatures are magnificent." They walked on a little further until Arianne became fascinated by a group of ants. "Look at their camaraderie! Aren't they amazing."

Arianne saw the brilliance in everything and had a reverence for all of God's divine handiwork in every molecule on Earth.

The next visit came on an intense keep-an-eye-on-Katrina Saturday. David was chopping wood. Roxy puttered around the house, every few minutes checking on Katrina, who was studying in preparation for fall semester.

Then Katrina disappeared.

Roxy ran through the house. No Katrina. "DAVID! KATRINA'S GONE!"

David, their finder of lost lambs, dropped his ax and ran.

Roxy freaked out, pacing back and forth in front of their house, looking in all directions. She had failed. The minutes ticked by. "Katrina!" Roxy yelled, to no avail. Back in the house, she looked in every corner, every closet. No Katrina.

David sprinted down the driveway. He peered deep into the forest, then to the left into the open field. "Katrina!" Still no Katrina.

Roxy went to the backyard that abutted the creek. No Katrina. Then back to the front yard, "Katrina!" she yelled, begging, "God, please help David find her. Shit, I blew it. I should have been more attentive."

David passed the furthest point where he'd previously gone in search with no luck. He picked up his pace as urgency rose. "Where could Katrina have gone?"

Roxy's breathing was labored. The minutes lasted forever. Seven … eight … nine eternal minutes passed. Roxy paced, squinting her eyes to see as far as possible. This was the longest it had ever taken David to find Katrina.

Ten torturous minutes later, David and Katrina walked down the drive. No, wait, Roxy thought, that's not Katrina. It's not Zeeq, either. That's Arianne!

As they had reached the front door David said, "This is Arianne."

"I know," Roxy sighed. Arianne was dubious and always wore a glow. Katrina was physically sure of herself and wore a forlorn look. Arianne continued to experience everything around her as fresh and new. Time and daily stress meant nothing as she paused to marvel at God's creations: the pear tree David had planted, the beautiful purple pansies, the billowy clouds, the goats chewing on a can in the meadow. Nothing was taken for granted—dirt, rocks, sky, chipmunks.

"Where did you find her?" Roxy asked.

"She was down on the neighbor's property, about three blocks away. She was just about to let the horses out of their corral."

"Yikes! What were you doing there?" Roxy asked.

"I heard the horses calling for help. I followed their voices, 'til I found them. They told me that they did not want to be held captive. I was just about to set them free when David came and stopped me. I do not understand." Arianne looked bewildered, sad for the horses.

David shrugged his shoulders.

Here we go again, Roxy thought. Ignorance can be bliss. So the horses are unhappy? What to do, what to do?

"I'm sorry for the horses, Arianne. Really sorry, but they belong to that farmer and we cannot set them free," Roxy explained.

"Belong? How can one soul *belong* to another soul?" Arianne was baffled.

"It's man's law! If we set the horses free, we will be breaking that law. And if we do that, we could get into trouble."

"The horses do not wish to belong to that man!" Arianne persisted. "Is there not something we can do to help them?"

It pained Roxy's heart. "I'm sorry. They have no choice," Roxy insisted. "We must leave them where they are."

"Very well. The horses must have karma [lessons] to learn." And Arianne put it to rest.

"Arianne, you scared us half to death, disappearing like that," Roxy pointed out.

"I am sorry. I did not mean to worry you," Arianne said, surprised.

"Will you tell us before you wander off again?" Roxy asked.

"Yes, I will tell you," she smiled.

Katrina's school was due to begin in a month and Arianne needed to be familiar with the campus. Acting on Tenaiia's suggestion, David and Roxy planned to stroll around the campus with Arianne on a Saturday before school began. The first priority of the day was proper attire.

"What shall I wear?" Arianne asked Roxy. She was naked in her bedroom.

"How about jeans?"

"Jeans?" Arianne questioned, bewildered.

"Here." Roxy offered her Katrina's favorite pair of comfortable jeans, guiding Arianne into the pants. "You'll also need a bra."

"What is this for?" Arianne asked, looking at the large bra.

"Here, put your arms through these holes. There. Now bend over and put your breasts into the cups."

"Cups? Does Katrina usually do this alone? This is very awkward."

Breasts inserted, Roxy said, "Stand straight. There you go. Here, I'll hook the back up."

"Yes, this does feel familiar to this body," Arianne conceded. Then on with a top and she was dressed. Whew! They packed a picnic and off they went.

David drove. Roxy sat in the front seat, Arianne in the back. As everyone commented on the vivid blues and greens of the forest, Arianne asked David, "Does it not bother you to drive so slow?"

"Slow? What do you mean? I'm going sixty-five miles per hour," David said.

"You usually drive at the speed of light," Arianne told David. "This is so much slower. Are you not bored?"

"So, David's Higher Self drives a spaceship?" Roxy perked up.

"Oh! yes. He is a master navigator!" Arianne announced. "With the battle going on with Zeeq, David's Higher Self will not allow me to fly on my own, even though I am an experienced navigator."

"No, I'm used to it," David smiled.

"So the battle is also being fought on the ethereal plane as well?" Roxy asked, intrigued.

"Yes. Zeeq is unrelenting in both dimensions." Arianne sighed, exhausted.

"So David's Higher Self is a master navigator," Roxy said. "That sure makes sense, huh, David? You're as masterful as anyone I've ever seen at finding your way around, even in brand new cities. Even when we move to new cities, you act like you've been there before."

"This is quite common," Arianne said. "You each carry many essences of your Higher Selves—all humans do. For example, Roxy, your Higher Self is extremely competent at being organized. The room where she lives on the ethereal plane is always impeccably clean, just as you keep your home."

When they arrived on campus, Tenaiia telepathically guided Arianne around, telling her the exact location of each class she would be attending in one week. When Arianne was as grounded as Katrina regarding the location of all the rooms that she would need to find, they left for the park.

"Can you see the fairies over there?" Arianne asked.

"No," Roxy said, "but I can sure feel their presence."

After a time, Leviticus channeled through David. The conversation turned to recalling a job David and Roxy had where they rolled dice to win money. David and Roxy had used a thoughtform to roll high numbers, winning more money. As Roxy shared the story,

Arianne's facial expression soured. Alarmed, she turned to Leviticus and said, "This is a dark use of thoughtforms!"

Roxy looked at Leviticus, bewildered.

"She is correct! You used it for greed!"

Roxy paused, and then realized that she and David had used a tool of Light, a thoughtform they had created of Light, to forward their dark side, their greed. Their intent had been focused on self-gain. A lesson well learned.

The final visit with Arianne came during the Harmonic Convergence. Katrina and Roxy took a rare venture out together to listen to Saint Germain speak through a new local channel. Saint Germain, a gentle, refined Guide-of-Light, works in team with Jesus/Sananda on the ethereal plane and with many spiritual seekers on the physical plane. This was the channel's first public appearance.

As Katrina and Roxy sat in the theater waiting, Roxy whispered in Katrina's ear, "Would Arianne discern for us just how pure this channel is?"

After listening to the channel say questionable phrases like "party hardy" and looking like an archaic version of King Henry VIII stomping around the stage, the session ended.

Roxy turned to see the dancing eyes of Arianne present. "What did you think of the channeling?"

"She did not channel," Arianne announced.

"You mean, at all? Saint Germain never came?"

"That is correct. It was merely an act, a performance."

"I remember Leviticus talking to us about this, but I didn't think it was this widespread. Does this happen often?" Roxy wanted to know.

"Often enough."

Who Are Lightworkers?

They are people who see others as
Not better than nor less than,
But rather different than themselves,
Yet part of the same whole.

—Jack Clarke

20

Eternal Love

Before The Melding, Katrina was competent and independent, functioning perfectly on her own. But with The Melding came spaciness, occasional confusion, and Zeeq.

David and Roxy were caretakers whenever possible, and, in their absence, Tenaiia filled in. Tenaiia drove when necessary, ate as needed, attended classes, and even took tests. Moreover, Tenaiia picked up a conversation—mid-word if necessary—when Katrina floated out into the ozone, a frequent occurrence. Tenaiia could resemble Katrina with such perfection that no one ever suspected. She even snuck past David and Roxy.

Katrina disliked the caretaking. The fact that simple things sometimes eluded her, like forgetting to eat, putting her clothes on backwards, or placing a plate only half way on the shelf so that it crashed to the counter, drove her nuts. She'd fallen into the habit of calling this state "jell-brained." As long as Katrina could remember, she'd been competent. Sometimes she wondered if she'd ever get all of her "brain" back. Looking into her eyes it was obvious when this condition was present; her eyes, her presence were elsewhere.

In the company of David and Roxy, Katrina was always jell-brained. It served everyone's lessons. Katrina had to let go of her control issues. Roxy had to let go of her selfish side. David had to neutralize the inevitable sparks. These lessons were the current focus of the three of them. For that reason, David and Roxy were surprised when Katrina announced that she was going to see her mother for the weekend. This meant a vacation from their constant dance with death. And a weekend free from crashing through emotions.

Katrina had resisted the notion of visiting her mother; it brought up even more issues. She loved her mother, but she didn't like her much. And she didn't like standing up to her. Leaving David to Roxy broke her heart.

Still, Athena urged Katrina to go. "Your caretakers are in need of rest. It would be wise for you to face your mother. It is time to hold to your truth."

"Okay, I'll go," Katrina caved in, "but only for the weekend!"

The next day Katrina's eyes screamed, "I love you," into David's as she left.

Vacation! Vacation! Vacation! David and Roxy breathed for the first time in months. Layers of exhaustion melted off their auras. Even David, more in love with Katrina than ever, was exhausted and grateful for the break.

Saturday was playtime. They splurged on wine, made a picnic, and headed to a beautiful Mt. Shasta glade. The sun was bright and warm and birds chirped everywhere. Wild flowers of purple, yellow, white, and pink were profuse and a sweet aroma filled the air. Car-sized smooth boulders were speckled across the meadow. They found one with a flat top and set up their picnic.

They chatted, walked through the meadow holding hands, and stopped to hug now and again. Calm for the first time in months, they noticed that their love and friendship was intact.

That evening they built a campfire in their backyard, toasted marshmallows, and relaxed in peace. Leviticus channeled through David to talk and share in the vacation merriment.

"I have the answer to a question of yours which you have had for a long time," Leviticus began.

Roxy perked up.

"The reason, Dear One," Leviticus continued, "that you yearn for me, is that I love you unconditionally. What you experience in my presence is unconditional love. It heals you. Indeed, Dear One, my love for you is eternal."

"That's what it is," Roxy mumbled, shaking her head to and fro, "unconditional love. God! That's what unconditional love feels like? When you come into David's body, an energy fills the space that soothes me like none other. I feel safe and loved. It's peaceful and calm. When you leave, the space feels empty."

"This is my gift to you on your vacation, this knowledge. It is not that David does not love you, Dear One."

"Yes, he does love me," Roxy agreed, "but not like this. Not unconditionally and to the bone. What a great gift. Thanks. I love you, Leviticus."

"Indeed, and thank you. Now I must go. In Love and Light."
Leviticus bowed his head in namasté and was gone.

David and Roxy watched stars for hours. There would be no battle
tonight.

On Sunday, Katrina called, lonely for David. "My jell-brained condition isn't permanent!" she triumphantly declared. "I've only needed
a little assistance from Tenaiia." Her worst fears, that her condition
was permanent, were eased.

For the rest of Sunday, David and Roxy rested and made love numerous times as they had so many years ago. Months of weariness
dissolved from their bodies. Roxy desperately wanted to be ready for
Katrina's return on Monday. But she wasn't.

She awoke Monday morning with the realization of Katrina's impending return thundering into her consciousness. Her stomach went
sour. She felt overwhelmed and exhausted.

As to Katrina, she was ready to climb into the car when Athena
came to talk to her on the screen of her third eye. "David and Roxy are
in need of further rest. And you need more time with your mother.
Your process here is not complete. It would be wise for you to remain
until Friday."

Katrina forced herself to call home. "Mom is thrilled. I've decided
to stay until Friday. Can I talk to David?" Katrina blurted out in one
breath.

The rest of the week was slow and easy as Roxy resolved to peacefully allow them more time alone upon Katrina's return. However, when
Katrina's first desperate request was for time with David, Roxy's vow
vanished! As David and Katrina walked back to Katrina's bedroom,
the perpetual strain returned.

Who Are Lightworkers?

Anyone who routinely experiences
A oneness
With All That Is.

—Jack Clarke

21

Trusting The Guides

Roxy was desperate for self-worth as she sobbed to Leviticus. "Maybe if I knew more about who my Higher Self is, it would help."

"There are certain responsibilities in being given such information, Dear One. We are not so sure you are ready to take on the responsibility of knowing more information," Leviticus cautioned.

But Roxy was despondent. "Please! Please tell me something more of Shining Star," the name she believed to be her Higher Self's name.

"This decision does not rest in my hands. I shall have to ask another if the time is right for you to be given further information, and to decide what information. One moment please, while I go check." Leviticus closed his eyes. Roxy waited, sobbing.

After several moments, Leviticus began to mumble aloud what he was telepathically communicating to Master Merlin above. "I see ... very well ... just those words? Yes, I see." Then, looking into Roxy's red glistening eyes, Leviticus said, "Shining Star is a counselor."

Counselor. The word reverberated through Roxy's entire being. Her life passed before her eyes, delivering scenes beginning early in her life where her counseling skills had oozed out. "Of course, Shining Star is a counselor. It all seems so obvious now."

"You have been told this information, Dear One, for a reason," Leviticus said. "You have earned it. Your intent to transform your issues and the transformation you have accomplished have earned you this knowledge. Now you shall be expected to use it wisely. Know that the clearer you become within yourself, the more effective you will be at accessing the skill inherent in Shining Star. It comes to you bearing certain responsibilities."

"Like what?"

"You shall know soon. Now I must go. In Love and Light."

Four days later, while Roxy still basked in euphoria, Antonomn channeled through Katrina and said, "In three weeks, your first client will come to you."

"Client? How will I know who it is, or what to do?" she gasped.

Antonomn, a Guide of few words, replied, "You will know." And he was gone.

It was August. With Katrina home all summer, Roxy and David had no time alone. Roxy's body ached from a lack of touch, as Katrina's had in the past. Roxy went in search of a massage on trade. On her fifth phone call, a woman named Monica asked, "What do you have to trade?"

"I'm a great organizer. Do you need organizing?"

"No," Monica answered. "What else?"

"I clean houses."

"No, I don't need that. What else?" Monica persisted.

From out of nowhere Roxy heard herself say, "I'm a writer."

"Yes, that I could use. I could use some help organizing some of my thoughts. I could use a writer. When shall we meet?"

After housecleaning the next day, Roxy walked to Monica's, a small house of immaculately kept space. The living room had a beautiful, thick, cream-colored wall-to-wall carpet. The off-white walls were accented with lavender curtains. Several small altars on low tables displayed treasures of amethyst, rose quartz and clear quartz crystals, placed in symmetrical groupings. An empty walnut shell housed a delicately placed scepter crystal cluster. Other crystals and miniature figurines of Buddha, Mother Mary, and Jesus/Sananda were mindfully placed here and there. Lavender and pink pillows dotted the floor. There were no chairs.

"Let's sit in the backyard." Monica suggested. A giant oak tree boasted an elaborate tree house, with Mt. Shasta towering above.

Monica was petite, with dark hair, dark eyes, and an olive complexion. Her heavy Hungarian accent was harsh and she spoke to the point.

Roxy listened to Monica. After a few minutes she realized that Monica didn't need a writer, she needed a counselor. Out of nowhere, Roxy heard herself say, "I can help you break through your blocks."

Roxy was shocked. She hadn't thought those words—someone else had said them through her. As her mind rocked from the implications, in the distance she heard Monica say, "Okay. You're on."

Roxy reeled. Antonomn's prediction had come to pass.

Two days later Roxy left David and Katrina alone while she went to the masseuse. Roxy returned in a peaceful state. David and Katrina were grateful for Roxy's progress.

Roxy's first counseling session was due five days later. The evening before, she asked to talk to Leviticus.

"Greetings, Dear One."

"Is this Leviticus of the Light?"

"Indeed, it is I. What can I do for you today?"

"As you already know, my counseling begins tomorrow," Roxy began.

"Yes?"

"Well, what am I supposed to do?"

"You will know what to do in the moment," Leviticus said. "Listen to your Guides. They will tell you."

Though Roxy and David had developed their telepathic skills several months earlier, Roxy had never relied on those skills. She was frightened. What if she heard wrong? What if she sent Monica in the wrong direction?

"But how will I know if I'm listening to the dark ones or the Light ones?" Roxy asked.

"Use your discernment."

Still nervous, Roxy pleaded, "Can we begin with all the Guides speaking to you and then you tell me what to do? I know your voice and your syntax."

"Very well, we shall begin that way."

"So, what are we going to do tomorrow?"

"Dear One! Do not seek pictures," Leviticus snapped. "Simply flow with your guidance. Do not try to figure this out ahead of time. That is how you get too many of your filters in the way. Simply listen tomorrow and follow your guidance. You shall see; you will be fine."

Recently Leviticus had been nudging Roxy to release her many "pictures." Roxy would get a notion or guidance on some future event or possibility and lock onto it, leaving no room for flow or choice. She wanted to know ahead of time how situations were to turn out and what she should do. Following the flow frightened her.

Leviticus endeavored to break her destructive, insecure habit by encouraging Roxy to use windows instead of pictures. Pictures stay constant, while the view in the windows is ever-changing. He urged Roxy to flow with the possibilities of the various views through the windows.

"*Listen*, Dear One, and you will be fine!" Leviticus reminded her. "This is your destiny. You have a natural ability. We shall help you tap your gift. Trust us."

Roxy left to meet with Monica the next day. Tense, she "jumped off the cliff into the void" with total faith and trust in Leviticus and the Guides to show her the way.

She and Monica sat facing each other in Monica's tiny living room. Magic began to happen. Roxy telepathically heard Leviticus as clearly as if he were in the room next to her.

"Have her lie down," was the first instruction in Roxy's head. "Lie down, Monica," Roxy instructed. Then came specific instructions regarding the laying of crystals on various parts of Monica's body. Monica regressed into a past life that lasted most of the hour. The Guides had come through.

The next counseling session was a test. Monica wasn't home. Roxy was to go home and embrace David and Katrina's private time with love. A lump formed in the pit of her gut. After resisting her test for twenty minutes, Roxy returned home edgy.

She drove into the yard. The house was still. She went around to the back to the sliding glass window that opened into The Trinity bedroom. The heavy red velvet drapes were closed tight. Still nervous about going inside, she went around to the front of the house. There was David standing at the door, naked.

"You're back early! What happened?" David smiled.

"Monica wasn't there. Are you in the middle?"

"No, we're finished. Wanna come in?"

"Sure," Roxy lied. To pass the test, she had to go in and remain in peace.

She followed David into the house, back to where a satiated Katrina lay goofy-eyed in bed.

David snuggled back up to Katrina as Roxy sat on the edge of the bed. Her jealousy was fragile, like the hurt feelings of someone left out, and she was amazed at the calm within her.

Roxy's new-found strength impressed Katrina. David glowed with pride at Roxy's progress.

In that moment Roxy made a decision: if Katrina was going to win David's heart through weakness and need, then Roxy was going to do it through strength and mastery. It was the most potent attribute she had to contribute to keeping Katrina alive.

The counseling work with Monica continued to progress. In their second counseling session, Monica revealed that her uncle had molested her when she was a child. Roxy knew that Monica's freedom lay in forgiving her uncle and taking responsibility for her own victim pattern, the pattern that drew in the abuse.

Monica struggled with the concept. "But I was only a child!" she insisted.

"Yes, Roxy agreed, "you were just a child. However, at some point in a past life, Monica, you violated someone and the abuse in this lifetime is there for you to learn how it feels to be abused so your soul learns not to abuse others. It is your karma. An ugly experience, but still your karma, your lesson. You must forgive your uncle who will also have his karma to deal with at some point, in this life or another. And you must forgive yourself and promise not to treat others similarly in the future. Your victim pattern stems from you victimizing others in the past."

Again Roxy suggested that Monica forgive her uncle.

Monica looked at Roxy. At the Guides' urging, the suggestion was repeated. Once more Monica looked at Roxy in disbelief. Then something inside Monica that yearned to be free guided her forward. Softly she said, "I forgive you, Uncle Jim." Then, "I *forgive* you Uncle Jim." Then, screaming with solid conviction, "I FORGIVE YOU, UNCLE JIM!" With that, the dam broke and a flood of tears rushed forth.

Roxy was told *not* to hold Monica. Monica released torrents of pent-up grief, pain, and agony as the memories flooded into her mind.

After several minutes, Leviticus guided Roxy to hug Monica, who was spent.

Months later, Monica recalled that session. "You let me have my pain." Roxy's empathizing, rather than sympathizing, had allowed Monica to experience her pain and release it out of her body. A powerful experience for both women.

A few days later, David brought home an out-of-town woman who had walked into his office. David felt that Karen, on her own spiritual path, would enjoy Roxy's and Katrina's company. He was half right: Karen and Roxy hit it off immediately. Katrina went into a frump over David's spending *any* time with another woman.

As Karen talked about her current process, Roxy saw how she could help her. She prescribed specific Bach Flower Remedies for Karen and wrote down some effective subconscious programming that pierced into the heart of Karen's problem. Karen was so grateful that she paid Roxy thirty dollars, the first payment Roxy had gotten for her counseling skills.

Roxy's confidence grew.

Truth That Sets You Free.

As talents flow through you, remember:
They are not yours, or from you.
And you are not great because of them.
Be grateful to your creator.

—Keith Amber

22

Psychic Brain Surgery

Katrina was frantic for a breakthrough of her own, allowing David and Roxy to spend time alone while she was home. She picked a Saturday to announce, "You two can make love today. It's okay with me, really!"

But they didn't trust Katrina's offer. This would be a perfect opportunity for Zeeq to come in through Katrina's jealousy and wreak havoc. The only way it could work was if Katrina remained centered and love-filled in their absence. David and Roxy doubted she could do it.

Katrina wouldn't let go, determined to make progress. She offered again and was declined once more. But Katrina's persistence did not easily quit. "Really, I *want* you to."

"No, that's okay," David said.

"No, I mean it. I'm going to be fine. I want to let you two make love. You've hardly had time all summer since I've been home. I want to do this for you. Please, I'll be just fine."

"Are you sure you really want this?" Roxy asked.

"Yes, I'm sure. Really. Go!" Katrina said with confidence.

"Okay, fine," David said, surprising Roxy.

It was mid-afternoon and off to bed they went, but neither David nor Roxy totally surrendered to their lovemaking. Both cocked a vigilant ear in the direction of Katrina.

As a diversionary tactic, Katrina talked on the phone in their absence. When David and Roxy rejoined her they noticed that she was strange. Though Zeeq had not whisked her away, something was not right. Her voice was softer than usual, sort of childlike. She was calmer than normal. David and Roxy looked at each other and called, "Tenaiia," who immediately entered Katrina's body.

"Is this Tenaiia of the Light?"

"Yes! How was your lovemaking?" Tenaiia beamed.

"Preoccupied!" Roxy answered. "What's going on with Katrina?"

"Katrina has … um … how shall we say? Ah, yes. She has blown a fuse!"

"Blown a fuse?" David shrieked.

"Ah … your term would be … insane. Yes, that's it! She has gone insane." Tenaiia said, undisturbed.

"Why? How?" David moaned.

"She was unable to remain centered as she promised. With the overwhelming force of her jealousy raging inside, the pressure had to get relieved somehow so it blew a fuse in her brain, causing your lovemaking to not matter to her anymore."

"Great! Just great!" Roxy was exasperated. "We shouldn't have accepted her offer. Now what?"

"Master Zoozer is discussing this with Arianne and Athena as we speak. One moment, please."

A moment passed then Tenaiia mumbled aloud the responses that she was telepathically sending out. "Very well … yes … I see … very well." Then she focused on David and Roxy. "Tonight, after you all go to bed, Master Zoozer will send forth a team of etheric surgeons to perform surgery on Katrina's brain. They will require a space of total love so that Zeeq will be unable to interfere with their work. The surgery will take place each night for four nights. It must be done in stages. In the meantime, you must take care of Katrina."

"How old is she?" Roxy asked.

"In her mind, she is four years old."

Roxy marveled at the notion of the etheric surgery. Months earlier, Katrina had broken her ankle and was unable to walk on it. The etheric surgeons had performed the surgery on Katrina's Light body which bled through and healed her physical body. The ankle was mended in twenty minutes.

Roxy knew they were living on the cutting edge of high-tech etheric or psychic surgery on Earth. Yet it made her wonder why others, like those in mental institutions, did not also have such technology available to them. She asked Leviticus later that day as he channeled through David.

"They do not believe, Dear One. If they do not believe, then they block all such possibilities. Belief is indeed a strong barrier—and then there is the question of karma. You would not want to violate their karma would you?"

"No,"

"That is the path which they have chosen. Your circumstances here are different. It is a part of your contracts to have such technologies available to you. And, of course, you three believe; therefore, you allow for the possibility."

"But wouldn't the etheric surgeons like to make such technologies available to humanity as a whole?"

"Yes, in time, Dear One. There are not enough people ready yet to embrace such possibilities. It will require a mass consciousness shift, with an openness to *all* possibilities. We are certainly ready and available; however, we do not violate an individual's choice or beliefs."

"But what about those space-beings who abduct people all the time and do medical stuff on them?" Roxy asked.

"Those space-beings are certainly not of the Light. They are violating people. If people realized that they have a right to say no to them, to call for protective help, to call on Lord Michael, or the Great White Brotherhood, or Sananda himself, they could avert such unnecessary experiences. It falls back on discernment. People must learn to discern."

Roxy wondered when humanity would be ready to embrace the greater universe.

The surgery was another major challenge. They all went to the bed at ten o'clock. David nuzzled next to Katrina, holding her head and soothing her, creating a space of love. Roxy squirmed as she sat in a chair watching David cuddle up to Katrina while she attempted to hold a space of love. Her jealousy raged. She forced herself to focus on love.

Then Katrina went into "loudspeaker" mode as she observed the etheric surgeons. This is similar to a person who speaks in a lucid sleep state, except that in Katrina's case she reported the events occurring to her Light body on the ethereal plane.

"Who are you? What are you going to do? OUCH! ... Stop! ... Stop that, you're hurting me! ... Stop!" She thrashed about. David snuggled in closer, holding her even tighter. Roxy fought back her jealousy. What a workout.

Then Katrina went still and a deep scratchy voice boomed. "I am one of the surgeons present."

"Are you of the Light?" Roxy tentatively asked the authoritative voice.

"Yes," he said, "we are *all* of the Light. We require you to keep her head still. Have you been informed that we require a complete space of love to perform the surgery?"

"Yes." Roxy sighed.

"Very well. Then know that if this space is violated, we shall leave and not return. Do you understand?"

"Yes,"

"Very well."

David cradled Katrina's head and Roxy focused on beaming love. The tension was thick.

Then Katrina's head moved as she screamed and writhed in pain. Roxy yelled at David, "Her head's moving too much!" Anger filled the air. The screaming stopped and the room went still. Roxy gasped in fear.

"What is the problem?" the deep scratchy voice boomed. "The space has been altered!"

"I'm sorry. It was my fault." Roxy babbled. "Katrina's head moved. I thought it was a problem for you."

There was dead silence. Roxy's heart pounded in her throat.

Then the deep scratchy voice said, "We understand that you had good intent. He is holding her head sufficiently still," and he went silent.

The screaming resumed for another twenty minutes. Total surgery time was thirty minutes.

Katrina remained childlike the next day and surgery was easier the next two nights. The pain was reduced, so Katrina wiggled and squirmed less, making David's job easier. Roxy forced herself to think of nothing except love and Katrina's well-being. By the third day, Katrina was back to her normal behavior. The final night the surgery lasted a brief ten minutes.

Katrina never attempted such a breakthrough again.

Who Are Lightworkers?

People who recognize that
The Unknown
Is a part of God yet to be discovered.

—Jack Clarke

23

Discovering Humility

Out of all the Guides involved with The Trinity, Antonomn was chosen for the job of dealing with Roxy. With his intense personality and to-the-point nature, he was the perfect candidate for corralling Roxy's out-of-control ego.

The blasts, channeled through Katrina, were frequent, hard and direct. At every arrogant infraction, Antonomn would come through Katrina, aggressively pointing out where Roxy had been arrogant and her behavior inappropriate. He made it his business for a period of time to know every word or energy that came out of Roxy's mouth or was displayed in her aura. Every sign of arrogance was pointed out in loud blasting declarations.

"This is not Katrina's issue. It is yours," Antonomn declared after Roxy had pointed out to Katrina something she thought Katrina needed to handle. "You are the one with the problem!"

Roxy's eyes grew wide and a permanent lump formed in her throat. She made no comment; she could not find her voice. After three or four such sessions, Roxy feared her meetings with Antonomn. Her mind raced. She felt cornered, trapped and lost. Leviticus had warned her that her ego was a problem; Tenaiia, too; yet Roxy thought she had got it under control.

Over the weeks, Antonomn's intensity persisted. "Your ego is out of control," he'd say, using Katrina's piercing eyes to stare right through her. "Get control of your ego!"

Roxy would bolt from the channeling sessions before Katrina returned, never a wise move with Zeeq around. Or she became a crumpled, sobbing mess. The process was wrenching. Roxy had no idea what "being humble" meant. She didn't know how to recognize egocentric comments when they poured from her mouth. She was defeated as the frequent, intense assaults broke down her ego one blast at a time.

Roxy's first introduction to humility came two months into the ego-blasting process. At one of her housecleaning jobs, she found and read a paragraph about humbleness. She took a copy home. That evening, she and Leviticus talked about ego and ego-management.

"Dear One, you must begin to notice when you are defending yourself. Is that not ego?"

"Okay."

"When you think of yourself as important, is that not ego?"

"Yes, okay. I see what you mean."

"How about when you promote yourself to others? Or when you interrupt others, mid-sentence so that you can speak, is that not ego?"

"Okay, yes."

"And when your whole focus is around yourself and your needs, is that not your ego?" Leviticus hit below the belt.

"Yes, I guess that would be ego," Roxy admitted.

"Self-focus, self-aggrandizement, making others wrong, a need to be right, or a need to be heard—those are overactive egos, are they not?"

"So, how do I change the pattern?" Roxy asked, realizing the huge job facing her.

"Remember our conversation on emotions, how you are to notice your thoughts before you say them?" Leviticus asked.

"Yes, I'm still doing that."

"Well," Leviticus said, "this is the same direction to go with ego-management. You must notice your thoughts before they are said, then decide if you wish to say them. When you say comments which feed your ego, it grows. When you stop yourself from saying them, you begin to starve the ego out. Over time, the thoughts stop forming. It's a management job over the long haul. Do you understand?"

"Yes, I believe so. If I go to promote or defend myself, or make someone else wrong, I feed my ego. And excessive self-focus is a problem, too," Roxy acknowledged.

Gently, Leviticus added, "In part, your ego is out of control because of your low self-worth. Are you not seeking self-worth from outside yourself when you seek another's approval? Dear One, you must seek approval from within. Do not look to others."

Leviticus was right. The task at hand seemed enormous, though at least she had a solid direction in which to go.

In the weeks that followed, Roxy was amazed to discover the actual physical pain she experienced from parts of her ego dying. No wonder, she thought, that so few people tackle this lesson.

After two months of concentrated focus, Roxy felt confident about her progress. She relaxed her ego-management. Without management, her ego exploded overnight. Two months of aggressive effort was expunged. When she realized what was happening, she was horrified. Anything that popped into her head spilled out of her mouth. The proper intent was absent. She asked David if she could talk to Leviticus.

"The ego does not voluntarily die or stay at bay without management, Dear One."

"So you're saying that it's a life-long management process?"

"Yes, that is the nature of the ego. If you do not consciously manage it, it grows—period!" Leviticus confirmed.

So it was. Ego-management was locked into place, never to be abandoned again.

Truth That Sets You Free.

Humbleness is to crawl back to rightness,
Against the well-established self-serving compulsions of the Ego.

—Keith Amber

24

Regressing Katrina

Katrina had her plans and the Guides had theirs.

Labor Day weekend Katrina wanted some intimate time with David on Saturday, search for lichen and moss in the woods with David and Roxy on Sunday, and catch up on her enormous homework load on Monday. Even though she was only in school Tuesdays and Thursdays, she'd somehow managed to squeeze twenty-two credits into her schedule.

On Saturday, Katrina and David played, while Roxy held her reactions in check. On Sunday life shifted. David and Roxy woke to a bewildered, young-looking Katrina. Her face was that of an angelic child, soft and innocent. After their recent Katrina-blew-a-fuse episode, they grew concerned and called on Tenaiia.

"What's going on with Katrina? Has she blown another fuse?" David asked.

"She has not 'blown a fuse.' She is fine! We began a regression process on her during the night. She is three now. She completed ages one and two during the night," Tenaiia said, smiling.

"Regression process? Is she going to go through each age?" Roxy asked.

"She will go through each age that holds a meaningful or traumatic event for her."

"How long will it take?" David wondered what this process would be like.

"It depends on Katrina, on how long it takes her to work through the pain of her traumatic memories."

"What's the purpose of the process?"

"This process will allow Katrina to reexamine the traumatic events in her life. These events have influenced her way of thinking, helping her form her 'thought structure foundation,' or what you call her belief systems. As she relives the traumatic moments, it is hoped that she will be able to see deeper into the perfection of those events, which The

Melding connection can help her to do—heal and release the pain, and free up the associated limiting belief. It is the intention of this process that Katrina will release many of the beliefs which are limiting her.

"You see, people often make decisions as a result of traumatic events. These decisions are the very fabric of the belief systems which affect the rest of their lives. At the time, these decisions become protection or armor; however, as an adult, the protection is no longer needed, yet people keep the beliefs, usually without thought, and frequently long past their usefulness."

"Are we supposed to help? What are we supposed to do?" Roxy felt she was in over her head.

"She will look to you mostly, Roxy. You will need to be there for her, to offer support and listen to her. Her pain shall be released as she relives the old memories in her mind. Do you have any questions?"

"Tons! but I have no idea what they are right now!"

"You will do fine, Roxy. Relax, have fun. I must go. It is best for Katrina's consciousness to be present during this process as much as possible."

When Katrina returned, Roxy asked her how old she was.

"Three," came the soft, childlike answer.

The Guides, with their infinite abilities, transported Katrina back in time. Her current consciousness was not regressed, as in hypnosis or a past-life regression, but rather her current consciousness was *replaced* by her earlier consciousness.

It was noon, time to gather the lichen and moss for the new crystal light-boxes they were making for Christmas presents. Katrina, craving fun, had made David and Roxy promise to include her. Roxy and David wondered whether the regressed Katrina would remember. Should they wait?

"It's still Katrina," Roxy offered. "This might be really fun at her current young age."

"Yeah," David said. "Let's just take her and go."

Once in the woods, Roxy asked Katrina, "How old are you?"

"Five. See?" Katrina held up five fingers. "Five."

"What's ya doing?" Roxy nudged.

"I'm playing with my friends in my bedroom."

"What are their names?"

"Joshua and Jerry. No one can see them but me. We play dolls and sing. Can you hear the music? They're here most the time."

Roxy was astounded. Joshua and Jerry were two Guides-of-Light who frequently channeled through Katrina. Tenaiia had told Roxy that when she was four years old, her nightly protector had been Antonomn. Even as an adult, Roxy could still remember waking in the night and seeing the strange man sitting in the chair, watching over her. Now she realized that everyone is watched over and cared for by their Guides and Guardian Angels, sometimes even as children's invisible playmates.

"How old are you?" Roxy asked Katrina again.

"I'm six."

"Wow. You're getting big huh? Are Joshua and Jerry with you?"

"I don't know who that is," young Katrina answered.

Minutes later, "How old are you?"

"I'm nine," came a more mature voice. "My daddy just told me that big people don't have to talk loud."

"Were you talking loud?"

"Yeah, but daddy says we can talk loud or soft. He says when we're big people, sometimes it's best to talk soft. Other people like it better."

"Is that what you're going to do?"

"Yeah. My daddy's pretty smart. He'd know what to do. If he says talking soft is smart, then that's what I'm gonna do."

That decision still plagued Katrina because Roxy and David had to strain to hear her, often requesting her to repeat a statement, irritating her in the process. It added fuel for the likes of Zeeq, who magnified Katrina's annoyance. Katrina needed to be flexible. Arianne needed to have both soft and loud at her disposal.

"I don't like these boys," Katrina mumbled, barely audible, an hour or so later. "I'm supposed to like them, but I don't. I know dad wants me to say I like them and want them as my brothers, but I don't. That lady in that office, who was real nice to me, said that if I don't like them, and if I don't want them to live with us forever, that I can tell the judge when he asks me. But the judge never asked me. He was supposed to ask me but he never did. Every time my dad asked me, I lied cuz I didn't want him mad at me. The judge was supposed to ask me, but he never did. Now those awful boys live with me and my brother Jake all the time. Daddy says they're our legal brothers. I hate it! I hate them! They're always in trouble. They get all daddy's attention. I just hate it!"

"How old are you, Katrina?" Roxy asked again.

"I'm ten. That judge was supposed to ask, you know. He never did."

Young Katrina's life was changed forever.

Katrina's soul, Arianne, had a negative soul pattern. She craved being on a pedestal; she wanted things her way. Katrina had contracted to transform that pattern during this incarnation. To that end, her father, Bill, doted on her. She could do no wrong. This helped to anchor Arianne's dark soul pattern in Katrina and her spoiled side blossomed. This continued until around age five. Then Jake, Katrina's brother, began to be a problem. He was an agitator and not too bright. Her daddy's time was now split: he needed to help Jake out. Spoiled Katrina had to share the limelight.

Then came the addition of the three adopted brothers. Katrina was bumped further from the forefront. Since her grades were exemplary and she never got into trouble, she received precious little special time from her used-up parents. Her spoiled side was starved out, as her Higher Self had desired.

Evening arrived and it was time for David, Katrina and Roxy to go to bed. They guided Katrina to her usual spot in bed, next to David. Then, out of the blue, young Katrina declared, "I've been here before!"

"You've been where before?" Roxy asked.

"In bed, with you guys. I remember. It happened a long time ago. You know, when I was little. I woke up one night and I was in bed with you guys. I remember."

Through that experience, young Katrina's fears of being in bed next to a strange man were alleviated. Little Katrina laid her head on her pillow and peacefully went to sleep. David and Roxy gazed at each other in utter amazement.

Later Tenaiia told David and Roxy that when Katrina was four, the Guides transported her consciousness forward through time, placing her in her future body, who was lying in bed next to David. Young and receptive, Katrina felt the safety of David's presence and his love for her. After a few minutes of this experience, the Guides transported her consciousness back to its early age. This experience was designed to prepare Katrina for this precise process slated to occur years later. Now, at age ten, little Katrina remembered the experience and it allayed any fears she might have had.

In the morning, after breakfast, Roxy found Katrina mumbling to herself.

"Dad's moving out. God, I'll miss him! I can hear him and mom yelling at each other. They don't know I can hear them. Dad's been seeing men on the side. Mom can't believe it; she's really pissed. I think she's really hurt, too, but she won't admit it. She's really embarrassed. It really matters to her what people think. She thinks people won't look kindly on dad sleeping with men. No one tells me and Jake anything, like I guess we're not supposed to know."

"How old are you?"

"Thirteen. Mom and dad are getting a divorce. Dad says I have to stay with mom. I really want to be with dad. I *really* want to be with dad. Mom and I don't get along so well. Mom says I have to stay with her, though she won't say why. I think it's cuz she doesn't want me to be with dad, in case he has any men around. I wouldn't care, you know. I love my dad. It doesn't matter to me what he does, I just really love him. But my Mom absolutely refuses to talk about any of it. Dad has been sort of keeping his distance lately. I *really* miss him."

Hurt feelings abound. Her innocence was replaced by skepticism. At this point in the process, David's presence made adolescent Katrina nervous. He stayed out of sight. She wasn't so sure who Roxy was either. Roxy's repeated attempts to assure her that she was a friend of her Mom's only temporarily satisfied her. Katrina's mind grew quicker; appeasing her grew tougher by the minute.

For a year and a half, Katrina got to share her mother's time with four difficult boys and her mother counted on Katrina's help. Finally her mother, Lanna, exploded. She demanded that Bill remove the three boys, permanently.

Katrina was again one of two children living with her least favorite parent. By early afternoon, Katrina began smoking.

"How old were you when you started to smoke?" Roxy asked.

"Sixteen," Katrina squirmed and trembled.

"What's wrong?" Roxy asked.

"Dad just died of AIDS. Mom won't even talk about it. Every time I bring it up, she goes ballistic. I don't know what to do with all the mixed up feelings I have." Tears rolled down Katrina's face. "He was my favorite. I didn't care if he was gay. Mom explodes at even the near mention of it, so I stopped talking to her, or anyone, about it. Mom is ugly to be around so I just go be by myself. It hurts so much inside, I could just explode. I miss my dad. God, I miss him!"

Shutting-down infiltrated every aspect of Katrina's life. Speaking her truth became abhorrent, though Arianne needed these channels re-opened so that Katrina/Arianne could speak the truth with grace and ease.

The tension grew thicker as Katrina demanded, to know where she was, why was she there, and who Roxy was? Answers satisfied her for only seconds, until she asked again. The situation was impossible.

"Are you sure my Mom knows I'm here?" Katrina asked for the hundredth time.

"Yes. She'll be back to pick you up in a while. Really, it's okay," Roxy tried. The Guides had a difficult time preventing Katrina from seeing her image in the mirrors, which would have blown her regressed reality.

"How old are you?"

"Sixteen. Mom married Bruce. Mom, Jake, and I just moved in with him and his four kids. Shocking, the difference between being an only child to being one of six."

Her spoiled side was forced to share again. She lived in this chaos for two years, then left home to attend college a long, long way from home.

Relief spread through the house when Katrina lay down for a nap at four o'clock on Monday. She awoke at six in her current conscious-ness of a twenty-two-year-old. Everyone went out to the garage so David and Katrina could have a smoke.

"What time is it?" Katrina asked.

"It's six-fifteen on Monday," Roxy braved.

Katrina squinted her eyes in disbelief. "Say what?"

"Six-fifteen, Monday evening," David said.

Confused, she looked around the garage. She saw the lichen and moss. "You *promised* to include me!" she blasted.

"We *did* include you. You just don't remember," David exclaimed.

David and Roxy realized then that Katrina had absolutely no memory of the entire regression. Two days of time lost, the lichen was gathered without her, and none of her massive pile of homework was done.

Over time, David and Roxy noticed changes in Katrina. She learned how to speak her truth and she became more flexible in her speaking volume. Her spoiled side, "I want what I want, when I want it," remained a challenge. However the dynamics of The Trinity forced Katrina to deal with her selfish side. She had to get permission before she got her most basic need met—time alone with David.

Although Katrina never remembered one minute of this amazing process, the subconscious effects rippled outward for years.

Who Are Lightworkers?

Those striving again to be free
Particularly from
Our self-imposed limitations.

—Jack Clarke

25

Zeeq's Ongoing Antics

Zeeq's strategies began to bridge into horrifying new realms. He had creative, unlimited universal knowledge at his beck and call, plus an added measure of his own evil. Failing wasn't an option. To that end, he was up for doing anything to win.

Failing wasn't an option for David and Roxy either. Zeeq's fierce opposition challenged their convictions hundreds of times as the hours, days, and months unfolded. They stretched mentally, physically, and emotionally, attempting to keep Katrina alive.

Zeeq's schemes progressively intensified, and some there was nothing they could do to prevent.

"Here comes the snowwwwwwww...." Katrina reported as her mind was whisked off. Then her body went rigid from head to toe. She lurched off the bed in uncontrollable spasms. Her face was contorted in pain. Though it looked like an epileptic attack, Katrina had never had one before. There was a horrendous feeling that whatever Zeeq was doing was hideous.

"Tenaiia!" David shrieked.

But Tenaiia couldn't come through Katrina's body while it was frozen and jerking out of control. The twenty seconds lasted forever before the bed stopped shaking and Katrina collapsed like a rag doll. Tenaiia came to talk through Katrina.

"You called?"

"Is this Tenaiia of the Light?" Roxy was all choked up.

"Yes, it is Tenaiia." She was less than her usual bouncy self. "You are wondering what Zeeq is doing?"

"It feels horrible," David's voice cracked. His face was red and contorted.

"Yes, this is certainly Zeeq's cruel side," Tenaiia confirmed. "He is sending electrical charges through Katrina's body into her uterus. It is his intent to render her incapable of having children. He will be successful if he continues this process for more than two or three days."

"Can't you do etheric or psychic surgery to repair the damage?" Roxy pleaded, knowing how Katrina adored kids and wanted some of her own.

"Surgery is not permitted at this time," Tenaiia said. "You see, Zeeq is acting within the parameters of your contract. Although this strategy will not damage The Melding, he knows it will wear you all down. Since he does not care if he ruins Katrina's chances of bearing children, then wearing you all down is reason enough."

"How can we stop him?" David asked.

"You cannot."

"You mean there's nothing to do but watch?"

An unbearable thought.

"I'm afraid so. I cannot stop him from here and there is no way for you to prevent him." Then, looking into David's eyes she said, "This process will devastate Katrina. She will need much loving support. I must go now."

"Thank you," they mumbled.

Upon Katrina's return, she doubled over into heart-wrenching sobbing; she was bereft. David squeezed her in his arms. A tear trickled down his cheek. Roxy watched, eyes moist, lying next to David. Time halted; grief was thick in the air.

Abruptly the crying stopped and Katrina was jerked out of David's arms. Then, as if she were a mere puppet, she was thrust, a second time, into that awful rigid twitching. Her face was flushed and gnarled in pain. She looked like someone receiving shock treatment. Her body was inches off the bed, shaking and thrashing about.

"Oh God, Katrina!" David gasped. "How can I help?"

There was no response. The twenty seconds felt like an eternity.

Then, without notice, Katrina fell limp and began wailing. Everyone began sobbing as pain consumed the room. Katrina's tears outlasted David's and Roxy's by hours. Late into the night they all drifted into a fitful sleep.

Zeeq persisted with this appalling tactic for two grueling weeks, long past rendering Katrina too damaged to ever bear children again without the assistance of etheric surgery.

With Zeeq's next strategy, the instant Katrina's head hit the pillow she went into "loudspeaker" mode. She reported events that were occurring to her Light body on the etheric plane. Though Katrina spoke with clarity and could hear David and Roxy, she was unable to respond to their questions until her Light body rejoined her physical body.

"I am in a large dungeon-like room, with walls made of stone. It's eerie and cold." Katrina's body quivered as her experience bled through to the physical plane. "There are people in tattered clothing. They're glaring at me. There's an aisle in the middle of the crowd. I'm walking down the aisle."

"Something's wrong!" David exclaimed, sitting bolt-upright in bed. There was a fear in his voice Roxy had never heard before.

"Katrina!" he yelled.

Her consciousness jerked back into her body. Her eyes abruptly opened. She turned her head toward David. "Yes?"

"What's going on in there?" David gasped.

"Zeeq has this book. It sits on a podium at the end of the aisle. You know, the isle between all the people wearing bedraggled long robes. They look like homeless people. It's eerie." Katrina shuddered. "And they're all staring at me for some reason. Zeeq said that I have to sign the book that he has. He said that when I sign it, I'll be signing my soul over to him. Then I'll die and Arianne will go to his ethereal camp."

David and Roxy's eyes went wide.

"How do we stop you from signing?" David asked Katrina.

Before she could answer, she was whisked off, back to her life-threatening ethereal experience.

"We've got to stop her from signing that book!" David yelled, trying to jolt Roxy out of shock. "I've got a really bad feeling about this!"

"How? The book, and whatever she's going through, are all in the other dimension. How do we even touch it?"

"We've got to do something!" David was lost with fright.

They were horrified and out of control, their minds frantic.

"I'm walking down the isle …." Katrina began.

"Shake her!" Roxy urged David.

It didn't work.

"Katrina! Come back!" Roxy yelled. Then she became aware of a small terrible side of herself that wanted Katrina to die. Roxy shook the thoughts from her head. She willed herself to beam love into Katrina. It had no effect.

"It's not working! Nothing's working!" David wailed.

"Let's call for Tenaiia!"

But there was no response.

"Try Leviticus!" Roxy urged.

"It's no use! He can't help!" David said, sinking deeper into the pit of despair.

Leviticus and the other Guides were not permitted to help. Neither could Katrina or Arianne. Katrina's life was in David's and Roxy's hands. They were lost as to how to proceed as precious seconds, then days ticked away.

Katrina inched closer to the book each night before David's and Roxy's attempts brought her back. Screaming at Katrina, shaking her, beaming love, begging—each worked briefly, then she'd be yanked back, ever closer to signing, to certain death. Nothing worked long enough to matter. The closer she got to the book, the more intense David and Roxy became. Their intensity was all they had left in their arsenal.

On the seventh night, Katrina, again on loudspeaker, described the events. "I have reached the book. Zeeq is telling me that I must sign it. He handed me the pen. He is urging me to sign it ...."

"STOP, KATRINA!" David pleaded. It had no effect. They were lost. Roxy beamed love with a fury. Still, no effect.

David shook Katrina like a rag doll. It didn't work. Nothing worked. "I am signing the book."

David crumbled, sobbing like a frightened child. They thought it was over. Katrina was going to die. Pain surged through David. His cockiness was dissolved as tears streamed down his red, twisted face. "I love you, Katrina! You can't die this way! Please don't sign the book! Can you hear me? I love you, I love you! Please don't die! You can't leave me, Katrina. Oh God, what have we done?" His deepest feelings were revealed. Roxy watched, mouth agape.

As David's love for Katrina poured forth, it broke the spell. Katrina, who had not finished signing her name, was set free. David stumbled upon the magical key, the display of his love for her.

Katrina's consciousness returned, "You did it, David! It was your love for me that set me free. It's over! This strategy won't work any-more!" She gazed into David's sobbing face. Grinning, bold eyes shimmering, she declared, "You do love me ... you really *do* love me." She was swept away by his tearful, loving eyes. Her insecurities vanished for the moment. Roxy, six inches away, didn't exist.

Ripped to shreds, Roxy witnessed the depth of the love her husband had for Katrina. She had never seen David display this kind of love. How could David feel such a depth of love so fast? Roxy was terrified.

If it was love that motivated David to keep Katrina alive, it was fulfilling a mission that motivated Roxy; she did not experience anywhere near that level of love for Katrina. Roxy was on a mission of God's, to deliver to Earth a Melded Being to care for the ailing educational system. Her deepest desire, to make a difference in this world, kept her rooted in her commitment.

It was now painfully clear to Roxy that if she had allowed herself to react to David's display of love to Katrina, stopping him through an explosion of jealousy, they would have lost Katrina. Zeeq had counted on Roxy to lose control and stop David from expressing his feelings. Out-of-control jealousy had no place in their home anymore. It was too dangerous.

Zeeq's focus was not isolated on Katrina, either. Disabling a caretaker would put him one step closer to accessing Katrina. To this end, he frequently took shots at David and Roxy.

One evening, conditions were ripe for Zeeq. Leviticus, through David, pressed Katrina on one of her irritating issues. Roxy sat next to Leviticus, across from Katrina. Nervous, Katrina fumbled with a small piece of green tourmaline. There was a pregnant two-second pause. Katrina got the Zeeq-gleam in her eyes, dropped the tourmaline, picked up a small smoky quartz ball, and threw it at Roxy. It broke Roxy's left eye tooth in half. Zeeq disappeared.

Katrina returned in time to see Roxy's eyes bulging. Guilt swept over Katrina. She plummeted into low self-worth but the attack had little to do with her. Katrina possessed her nasty feelings toward Roxy, but not to that extent. It was Zeeq who had come through Katrina's dislike and had thrown the ball. And it was Roxy's energy pattern, or attitude, underneath it all that was responsible for drawing the experience to her.

Searing pain throbbed inside Roxy's mouth. Even so, the Guides reminded her that Katrina needed care first. With Katrina's self-worth plummeting, Zeeq had another perfect hole to come through to sabotage their efforts. Although the Guides-of-Light kept Zeeq occupied during the emergency dental work, after they returned home, David put Roxy to bed and went to Katrina.

Hurt, Roxy realized those were her lessons. Her needs were no longer top priority. Service to another, despite great pain and strain, came first.

The next day, Roxy searched for answers. She opened her Hilarion book entitled *Symbols*, an ethereal version of Louise L. Hay's *You Can Heal Your Life*.

Hilarion's book revealed that the left eyetooth symbolized "an instinctive, violent tendency toward the spouse." That hit home. As David's loyalty inched toward Katrina, a deep resentment grew in Roxy. That resentment had drawn the crystal ball to her eyetooth.

Katrina's new school schedule provided Zeeq with another prime target for undermining. With her new Tuesday and Thursday timetable, she had to leave the house by five-thirty in the morning, after three hours of sleep.

Waking Katrina at five bordered on the impossible. Zeeq enjoyed magnifying the problem; that was his job. The predicament was even worse when Katrina left the 45-minute task of bathing for morning.

Mornings were a comedy. It was as if David and Roxy were trying to wake a dopey drunk. At a quarter-to-five, in a groggy, exhausted, hoarse voice, Roxy nudged David. "It's time."

David stroked and cooed, "Katrina, wake up."

Katrina opened her eyes, then—wham!—Zeeq would put her back to sleep. David touched her again; Zeeq knocked her out once more. David and Zeeq played this game for thirty minutes, until David became frantic.

"Katrina! Wake up!" he shouted.

Zeeq allowed Katrina to receive that jolt full strength.

"What!" Katrina shrieked. "Why are you screaming at me!"

"It's five-twenty! You're late!"

Katrina hit the roof. "Why didn't you wake me sooner?" Storming out of bed, she threw clothes on at the speed of light and flew out the door. The circus was over until evening.

Weary of the strain, David sought an alternate approach. He sent Roxy off to meditate, then he began sucking and kissing Katrina until she was awake and moaning in delight. They would consummate the act in plenty of time for Katrina to depart on schedule and in a great mood. Zeeq couldn't get past this approach. There was too much love in the space. David used this effective strategy for months.

Roxy forced herself to learn how to meditate while listening to them make love. Even for Roxy, this solution beat the alternative fiasco with Zeeq.

Who Are Lightworkers?

They are people honoring
Your right to your own path,
Not theirs.

—Jack Clarke

26

Ask For Protection Daily

Roxy was working on a day not long after Katrina's summer jaunt to her mother's, when a creepy feeling overtook her. It felt like the dark ones were hovering about, even in Katrina's absence. This apprehension persisted until the phone rang.

"They came and took the car," David said, his voice heavy with weariness. David and Roxy had no money; the loss was inevitable.

"So they just came and took it," Roxy sighed.

"Yeah. I looked out the window and saw two men in dark suits hovering around the car. I ran out and they said, 'We're taking the car' and that was it."

"Did you get our stuff out?"

"Barely. They weren't exactly patient guys. I was able to grab my coat and some tapes."

Later, Leviticus told Roxy, "We are pleased that your awareness of the dark ones is expanding beyond the four walls of your cabin."

Katrina graced David and Roxy with the use of her car for a couple of weeks. Then she used her credit card to fund a used, faded and dented light-blue Rambler. The car was delicate and required David to check its fluids often and to adjust the carburetor every other day. It consumed oil as though it were gas. Nevertheless, David loved that car. Roxy did not. Nor was she grateful.

In early September, Athena announced, "It has been decided that you are to make a journey to see your friends, Tom and Jenny."

"When do we go?" Roxy asked.

"You are to journey on the third weekend of this month of September."

"Why are we going? What are we supposed to do?" Roxy was baffled.

"You will be told at the appropriate hour."

Katrina, having listened to the conversation with Athena, returned to her body. Her eyes were wild with fear. Without a word, she sprang from her chair and disappeared into her bedroom.

David followed. "What's wrong?" he asked, rubbing her shoulder.

"Just go away! Leave me alone. All you care about is Roxy anyway!"

"That's not true and you know it, Katrina," he insisted.

"Well, you'll get three days alone with her while I get to deal with Zeeq alone," Katrina retorted.

"We'll see, Katrina. The Guides know what they're doing. I don't really get why we're going anyway."

Tom and Jenny, also on a spiritual-metaphysical path, had known the Plumbs for five years. Tom, an OB-GYN physician and surgeon for more than twenty years, had shifted his focus from drugs and scalpels to counseling. Interested in helping patients learn how to heal from the inside out, he had successfully empowered several patients to "dissolve" cancer by uncovering the underlying attitudinal cause and transform it.

Tom had been Roxy's and David's counselor for about a year; then the relationship evolved into friendship.

Roxy called Tom.

"Why are the Guides sending you, Roxy?" he asked.

"I don't know, Tom. The Guides told us to make the journey. They said that we would know why soon enough."

"All right, fine. We'll see you then."

On Tuesday, three days before the scheduled departure for Portland, Athena came to talk. "It was never stated that you and David were to journey together. This assumption, although made by all members of this Trinity, *was* an assumption. It is the suggestion of the ethereal Melding Team that you, Dear Lady, make this journey alone."

Roxy's mouth fell open. Shock flooded her body. It had never occurred to her that she would go unaccompanied, leaving them alone. She was appalled.

"This is an opportunity for you to be tested in what you have accomplished in this Trinity to date," Athena said. "And also in your newly budding counseling skills. We leave the choice in your hands."

"Oh right," Roxy lashed out, "like I have a choice!"

"You do have a choice," Athena said. "You must do what you feel is wisest."

Wisest, yeah right, Roxy thought. Take David and fail the test, or go to Portland and take a shot at passing the test. Despite the stress, there was no choice.

Athena left Katrina's body and Tenaiia took over, coming into the thick, queasy energy. Confronted to her limit, Roxy requested that Katrina not be told of her good fortune. Roxy would tell her herself, once she was able to stomach Katrina's look of joy over the news. As soon as Katrina returned, Roxy ran to her bedroom.

Roxy spun in agony. The emotional task seemed insurmountable. She cried, then fumed, then fought nausea, then cried again. It took hours for her to work through the initial trauma. Then a glimmer of light began to dawn. As the numbness wore off, Roxy noticed an inner strength emerge.

The underlying layers of truth were a different story. *Subconsciously*, where jealousy still raged out of control, the only way Roxy could successfully leave was to render David incapable of intimacy over the weekend.

On Wednesday evening, while David was up in the rafters in the garage, he slipped and fell to the concrete floor. Though Roxy didn't *consciously* psychically attack David, she noticed that she was relieved by the outcome of his unfortunate accident. David pulled the muscles in his back. There would be no lovemaking over the weekend. Leaving became tolerable.

On Thursday evening Roxy announced, "You'll have a weekend alone with David; I guess your first ever?"

Katrina sighed. "And I don't have to fight Zeeq off alone!"

On Friday Roxy packed a few clothes, some crystals, food, and water. She loaded the car while David checked the fluids. "You can't drive over fifty-five miles per hour. Promise me that you won't go over fifty-five."

"Okay, I promise."

"I'm serious, Roxy!" David warned, knowing her. "This car will do just fine at fifty-five. It won't go over that; you'll blow the radiator if you do."

"Okay, okay! I promise," Roxy groaned.

"Check the oil when you get to Tom's—the water, too—and you should be fine."

As Roxy got into the car, new inner strength bubbled up. She turned the key and the engine started.

"Bye, Roxy," Katrina said, grinning ear to ear. "Good luck."

Roxy put the Rambler into gear and David said his final words. "I love you—and don't go over fifty-five. Good luck! We'll see you Sunday. Bye."

Driving through Oregon, Roxy noticed an unexpected sense of freedom; everything was out of her control. There wasn't anything she could do to influence what they did in her absence so what did it matter? The reality brought with it a sense of abandon.

Then Roxy broke her agreement and cruised at sixty-five to seventy miles per hour. She was soothed, yet haunted by her agreement. She watched the dashboard; nothing seemed amiss. She decided that David was being overly cautious and continued to speed.

"Where's David?" Tom asked when she arrived.

"Stuff came up," Roxy hedged. "He had to stay in Mt. Shasta."

After hugs, Jenny invited Roxy to join them in the living room. The pregnant question floated about: Why are you here? Roxy, not used to "living in the question," was embarrassed. Stiff and fidgety, she had no clue as to her purpose with Tom and Jenny.

After chatting for an hour, Jenny finally asked, "Do you have any idea yet why the Guides sent you, Roxy?"

"No," Roxy said, "but maybe sleep will help. I'm pretty tired. I'll meditate in the morning and see what answers I get. See you in the morning."

Roxy went to Tom's office, where she was to sleep on the large, cushy sofa. She was exhausted and lost. Then Tom appeared.

"I know why you're here," Tom began. "You're here to help me. You see, I've been suicidal for months now. The only reason I don't kill myself is that I know better. It's terrible karma, you know. Anyway, you're here to help me. I didn't want to tell you in front of Jenny because I didn't want to worry her. She doesn't know that I've been suicidal. I know that if I commit suicide, whatever I run from will only haunt me worse later."

"You're right, Tom. And I can feel the dark ones present here as we speak. They are magnifying your suicidal thoughts. Do you ask for protection from your Guides-of-Light?" Roxy asked.

"Well, I did once, years ago. I thought that that was all I had to do. Do I need to do it more often?"

"You must ask for protection every day. The Guides-of-Light, according to *God's Universal Laws of Fairness*, can only honor your request for protection for a short period of time. Then you must ask again."

Surprised and skeptical, Tom decided to take Roxy's advice. From that day forward he asked for protection daily. Roxy gave him the Father/Mother/God Prayer of Protection, along with other techniques. Years later, Tom told Roxy that from that weekend onward, he'd never been suicidal again. Roxy was grateful to have been able to help.

But that night was an awful combination of erratic sleep peppered with nightmares. The positive feelings Roxy experienced on her journey battled with the subconscious part of her that caused David's fall. The internal fight raged on.

On Saturday afternoon Roxy went for a drive. David's warnings manifested: the radiator developed a leak. Roxy put some ground ginger into the radiator, hoping it would plug the holes. It didn't.

On Sunday she was asked by the Guides to give Tom her prized citrine crystal cluster. Then, as Roxy prepared to leave, Jenny came down the stairs. Nestled in her hand was a beautiful, clear, double-terminated quartz cluster with a small slice of watermelon tourmaline lying in a crevice on top. The cluster is used for empowering internal balance. Watermelon tourmaline is used for healing heart wounds. A tear rolled down Roxy's cheek.

"Thanks!"

"Thank your Guides, Roxy," Jenny smiled.

At ten o'clock that morning, Roxy was ready to go home but problems prevailed. She had to stop every half hour to fill the radiator. The leaks grew. As Roxy went up the mountain pass, the engine steadily lost power. It was impossible to keep water in the radiator.

Then, near the crest of the pass, the radiator exploded. Steam and water sprayed into heaven. Visibility vanished and Roxy freaked. She'd broken her promise and now she was nailed.

She watched in horror as the gallon of water rushed out a hundred holes. She crept up over the pass at three miles per hour, adding a blown engine to the list of problems. The dying Rambler glided its last mile down the mountain into a motel parking lot. She phoned home.

"Hi, David. I've got car trouble."

"You sped didn't you?" David snapped.

"Yes."

"I told you not to do that. Damn it, Roxy, why couldn't you listen to me? Where are you?"

Roxy described her location. Then David asked Katrina, "Do you want to go with me to get Roxy?"

Roxy had never heard David ask Katrina what her choice was before. As caretakers, they simply made decisions for her, around her.

Roxy waited what felt like days for David and Katrina to arrive and rescue her. After David listened to the bleak story, it was clear that the car was beyond repair. They had the car towed to a nearby junk yard and headed home.

Katrina spent the three-hour journey in the back seat in a silent, numb stupor. Her time with David had been as glorious as her fantasies had promised. David had listened to Katrina's needs and promised to give her more say in her life. Over time, he honored his word. And again, she had to share David. She was horrified and nauseous.

For the two nights of Roxy's absence, Zeeq fell back on his old strategy of stopping Katrina's heart. As David endured full nights of CPR, his bond with Katrina strengthened. David and Katrina grew closer. David and Roxy shifted to being less a couple and more a team of caretakers. David also remained angry at Roxy for a long time about the car.

The car lesson was strenuous. After the dead Rambler, Katrina refused to fund another car and they had no money to buy one.

On the walls of the garage hung two old bikes that became David's and Roxy's transportation to and from work on Tuesdays and Thursdays. Up on the mountain, the cold rain was due soon. Biking into town took tons of extra energy, energy neither one had.

David's resentment filled the air. Roxy too was angry and resentful. Biking seven to ten miles in the cold, sleeting rain up and down hills helped in the area of attitude adjustments. With every push of the pedal, Roxy embraced the result of her arrogance.

One day in December, David and Roxy bundled up and put on torn plastic rain gear. As they pedaled into town, the wheels of their bikes spit sleet at their legs, and the freezing wind pushed against their chests. Even biking downhill was a laborious task.

Roxy realized that her thoughts were no longer focused on resentment. Instead, she was grateful that she was alive and well and, at worst, wet and cold. She no longer yearned for a car. She'd forgiven herself. She would not repeat that error again.

When they arrived at the place where their paths split, Roxy shared her experience with David. "Me, too," David said. "I'm not angry anymore! I don't care when we get a car."

Once they learned their lessons of gratitude, humbleness, and forgiveness and let go of their yearnings, God provided the money to buy a car. In mid-January, four months after Roxy's debacle, David received a large commission check. Roxy was deeply grateful to have a new, albeit used, car.

Who Are Lightworkers?

People who change their behavior
To create new ways
Of acting and reacting to the world.

—Jack Clarke

27

The Apathy Implant

Roxy still battled internal demons. She'd worked her way up to blessing their time alone here and there, and she contained the explosions better. However, surrendering control for a weekend, when David was whole and healthy, was still insurmountable. Indeed, there was progress, just not enough of it.

The counseling/massage trade with Monica had continued. In September, Monica decided to lead a workshop slated for mid-October. She invited Roxy to co-lead.

Monica wanted six couples. She wanted to duplicate the number twelve-plus-one, like the twelve disciples plus Jesus. Though Roxy never understood its meaning, one thing was clear: Monica wanted David and Roxy to be one of the six couples, and Roxy wanted to co-lead.

David remained aloof. He didn't feel a need for outside assistance with his process. Neither did Roxy. But she wanted to co-lead and Monica continued to apply an enormous amount of pressure for them to attend together.

On Friday evening before the workshop, David was still undecided. Then Tenaiia added to the mix. "There will be no protection for Katrina if you both attend this workshop."

The words hit with the force of a level four hurricane. Roxy had made an assumption that ethereal protection would be forthcoming. But the Guides wanted Roxy to go alone. It was her next test: to leave David and Katrina alone with grace for the weekend.

Roxy felt ambushed and incapable, and Monica wasn't helping.

Monica exerted a tremendous force, including psychic and verbal pressure, to have the Plumbs attend together. Not understanding the complicated dynamics of their home, Monica felt that David and Roxy were all too protective of this adult "cousin," Katrina. She believed that Katrina had everyone wrapped around her little finger. Monica condemned their actions. Her pressure and psychic force magnified Roxy's desire to have David attend.

Roxy desperately pulled on David to go to that workshop with all the psychic force she could muster, in spite of Zeeq's sinister presence. Roxy wondered if Katrina didn't exaggerate Zeeq's presence. Couldn't Katrina take care of herself for thirty-six hours?

David, still undecided, headed out into the yard with Roxy to make a final decision. In a moment of inspiration, David found a feather, picked it up, and said, "When I let go of the feather if it falls on the right side of that branch, I'll go. On the left, I'll stay."

He let go. The feather drifted down to the right side of the branch. Roxy felt a quiet, selfish relief. David agreed to abide by the feather. Later, Tenaiia told them that it was Zeeq who had guided the feather to its resting place.

Katrina was scared to death but she couldn't say anything. It was a test of commitment for the Plumbs. She thoroughly knew that she didn't exaggerate Zeeq's presence; she disliked his presence more than her caretakers. Hands down, Katrina would have preferred to get attention from David because he wanted to, not because he had to. Katrina also knew that Zeeq had been overactive all week long; something was brewing. For Katrina to even hint to David or Roxy the trouble she sensed forthcoming would be breaking the rules. They needed to make the decision on their own and live with the consequences. Tenaiia wasn't permitted to help, either. Those were the rules: no cheating while being tested.

The ominous Saturday morning arrived. David and Roxy departed as scheduled. Katrina bit her tongue, hiding her enormous fears. Roxy sensed something amiss but blindly trudged forward anyway. A psychic fog clouded David's mind.

The workshop was a flop for the Plumbs because a part of their consciousness remained with Katrina. Something wasn't right. They never settled.

By late Sunday afternoon, the nervous tension in David and Roxy had reached intolerable proportions. Something was very wrong. They called Katrina at home several times, letting the phone ring more than twenty times. Their guts began wrenching. At every phone call, Monica beamed more judgment; but judgment or not, they chose to leave the workshop four hours early, despite the verbal lashing delivered by the group, spurred on by Monica.

Once home, they found Katrina lying in bed, asleep. The moment both gingerly perched on the bed, Katrina's body, channeling Commander Ashtar, sat up and he began to speak. Stunned, David and Roxy listened.

"You have inappropriately left this one unprotected. The results were as follows: Zeeq came here in a physical spaceship. He took Katrina on the ship. They rode away en route to Zeeq's encampment. Zeeq then severed The Melding cord. That is when I intervened. I PERSONALLY scanned your contracts CLOSELY. I found, in fine print, a clause. I broadly interpreted this clause allowing me to legally intervene. We intercepted Zeeq's ship. I read the clause to him. RELUCTANTLY, he turned Katrina over to me. We then brought her back to this house.

"You, Dear Lady," his eyes pierced Roxy's, "are not progressing through your lessons consistent with your agreement. You are behind and the results are evident. It is time for you to put your selfish ways behind you and think of others first. I remind you of our conversation on ship one-zero during your contract negotiations. You told me that it was not necessary to test you in the area of commitment. You said that you come from a planet of commitment, that it was so ingrained you did not need to be tested. Yet I have tested you and you have failed.

"It is time to stop doing The Trinity for the purpose of getting the position you seek in the Ashtar Command. You must do The Trinity for The Trinity. I am wise enough not to make a ruling today regarding your position, as you would surely not get what you seek. You are now being given a chance to redeem yourself. *DO NOT LET US DOWN!*"

Roxy had never seen Commander Ashtar displeased; it was blood-curdling. His intensity woke something in her that never slept again.

"In order to give Zeeq a fair chance," Commander Ashtar went on, "in light of your error, we have allowed him to place an apathy implant inside of Katrina. Zeeq will not interfere, beyond the presence of the apathy implant. This will provide you with a four-day test. You have four days to get Katrina beyond her apathy. On the fourth day, you will be given a five-minute window in which you must get Katrina to say, 'I want to stay on Earth,' yet you are not permitted to give her those exact words. Do you understand?"

"Yes," Roxy gulped. "What about The Melding? Will it be reconnected?"

"That has not yet been decided." And Ashtar was gone.

Katrina's body went limp. Then Zeeq came calling. Katrina's head lifted and her muscles became stiff. Her long, red hair framed a menacing scowl as Zeeq spoke in a harsh, guttural voice. "You have been saved by your precious Commander Ashtar! I am not permitted to interfere, but the effects of my apathy implant will be evident, and hell to get past. You shall not win this one!" And he was gone. The chill remained in the air for hours. All of this over a useless workshop, judgment, jealousy and control issues. If Roxy thought one night away was difficult to embrace, she was about to discover how difficult four days present would be.

Apathy implant, Roxy thought. No Zeeq, just his apathy implant. Apathy is so totally debilitating.

"Hello." Tenaiia's voice pierced into the gloom after she had come into Katrina's body. Without judgment, she'd come to dislodge the shock from inside the caretakers.

"Is this Tenaiia of the Light." Roxy asked despondently.

"Bingo! It is I. This body is in need of nicotine. Shall we go to the garage for a smoke?"

Tenaiia popped out of bed and took Katrina's worn-out jeans and faded pink sweatshirt from David's hands. David and Roxy numbly followed Tenaiia out to the garage. Each found a chair. The stupor was thick. Tenaiia lit a cigarette. David joined her.

Roxy stared in a daze. The horror of having the Melding connection severed was more than she could bear. Why go through all of these painful Trinity lessons if they didn't end up with a Melded Being? And apathy. How do you get someone past apathy, especially someone who's life is as unbearable and confronted as Katrina's? Impossible! That's how Roxy was feeling when Leviticus channeled through David's body to help.

"Is this Leviticus of the Light?" Roxy methodically asked.

"Indeed, it is I," Leviticus smiled.

"Some mess I've gotten us into."

"Nothing you cannot get past, Dear One. You must find a strategy."

"Strategy? Past apathy? Sure! Every time David goes into apathy, it's a mess. I've never been successful at getting him out of it."

Leviticus moved his foot until it was touching Roxy's foot and then he began sending soothing energy into her body, helping her regain some semblance of balance. Finally, amid the reeling in her mind, a productive thought surfaced.

Leviticus smiled at her.

"What are you smiling at?" Roxy said, perking up.

"It is good to see that you are thinking again."

"Do you think my idea will work?"

"No, but you shall soon find one that will. I must depart. In Love and Light, I bid you farewell." And David was back.

"I should make love to her," David suggested the first of many times, not knowing what else to do.

Tenaiia went further. "Perhaps it would be wise, after what Katrina has been through, that she wake up in your arms, David. Then you could make love to her."

Roxy sighed. She was in no position to disagree, according to Commander Ashtar.

David, Tenaiia, and Roxy left the garage and went into Katrina's bedroom. Tenaiia and David undressed and climbed under the covers. When Tenaiia was snuggled into David's arms, she bid them farewell. Roxy left before Katrina's consciousness returned.

The ninety-six hour test began.

The clock ticked unusually loud, announcing every second as it passed. Roxy sat in the living room, straining through the numbness, trying to feel and think straight again.

Then the moaning began. Softly at first, then louder, Katrina said, "Oh! David, I love you."

Roxy noticed then that the numbness was gone. The minutes turned into hours. Roxy forced herself into a space of love. Silently she screamed at the out-of-control part of herself that kept trying to well up and explode. She refused to give it the time of day. The force was horrendous. Katrina made no effort to muffle her sounds. Roxy battled herself at every moan.

Three hours later, the door opened. Roxy had gotten herself into bed, though she remained wired and awake. She refused to allow the knots in her stomach any verbal expression.

Katrina entered the bedroom. Immediately upon seeing Roxy, she declared, "You lied to me, David. I don't love you any more."

Roxy looked to David, wondering what Katrina was talking about. David shrugged his shoulders in bewilderment. All David knew was that after three hours of lovemaking the funk was thick in the space of two minutes. David and Roxy glanced at each other. It was going to be an uphill battle all the way. Dread permeated their sleep.

Katrina woke in a grumpy, apathetic state. "Don't you need to go meditate, Roxy?" David urged.

Roxy forced herself to gracefully leave, Ashtar's words still ring-ing in her ears. Moments later the sounds began. David had cancelled work; Katrina's life took priority. Tenaiia had cancelled school, so there was no rush. After all, if David and Roxy failed in the next four days, then Katrina would die anyway.

Roxy left to go to work, leaving David and Katrina in the midst of making love.

She returned to the same sounds that she'd left, with Katrina scream-ing in ecstasy. Roxy hunkered down to begin the waiting game again, engaged in an internal battle that raged on. She wanted her turn. She wanted Katrina denied. Those ugly thoughts surfaced and Roxy re-peatedly told herself, "Your time is up. No more. No longer will you run—or ruin—my life. I find peace in their lovemaking" Roxy repeated aloud. "I *bless* their lovemaking," Roxy insisted. "I *release* all jeal-ousy," Roxy demanded. The pain, the torque, was astronomical. Still Roxy was unrelenting. The Light in her insisted that her dark side die. It was time; the game was up.

By the time David and Katrina emerged two hours later, Roxy was exhausted.

Katrina came forth aglow, then she saw Roxy. The memories she'd managed to forget flooded back into her consciousness: she had to share David. Her hourglass figure slumped over. She began mumbling, "I don't care if I live. No one else cares, either."

"*We* care, Katrina," Roxy encouraged.

"No. You say you care, but you don't. You're just saying that to make me feel better," Katrina glared.

Hearing Katrina's words caused David to look at Roxy in despair. Hours of passionate lovemaking had only produced minutes of posi-tive results. He was exhausted.

Roxy prepared a meal, blessing it with Light, and everyone ate. Then back to bed they went.

This time, the battle in Roxy was diminished. Progress against her own dark side was made. She forced herself to transform; there was no other choice.

Consumed with apathy, Katrina's tall stretch of body looked pa-thetic. By the day her curls became more tangled, her words more life-less, her shoulders slumped further. It was impossible to get her to eat and she barely visited the bathtub. She wore the same dirty inside-out clothes all four days. Sharing David was an insurmountable proposition to her. The intense, confrontational, highly responsible nature of her destiny was beyond what she could bear.

Despite Roxy's progress and David's fervently attentive life force, they were still losing the battle, all they had worked for.

Thursday evening at seven, the enchanting hour of do-or-die arrived. They had a five-minute window and no more. David had just finished making love to Katrina. It was time for Roxy to coach her, to get her to say those magical words, but Roxy was lost, with no clue how to proceed.

She tried by mentioning Katrina's mother, school, and, of course, beloved David. Nothing worked. She fumbled, "I know you want to be with David ...."

Katrina stared at Roxy, confused.

" ... and school. Don't you look forward to teaching?"

Katrina looked befuddled, bewildered. The five minutes were vanishing. Roxy felt doomed. Then out of the blue, Katrina said, "I want to stay on Earth."

Roxy's eyes bulged and her jaw dropped. The apathy implant was broken! David grabbed Katrina and hugged her." I love you, hon."

Arianne telepathically planted the words into Katrina's mind. Telepathy from Katrina's Higher Self was legal.

Ashtar channeled through Katrina's body and announced, "You have won, *this time*! Do not repeat your error. The Melding will be reconnected." And he left.

In a fury, Zeeq followed Commander Ashtar. "You think you have seen difficult times! I have been easy on you! I will build a web that you will never get past. I will make your lives miserable. You will wish that you were dead." And he left. The frost chilled their home for hours.

Their enormous mission was clearer: It was beyond personal challenge. A Melded Being meant advanced information to solve today's massive problems. Katrina/Arianne was capable of transforming an entire generation through the educational system. Failure was not an option they were willing to risk again. Their commitment had deepened.

After all was said and done, they were told that they'd had a *four percent* chance to succeed against the apathy implant. They were left wondering what Zeeq would come up with next.

Who Are Lightworkers?

People who radiate
Peaceful Serenity
In the midst of turmoil.

—Jack Clarke

28

Energy Vampire

As November rolled around, progress was evident. Zeeq was active as usual but David and Roxy were conditioned. Remaining always alert, they were rarely surprised. The ugly assault Zeeq had planned was slated for just down the road.

Leviticus was preparing for his new contracted destiny as a Walk-In. Soon he would be too busy in an Earth incarnation to channel through David. For now, his visits allowed him to practice his whittling skills. Leviticus wanted to resemble the old Soviet Bloc man he was soon to "Walk-In" to who whittled for fun. That way he could accomplish his mission quietly, without arousing suspicion from close family or friends. Those close to the old man would not be aware that he had died and that his consciousness had been replaced by a Walk-In. Anonymity was vital.

Walk-Ins can occur for a number of reasons. Sometimes, they slip into bodies that have been abandoned by their original soul, with that soul's permission. Such is the case on occasion with suicide victims who miraculously survive. They are, from time to time, Walk-Ins. Or accident victims who intend to die in an accident. A Walk-In can take over the body and carry on the new mission. Walk-Ins *never* walk into and take a body inhabited by another. The changeover is always by agreement, and is often planned before the birth of the physical body.

In Leviticus' case, he was due to walk-in to an eighty-year-old who also had psychic gifts. Leviticus' intent was to take the body over when the old man died and complete his own mission.

The old man gave psychic readings to his country's leaders. These leaders were due to attend historic peace talks with their adversaries and Leviticus' job was to portend peace to his clients, setting the mood for a peaceful resolve. In the end, his mission was to be a grand success.

"Hello, Dear One. You wish to speak with me?" Leviticus began after entering into David's body.

"Is this Leviticus of the Light?"

"Indeed. May we pause here for a time? I would like to practice my whittling." Leviticus picked up a soft piece of pine kindling, pulled David's jackknife out of the pant's pocket, and began smoothing off the rough bark.

"Tenaiia told us that you are preparing to be a Walk-In," Roxy said. "Are you going to still be able to channel after you're a Walk-In?"

"Initially," Leviticus said, "probably not. However, perhaps over time I shall better learn how to split my consciousness and do both— talk to you while I'm also present there."

"How is a Walk-In different from being Melded?"

"A Walk-In bypasses the birthing process and therefore the 'filter' process, just like a Melded person. The main difference is that the Melded person bridges both dimensions. The Walk-In is only physical, with a complete memory of their task. A Walk-In does not have access to all universal knowledge as Melded Ones do. However, the Walk-In certainly is aware of what is to be done and how to do it. All of the wounds and patterns of the body leave when the Walk-In replaces the original soul's consciousness, which sometimes can take a brief period to fully complete. Then the newcomer, after thoroughly integrating into the body, can begin with a clean slate. And, like a Melded person, the newcomer will seldom reveal their identity to others. This makes Walk-Ins also different from those who refer to themselves as ET's, who are often happy to announce to everyone who they are."

"And the point of a Walk-In?"

"To perform an isolated specific task, which requires fully awake consciousness. Now, you asked to see me for a reason?" Leviticus said, getting back to the business at hand, not wanting to overindulge Roxy's curiosity.

"Yes. I'm still struggling over pictures versus windows."

"Indeed. This is challenging for you, is it not?" Leviticus agreed. "Very well. Clear your mind for a moment, Dear One."

As Roxy did so, a poem popped into her head:

"*Pictures*

Pictures oh! Pictures abound

Boxes for all around

With each picture we hold

Disappointment unfolds

Reminding us again
Limitlessness wins!"
"Very good, Dear One. I shall leave you to ponder those words. I must depart. In Love and Light."

Thanksgiving brought a test for Katrina. Katrina's mother, Lanna invited herself to Thanksgiving in Mt. Shasta and Katrina had been told on a journey-while-in-trance that the Guides wanted Lanna to visit. It was time to test Katrina's advancing abilities to stand up to her mother.

None of them looked forward to the visit. Katrina and Roxy, still working on taming their over-controlling natures, were not looking forward to Lanna running her psychic force through the house. Not only was Lanna naïve to her controlling nature, she wielded more control over those around her than Katrina or Roxy, separately or combined, ever had. Lanna's every breath, every statement, had a control issue or position at its root. Roxy and David stayed out of the way, leaving Katrina to her tests.

Lanna arrived late Wednesday evening, unexpectedly accompanied by her friend's two young daughters. Tired from their six-hour journey, they were all ready for bed.

Without David, Katrina knew she would cry the night away in loneliness. Katrina was tired of her mother assuming, even demanding, that she give up her bed, so Katrina decided she would sleep in her own room.

Shortly after they arrived, Katrina announced, "I've prepared your bed for you." She pointed to the two wide sofa sleeper sections she and Roxy had assembled as a makeshift double bed.

"You'll be sleeping with the girls." Lanna said, matter-of-factly.

"No, Mom, you can. I need my rest. I'll be sleeping in my room." She hugged her mother, whose eyes were wide in disbelief. Lanna had never seen Katrina like this.

"Good night," Katrina said, and left.

Early Thanksgiving morning Katrina, bleary-eyed from weeping all night, came to The Trinity bedroom to announce, "I'd like to spend some time alone with David this morning."

"But what about your Mom?" Roxy asked.

"I'm sending her up the mountain with the girls."

"She won't like that much," Roxy warned.

"I don't care."

By then there was activity in the living room. The girls were bright and cheery but Lanna was grouchy and achy as she rubbed her back. After a breakfast of French toast and orange juice, Katrina dropped the bomb.

"Mom, why don't you take the girls up the mountain to Panther Meadows? I'm sure you'll all really enjoy it."

"You're coming with us, aren't you?"

"No. I have things to do for a while."

"Then we'll wait till you can come," Lanna flatly announced.

"Nope. I go up all of the time. You go. Really, I insist." Katrina wouldn't budge.

"But, Kat, I'm here to visit *you*. Why don't you join us?" The pressure was thick.

"No. You go. Take the girls. We'll visit when you get back."

Lanna begrudgingly agreed and the tone was set for the weekend; Katrina had changed. Repeatedly Katrina had held her own. Her strength took hold and Lanna lost control. Katrina had passed her test.

A few days after Lanna departed, Roxy scrounged up a little money and bought a cheap bottle of wine. Later that evening David and Katrina had planned to spend time alone, including sleeping together for the night in Katrina's room. Roxy wanted to use the opportunity to percolate on her life, to ponder how she could push forward with still more grace.

It was dark outside when Roxy went out into the cold, dressed in her warm winter coat and worn-out pink sweat pants. She found a comfortable spot on David's meticulous wood pile to perch. Something didn't feel right but it was eluding her.

Roxy had become aware of her cravings for David. It bothered her. She needed a regular fix, like an energy fix, from him. Too long away from David and she went a little crazy. The cravings, the yearnings, inevitably ensued. She needed to physically connect: like holding hands, her foot touching his, her hand on his leg in the car. It had never dawned on her that she was doing anything other than connecting with the one she loved, until tonight.

Thoughts crept in. There was more to it than that. As she sat on the cold wood pile drinking the cheap wine, the chill reaching through her thin sweat pants, Roxy noticed her energy was psychically pulling on David's. She craved him. She was dependent upon him, on his energy. Then the full impact struck: there was a hole in her aura, a hole that constantly required filling and only David's energy sufficed.

She was shocked and revolted. She shuddered as scenes of her getting an energy fix off David flashed before her eyes. "I thought that it was just because I loved him," she mumbled. "God! I'm dependent upon him." She was repulsed.

"How do I fix this?" she asked God. It was Athena who responded telepathically.

"You have a hole in your aura," Athena confirmed. "Under certain conditions, we shall agree to patch this hole."

"Tell me and I'll do it," Roxy telepathically replied.

"You must let go of seeing this one, David, as a source of fuel," Athena said. "You must learn how to fill yourself. You must vow to stop psychically pulling on David. Your yearnings for him must transform into a yearning for independent wholeness. Do you understand?"

"Okay. No more touching David to draw energy off him. When I yearn for him, I'll shift it to yearning for myself," Roxy promised.

"Very well, then go to bed. The etheric surgeons will arrive shortly to patch your hole. Remember your promises." Athena's presence faded.

Roxy followed instructions and went to bed. Within a minute or two the bedroom filled with the energy of the etheric surgery team. Roxy's body became very heavy and hard to move as she felt a drug-induced type of drowsiness come over her. She drifted off to sleep.

In the morning, Roxy could feel that she was different. She felt whole, more self-contained. Her need for David had been transformed. Now she had the ongoing task of managing and maintaining her new independent energy pattern, ensuring that she depended on herself and none other.

Who Are Lightworkers?

They are people
Knowing and loving themselves
In order to better know and love others.

—Jack Clarke

29

Zeeq's Fortress

Zeeq's physical attacks became increasingly violent. One evening, David went in search of Katrina, feeling something was amiss. As he bounded around the corner into the living room, he found her sitting by the fire, David's open jackknife in her right hand, the blade touching her left wrist. In a flash, David was behind Katrina/Zeeq, grabbing her right hand, and pulling the knife away. This was not an isolated event.

A few nights later she played with the red hot embers. "Fire sure feels good tonight."

"Glad you like it." David was peaceful and content.

Without warning, Katrina's face grew menacing. She turned as she shot upright, hot poker in hand, and thrust the poker at David's face. David felt the heat pass by. He sprung out of his chair, lurching into a better position, narrowly escaping Zeeq's second jab. Zeeq persisted, lunging Katrina's body forward, the poker aimed at David's chest.

David bent backwards and twisted around, sliding behind Katrina. He wrapped his arms around Katrina and held her tight.

Her cells remembered David's energy. It was soothing, safe, and loved. That rendered Zeeq weak. Katrina's body withered in David's arms as Zeeq surrendered her body. Katrina didn't remember a thing.

As was written in their contracts, the fight had to be fair. There were guidelines to which both sides must adhere. For Zeeq, this meant that his more rigorous physical strategies could only be used in proximity to David. Roxy just wasn't strong enough. Routinely, within seconds of David's arrival home, the heavy-duty physical combat commenced.

Katrina sat on her bed, devouring volumes of reading assignments that lay before her. Roxy was preparing food and checking in on Katrina every few moments. David, just home, was chopping wood before dinner.

"Have you checked in on her lately?" David asked Roxy as he flew through the kitchen en route to Katrina's bedroom.

"Yes, just a few minutes ago," Roxy answered.

"Something doesn't feel right!" David's voice echoed as he ran through the living room. As he bounded through the bedroom door, the view horrified him. There was Zeeq, in Katrina's body, making a meal of Katrina's arm.

"Roxy!" David screamed.

"Coming," she yelled. Roxy was confronted with David tackling Zeeq. There were round, purple teeth marks on Katrina's right arm but the skin had not yet been broken.

David flung Katrina onto the bed and pinned one arm down while Roxy grabbed her other arm to protect her. Zeeq struggled to get free. Katrina's arms were bruised from the fight. Then her body went limp.

"Wow! That came on fast," Roxy said.

"You have to watch her more closely!" David snapped.

They released Katrina's arms as her consciousness returned. She looked at her arms, red from being gripped with such force. It was a real question as to who did more damage, Zeeq or her caretakers. Against her preference, Katrina started wearing long-sleeved blouses to prevent suspicion at school.

"Sorry! He was biting you," David said.

"So I see," Katrina sighed, her gaze moving across the vivid purple and red bite mark.

Roxy rubbed White Flower Oil, a homeopathic remedy that stimulates the red blood cells to circulate and heal, on Katrina's wound. As she and David walked toward the living room, Roxy said, "David, you go ahead. I promise I'll check in on her—"

But before Roxy could even finish her sentence, they heard a loud, sickening thud. They flew toward Katrina's room as a second and third thud echoed through the house.

Zeeq, in Katrina's body, had the eyes closed and was pounding Katrina's head on the log wall. David charged over the bed and grabbed Katrina's arms just before the fourth blow connected. Zeeq snapped Katrina's body from David's grip and headed back to the wall. Roxy joined the struggle. She and David each grabbed one of Katrina's arms and flung her onto the bed.

Zeeq left. Again a deceiving calm came over the room. Katrina rubbed the large knots on her head. "Ouch! What happened?"

"Sorry," they both said outraged.

"I'll stay with you while you study," David insisted.

"No. I'll be fine, really. Go. I've got to get this studying done. Really, you can go."

"Are you sure? I'd feel better if I stayed here," David persisted.

"I'm sure. Please g— " and before the word got past her lips, Zeeq took over and began pulling her hair.

Again they vaulted into action, grabbing Katrina's arms and pinning her to the bed. Then Katrina's eyes snapped open. Zeeq's glare pierced into Roxy's eyes with a deep, dark fury. Fear was projected from his eyes into Roxy's soul. Zeeq used this strategy often because it was effective. Until now.

Fear was no longer a part of the equation for Roxy. Looking at the fury in Zeeq's eyes, it struck her as funny. She began to laugh. They no longer held any power over her. She could beam love into them with ease. She'd grown in her self-worth and faith in herself so that Zeeq's awful energy could no longer damage her.

"What's so funny?" David snapped.

"They're funny," Roxy said, nodding towards Zeeq's eyes. "They're supposed to scare me, but they don't any more. It's a tactic, nothing more. It's actually funny." Looking into Zeeq's horrific eyes she said, "It doesn't work any more, Zeeq."

Zeeq closed Katrina's eyes and was gone. He never used that strategy again.

Roxy could hardly grasp Zeeq's persistence. Why was Zeeq so adamant about remaining anchored in the dark? Even though his soul had begun out of God, anchored in the dark, it was long past time for him to experience a season in the Light. The universal law of balance decrees that all souls must experience seasons in the Light and in the dark, regardless of whether they come out of God anchored in the Light or dark.

Roxy wanted to understand her adversary better. One night, as she drifted off to sleep, she asked Zeeq if they could meet to talk. They both agreed to a neutral visit where Roxy could go to Zeeq's castle and would be free to return to her body in the morning. Zeeq's graciousness was most unusual.

The next morning, in a dream-like memory, Roxy recalled the events of her journey. She had found herself standing on steps cut out of well-worn rock that overlooked a large courtyard. The feeling was foul, damp, and still. Zeeq stood before her, dressed in a long, dark, velvet-like robe which fitted snug to the waist, then cascaded outward down to the floor, hiding his feet. The sleeves grew wider as they fell down his arms. A scowl from eons of battle, anger and fatigue was etched in his face. His presence declared that he was a powerful force, despite the fact that he was short and thin.

As he and Roxy stood on cobblestone steps, they viewed the round, dingy-looking towers that comprised the four corners of the fortress. The rock and mortar walls were rough and foreboding. Not much got past these walls that wasn't meant to, but then, who'd want to penetrate them? It was evident that those who lived there didn't much want to. In the distance, screams of anguish could be heard. It was creepy.

This was Zeeq's fortress. This is what he sank his pride into. Dank, chilly, and dimly lit, it was permeated by fear. No one else was visible, but the hidden stares sent a chill up Roxy's spine. She couldn't quite shake the eerie, unwelcome feeling no matter how deeply she breathed.

Roxy spoke first. "Why is it so important for you to win?"

"I have worked long and hard to earn this position that I now hold." Zeeq said. "It took eons of pain, torture, and endless battles, which I have overcome and won, to reach this pinnacle. Now I am in control. I have the power over all of this and my subjects." He swept his arm across to indicate his entire kingdom contained within the walls of his castle. "I have absolutely no desire to give this up and begin anew at the bottom in the Light. Surely you can understand my position?"

"Yes, but what if you lose?"

"I shall not lose!" Zeeq's voiced boomed as Roxy's Light body plunged back into her physical body.

Zeeq had reached the equivalent level in the dark as Commander Ashtar had in the Light. His resources were vast, his intelligence keen. He was a pugnacious and hostile adversary.

After Roxy's journey, it dawned on her that the worst was yet to come.

Who Are Lightworkers?

Those who know that
Fear has too long diminished
The love within us.

—Jack Clarke

ZEEQ'S FORTRESS

30

Katrina's Vision

Surprises abound from The Troops. On a recent journey-while-in-trance, Katrina had been encouraged to go south for Christmas. The Guides had their reasons, reasons that would be evident just after the first of the year.

For now, all David and Roxy knew was that Katrina was going to her aunt's house in San Diego for Christmas. She would be gone for over two weeks beginning December 18. No Zeeq, no anxiety for two-plus weeks.

But with the announcement, Katrina became jumpier and strange. With all the non-physical entities frequenting Katrina's body, she wasn't the picture of normalcy; but even for Katrina, she was beyond the usual agitated moodiness. Snapping at Roxy had already become a regular part of their daily diet but growling at David—that never happened. Since announcing her vacation, she began climbing down David's throat with increasing regularity. David and Roxy were baffled until a week before Katrina's departure. Katrina confided her troubles to David with threat of an ugly barrage of retaliation if he ever revealed her secret to Roxy.

Katrina's secret exposed, David felt compelled to spend even more private time with her. He soothed her with compassion, explaining to Roxy only that Katrina "needed" it. The sight of Roxy caused Katrina to burst into tears and dash from the room. The mystery had Roxy stumped, and concerned.

On Katrina's departure day, she announced that she had something to tell Roxy. The three nestled in front of the warm fire. A strange, uneasy feeling permeated the air.

Slowly, as if trying to find the right words, Katrina began. "I don't want to be a part of this ... Trinity thing anymore. I've thought it over for a long time. It just doesn't work for me and I don't believe it ever will. It's been a very difficult decision, one that I did not make lightly. I just thought you had a right to know."

Roxy's jaw dropped and she stared in disbelief. The words didn't quite register. Then, "How will you take care of yourself?"

"Zeeq only has the right to meddle as long as The Trinity is together. If I leave, The Trinity dissolves and Zeeq must also let go. I figure that, without Zeeq's interference, I can take care of myself."

"Are you sure?" David was not convinced.

"Yes, I'm sure. There are other tools that I will ultimately be getting, which will help," Katrina assured them.

"Tools?" Roxy asked.

"I'm not at liberty to say right now. Just suffice it to know, I'll be fine." Katrina's mind was made up. "I'll be leaving after next semester, which will be the beginning of June. Then you can have David all to yourself."

The air was as thick as foam. Roxy was dazed.

"I'm sorry," Katrina said and left the room.

That afternoon Katrina announced that Ashtar wanted to speak to Roxy. They all trudged back to the fireplace. Shock was still thick in the space.

"Is this Ashtar of the Light?"

"Yes, it is I. I am here to officially inform you that The Trinity is to be dissolved in five month's time."

"Yes. Katrina told me this morning. Who decided this and when was it decided?"

"Katrina has made this decision on her own. She made it approximately two months ago," Ashtar said.

That was just after the horrible mishap, when Zeeq whisked Katrina away in a spaceship. Roxy cringed. Her negligence haunted her again. "Why weren't we told sooner?" Roxy snapped.

Ashtar pierced into her eyes, mirroring her anger, and said, "Dear Lady, had you been told sooner, you would not have made the progress you have made in the past two months. Your energy has already shifted since this morning."

Ashtar was right. In the mere six hours since Katrina delivered the news, Roxy's entire focus had shifted from obtaining alignment in The Trinity to tolerating the final five months.

David and Katrina went off for a final rendezvous before her departure. During their extended absence, Roxy pondered the events of the day. No more Trinity, no more Zeeq. Twelve months of programming "The Trinity is forever" obliterated in one sentence: "I don't want to be part of this Trinity thing anymore." Roxy still couldn't believe it. Part of her was thrilled, another part shattered. We'll never experience our full potential and it felt like we were getting so close, she thought.

Three hours later, Katrina's bedroom door opened. Katrina emerged wearing a somber aura and face, as if she were forcing herself to go through the motions, of preparing to leave despite the fact that it was the last thing in the world she wanted to do—now or ever.

At nine o'clock, everyone climbed into Katrina's car and they headed down the hill to the train station in Dunsmier, resignation heavy in the air. Boarding time came too quickly for Katrina. To Roxy, it seemed like it would never arrive. Katrina delivered an automatic hug to Roxy. Turning to David, she wrapped her arms around him and held on for what seemed to Roxy like hours. When she pulled away, her eyes pierced love and longing into his, as though sending an ambiguous message for him to decipher on his own. She tore herself away and boarded the train. She took a seat overlooking the parking lot, where David and Roxy waited in the car for her journey to begin.

"Promise you won't tell Katrina I told you this?" David began.

"Yeah, sure. What's up?"

"Katrina had a vision for years, over and over again. It began when she was real young, thirteen or so, and it's stayed with her all these years. In fact, it was this vision that kept her from marrying that rich guy she was engaged to a couple years back."

David fidgeted.

"Yeah?" Roxy encouraged.

"All of her life she's had a really clear vision in her head of what her husband was going to look like."

"What'd he look like?"

"Me."

"*You!*" Roxy's eyes bulged.

"Yeah, me." David repeated. "She said that the day we showed up to rent the apartment in San Diego .... "

"Yeah?"

"... well, the moment she saw me she knew it was me, that I was the one in her vision. She said my beard was missing but she still knew for sure that it was me. She was confused as to why I had showed up with a wife."

"Wow!" Roxy kept shaking her head in disbelief, the words persisting in her brain. She knew the feeling. She'd had a psychic describe

David to her about a year before they met, telling her that he was to be her husband. Within a month of meeting David, she knew that he was the one she had been told about.

So, Roxy thought, there'd been two predictions made. What did Katrina's vision mean? It left her feeling violated and shaken to her core, though she didn't understand why. Katrina was truly meant to be here with David, yet twelve hours earlier she had declared her intent to leave The Trinity, and David, behind.

The train began to move. Katrina waved to David. Tears rolled down her face. Their eyes locked. Katrina's eyes spoke of a deep sadness, a yearning, and then she was out of sight.

Their number one priority in Katrina's absence was to rest their weary bodies and souls. The house was a different place without Katrina and the likes of Zeeq. David and Roxy lovingly and casually spent time together, reaffirming their love, their friendship. So much had changed between them, yet their love had held firm.

In Katrina's absence, they magically secured new housing, due to be available the first of June. Gary, their soon-to-be roommate, had just bought a house in Mt. Shasta. He met David while purchasing homeowner's insurance. Gary spent only one weekend per month in his Mt. Shasta house and chose the Plumbs to rent the place to prevent vandalism.

And as per the suggestion of the Guides-of-Light, they invited an old friend and business associate, Grant, to fly down for a visit. Getting Grant to agree to leave his family during Christmas, even for forty-eight hours, was a small miracle. Grant was the president of the small transformational consulting firm David and Roxy had worked with three years earlier. An unexplained, harmonious bond had always existed between Grant and Roxy.

Ten minutes out of the airport, Leviticus joined the party to get the conversation rolling. Roxy was startled by Leviticus' speed. Within minutes he had Grant talking about space-beings, the dark, spacecraft, and the like.

Grant was no neophyte to such subjects, though he rarely discussed this side of himself with anyone, including his wife. It became the foundation between him and Roxy. Their conversations ranged from God, mission, Lightworkers, the dark, and finally, the possibility of

Roxy consulting with his company. Grant saw the consultant emerging in Roxy. The possibility of a work partnership remained open.

After Grant boarded the plane to return home, Leviticus declared the trip a success. The year 1987 came to a deceptively quiet close.

Who Are Lightworkers?

Anyone who seeks
The truth
From any source.

—Jack Clarke

31

Deadly Ethereal Poison

Trepidation was thick at five in the morning when David and Roxy climbed out of bed. Their vacation was over; Katrina was due in at the train depot in forty-five minutes. They had no idea of what to expect. Roxy was anxious to get the final five months over, and David, who lived in the now, looked forward to seeing and hugging Katrina soon.

Over two hours late, the train pulled in at eight. Zeeq's next version of hell was already under way. Katrina emerged from the train, and headed straight for David. She was aglow as she climbed inside his eyes, silently screaming, "I love you, honey! I've missed you desperately! Please take me into your arms and hold me forever." Their hug lasted an eternity, until a horrendous hacking cough broke them apart.

For Roxy, there was an A-frame hug and a forced "Hi" from Katrina. Their relationship had eroded.

The deep, uncontrollable coughing continued as they drove home. "How long you been coughing?" David asked.

"Oh, a few days. It's nothing really," Katrina said, brushing it off.

"Did you see a doctor about it?" David persisted.

"No. You know I don't like doctors." Katrina smiled at David until coughing took over again.

David and Roxy glanced at each other. Their first priority was Katrina's health. As they climbed up the hill to Mt. Shasta City, Katrina slumped further in her seat, looking paler by the moment. The incessant coughing had already burrowed deep into her lungs.

Once home, David helped Katrina to bed and Roxy tended to the luggage. Moments later Zeeq came calling. "My attempts to ruin this Melding have been mere child's play. In your absence, I have woven a web in Katrina's mind that you will *never* untangle. You will probably not even survive it. I WILL WIN! I WILL HAVE ARIANNE. I have five months to win and I fully intend to succeed. BE PREPARED! You haven't seen anything yet!"

Zeeq referred to the clause in their contracts which stated that if The Trinity remained intact, then Zeeq had full rights to interfere until the three had mastered their ability to block him through love. That was anticipated to take about two more years. In the event that The Trinity dissolved for whatever reason, then Zeeq would be given an intensified but shorter period to accomplish his objective. So Zeeq crunched the schemes of two years into five months. That way the Guides-of-Light ensured that when Katrina left The Trinity, Melding intact, Zeeq could not complain that he'd not been given sufficient time or a fair chance to win, according to the agreement.

To that end, Zeeq set up "the weaving" inside Katrina's mind, a web-like structure that connected Zeeq's energy field into the very fabric of Katrina's mind and soul. This was due to remain intact until The Trinity dissolved. The weaving dramatically shifted the odds in Zeeq's favor. Now he co-inhabited Katrina/Arianne's body, mind, and energy for the final five-month stint. That meant that Zeeq could more easily magnify Katrina's existing negative emotions. He could, at any moment, remove David's and Roxy's words from her mind. He could take control of her physically faster than before. He could allow any of his emissaries to take his place when he tired, and he could detonate at any time—or unexpectedly in the distant future—one of several life-threatening bombs he had placed in Katrina's head. The onslaught would be unremitting for five long, drawn-out months. Now there were only extremely rare moments when the dark ones were absent.

Previously, Zeeq had come through as a channeled being. Now he was an inseparable part of the very fabric of Katrina/Arianne. There were no longer "clues" of Zeeq's presence, such as the "Zeeq gleam" in Katrina's eye, to warn them of his presence. Any flicker of Light Katrina had possessed was replaced by a constant dark glare. Zeeq was in her at all moments.

The continual offensive intensified daily. Though Roxy and David thought the battle had been fierce before, they hadn't seen anything yet. Creative, malicious, and determined, Zeeq's most debilitating strategies were yet to come. Their lives would become more miserable than either David or Roxy could have ever fathomed or imagined.

Still, it all remained legal, within the boundaries of their contract.

Katrina's school work was abandoned. She was so weak she could hardly get out of bed. It was a miracle she had survived the train ride.

Later that morning Roxy approached Katrina. "Mind if I use your car to go to work?" The money for their car purchase wouldn't manifest until about mid-month.

Thoughts rolled wildly in Katrina's mind. I don't want to share anything with you—ever! I don't like you. Can't you just leave me alone? God, I hate how I feel. What's going on inside of me? I don't understand. I didn't hate Roxy this much before I left for San Diego. I don't really hate her. Well, maybe I do. Force yourself to be nice, Katrina. God, this is a lot of work. "Yeah, go ahead," Katrina said, a small smile across her face. It was the weaving at work.

"Thanks," Roxy said and left.

"Would you like to make love, Katrina?" David asked.

"I've missed you so much, David." Her coughing took over. "I think Tenaiia wants to talk to you first."

"How was your vacation?" Tenaiia said after coming into Katrina's body.

"Is this Tenaiia of the Light?"

"Yep, it is." Tenaiia confirmed. "Some cough, wouldn't you say?"

"Boy, I'll say. Where'd it come from?" Concern was etched in his voice.

"Compliments of Zeeq." Tenaiia said. "He's been feeding Katrina deadly poison on the ethereal plane since the day she arrived at her aunt's. Her illness has gotten progressively worse over the two weeks. It has settled into her lungs."

"Lung problems? Like pneumonia?"

"It would seem."

"Hmmm, let's see. In Louise Hay's book pneumonia is"—David grabbed the book, *HEAL YOUR BODY,* and read—"Desperate. Tired of life. Emotional wounds that are not allowed to heal. Well, that sure fits."

"Yes. This is a weak area for Katrina. An easy target for Zeeq."

"What do we do about it? Take her to the doctor?"

"I'm afraid I cannot help you there," Tenaiia said. "You and Roxy must decide this for yourself. I cannot interfere, except to tell you what is causing the problem. And speaking of Roxy, Zeeq has also set up the weaving."

"Weaving?"

"Yes. Through the weaving, which Zeeq has placed into Katrina's mind, Zeeq has much more control over Katrina/Arianne. Other dark souls under Zeeq now have an easy access into Katrina's mind as well. Any one of them can take control over Katrina's consciousness in an instant. Through the weaving, Zeeq is magnifying Katrina's dislike for Roxy."

David realized the battle had just gotten nastier. Tenaiia left and he attempted to make love to Katrina. He figured that his love for her would help her to heal. The problem was, it made breathing too difficult.

"I'm really embarrassed about how I feel," Katrina confided after she was able to catch her breath.

"About what?"

"How I feel about Roxy. I don't understand it, but every time I see her, I about go ballistic. I feel really bad about it but I can't seem to help it. Just the sight of her makes me go bonkers."

"Don't worry about it, Katrina. It's okay. You just rest for now. I'll take care of everything." David kissed her and held her till she fitfully drifted to sleep. He noticed the effects of the weaving already.

Roxy returned home to a quiet house. David heard the kitchen door open, and quickly got up to intercept her before she came in and disturbed Katrina.

"Hi, how's it going?" Roxy asked.

"Shhhh. Not good. Here, let's go into the living room and talk quietly. I don't want to wake her," David whispered, weary from his morning. "Tenaiia told me that Zeeq has been feeding Katrina a deadly ethereal poison for the entire time that she was gone."

"Deadly? How much has he given her?"

"Enough so that it's already reached toxic levels in her body." David closed his eyes wearily. "Roxy, Katrina is really sick."

"So now Zeeq is using ethereal poison to try to kill her." Roxy groaned, trying to comprehend their new dilemma.

"Yep. I wonder if antibiotics would have any effect on ethereal poison."

"I don't know," Roxy said. "Remember what the valerian root did? It worked the opposite in Katrina's system compared to what it was supposed to. Remember, her body chemistry is the reverse of most. And besides, what if antibiotics did something weird when mixed with this poison? Maybe Zeeq has set it up so that antibiotics will kill her. God, what a mess. What do we do?"

David shook his head. "I don't know." His face was etched with worry. "What to do? What to do?" He sighed. "The other thing, Roxy, is that Zeeq has set up this weaving thing." He explained it as best he could, including the part about Zeeq magnifying Katrina's negative thoughts towards her. "He's trying to remove you as one of her protectors so that the burden rests on my shoulders. He's hoping I'll blow it somehow. You know, Roxy, every time you go into the bedroom, she gets emotionally agitated."

"Really? It isn't obvious." She remembered the smile on Katrina's face earlier.

"It's too confronting for her to tell you herself. She doesn't have the strength. Roxy, she's *really* weak. We can't afford to weaken her further. It's best if you stay away from her, out of her sight. You do the kitchen stuff and let me take it in to her. Okay?"

"I'll do my best."

David continuously applied hot packs, Vick's Vaporub, hot fluids, steam, White Flower Oil, and loads of TLC hour after hour for days on end. He was exhausted and Katrina grew worse. Still the question lurked: Would antibiotics help Katrina or had Zeeq set up his strategy in such a way that the medicine would actually kill her?

David and Roxy agonized over what to do as the days ticked by. The only thing that had become crystal clear was that they were faced with a life-threatening dilemma; her condition was near fatal.

"I'm dying, aren't I?" Katrina asked David. "I have AIDS. I'm dying."

"Shhhhhhh, Katrina, you're going to be fine," David lied with the best smile he could muster.

Katrina was dying, but not from AIDS. Convincing her that it wasn't AIDS was another matter. Every time David told Katrina that Zeeq was feeding her poison, Katrina would understand the problem and come to peace for two seconds. Then Zeeq would erase the statement from her mind and fear consumed her body. Zeeq knew what he was doing; fear debilitates the immune system. Having Katrina frightened of AIDS only helped forward his cause.

Their only recourse was to get her well and then take her to get tested for AIDS. But how?

One day while Katrina was asleep, Roxy decided to check up on her. As Roxy entered the room, her jaw dropped in surprise. Katrina was a mime drinking from an invisible glass. She was sitting up in bed, eyes closed, her right arm raised ninety degrees, fingers curved as though holding a glass. She brought her hand to her mouth, tipped her curved fingers upward, and began drinking from the unseen container. She was drinking Zeeq's deadly poison.

To make matters worse, another day Zeeq came and opened the sliding glass doors in the bedroom, dropping the temperature from the mid-fifties to close to zero. Then Zeeq put Katrina back into bed without any covers. By the time David found her, she was shivering uncontrollably.

Her condition continued to worsen by the hour. For the first time since the arrival of Zeeq, their conversations drifted into wondering what they'd do if Katrina died.

"She might die if we don't take her to the doctor," David warned.

"She might die if we do," Roxy countered.

Finally they could stand it no longer. If antibiotics were going to do her in, so what? She was dying anyway. Two weeks into Katrina's return, they bundled her up and hauled her to an emergency room. The doctor paled when he heard Katrina cough. Bypassing the normal procedure to wait for lab results, he administered a strong antibiotic. They took her home, and prayed. David continued to nurse her with love and remained at her side.

The waiting was agony.

It was seven days before improvement became evident. When she was well enough to travel, David took her to Redding for an AIDS test. The results were negative. She was ready to resume her studies.

Only then did Tenaiia tell the caretakers that they'd had only a two percent chance of succeeding. Had they done anything a little differently, Katrina would have lost her life. Zeeq was on a roll.

Truth That Sets Us Free.

If there is just one thing that will never settle in me,
Let it be that whenever I'm not right
With my Maker and my Higher Purpose,
That I cannot be Content.

—Keith Amber

32

Gateway To The Universe

The weaving in Katrina's mind warped her. The emotional roller coaster of days gone by was replaced by a depressed, sullen state. She avoided Roxy most of the time. Except in rare moments, Zeeq was always present, causing varying levels of trouble. How Katrina managed at school, even with Tenaiia's help, was a mystery. Tenaiia had become so credible at "being Katrina" that Katrina's few friends hadn't a clue that they were actually talking to a space-being most of the time. Incredibly, her grades never suffered.

Zeeq no longer had to come through Katrina because he was now a part of her. The vicious, Zeeq-like gleam in her eyes was always present. The weaving intensified the caretakers' need to keep an eye on Katrina when either one of them was home.

Because of Zeeq's increased presence, Roxy was amazed one afternoon to find Katrina, sprawled across the bed, in a rare talking mood.

"You nervous to move? Guess you'll be glad to get rid of the likes of Zeeq," Roxy began, trying to find new common ground.

"No, I'm not nervous. Actually, I'm kind of looking forward to it. You know, get away from the strain and all," Katrina said.

Roxy hoped Katrina would tell her about the vision. That brought assistance from a most unusual source. The room went silent. Katrina closed her eyes and began to speak. "Hello."

"Who is this?" Roxy asked, expecting the worst.

"I am Katrina's subconscious mind."

"Are you of the Light?"

"I am of both and I am of neither. I do not take sides. It is not my job to fight battles or take sides."

Roxy's curiosity lapped it up, "What is your job, subconscious mind?"

"It is my job to provide you with your chosen reality as stated in your contract. I also listen to your thoughts and your words and give you the reality consistent with what is said and thought, with no bias."

"So whatever we focus on, you make happen?" Roxy asked.

"That's correct. Whatever you focus your attention on is the reality I bring you."

"And you listen to our words?"

"Yes."

"Does it matter to you if we're joking when we speak?"

"No. I listen to your words and literally deliver that which you state."

"And you present us with our prebirth contracts?"

"Correct. I give you dreams to help you progress along in your intended destiny. I also give you visions for the same purpose."

"Do you care which reality we choose?" Roxy asked.

"I do not care what you choose. It is my job to provide you with direction yet allow you to choose whatever you will, without judgment."

"So you don't care if Katrina dies and goes to the dark?"

"It is not my function to care. I will be with her in the Light and in the dark. It matters none to me."

"Why have you come to speak to me today?"

"I have come to tell you of Katrina's vision. I have given her this vision many times over the years. It is a vision of David as her husband. She was shocked when he arrived at her door with a wife."

"And you gave her this vision because it was a part of her prebirth contract?"

"Yes."

"Why did you come to tell me?"

"Because this vision, and telling you, has been a great burden on Katrina. I tell you this in hopes that the pathway I am creating will make it easier for Katrina to tell you herself. I must go now."

Roxy realized just how literal the subconscious mind is. It knows no humor or sarcasm. What is lightly or jokingly said, the subconscious mind seriously delivers. What one allows one's mind to focus or dwell on, the subconscious mind makes manifest. Fear, joy, jealousy, happiness, blame, forgiveness—the list goes on. No wonder, Roxy thought, Leviticus and Tenaiia keep urging me to get control of my mind. It truly is the only way through the hell.

The subconscious mind, the gateway to the Universe, is an integral part of what draws a person's experiences to them. This is in tandem with the Guides-of-Light, who are also instrumental in bringing the circumstances that facilitate lessons, karma, and contracts in one's life.

The full implications made Roxy shudder. We literally are our thoughts, beliefs and words, Roxy thought. When we desire to be different, we can literally begin by thinking and speaking a new way of being.

In spite of this assistance from her subconscious mind, Katrina was never able to share her controversial vision with Roxy.

Who Are Lightworkers?

They are people who believe
We are what we think we are
And can change ourselves
By changing our thinking.

—Jack Clarke

33

Breathing Interruptus

Training and testing begins during the years of formal education and continues until death. Circumstances, obstacles, opportunities and problems become both the training ground and the tests themselves. Which specific lessons we are to learn is pre-chosen in prebirth contracts.

One morning upon waking, it dawned on Roxy that she and David were being tested. The pressure had been worse for about a week when the light bulb went on for Roxy.

"You notice an extra pressure lately, David?"

"Come to think of it, yes. What do you suppose it is?"

"We're in testing; I can feel it. I always get this feeling when testing hits. You know that no matter what, I don't want to slip up and fail. Well, that's how it feels right now."

"What are we in testing for?"

"It feels like we've been on an edge all week long. You know, of almost going into overwhelm."

"Yeah, so?"

"Well, that's the test—live on the edge of a state of overwhelm yet don't go into overwhelm."

"Got it! I think you're right. God! That's a fine line. Makes you wonder what Zeeq's going to come up with next." David shuddered.

Later that day while talking to Tenaiia, Roxy took the opportunity to ask, "What's the purpose of placing a person on a very uncomfortable fence, nearly in overwhelm?"

"You see, the point just prior to going into overwhelm is an extremely potent growth arena. Your natural defenses are weakened and transformation occurs rapidly. However," Tenaiia warned, "once the line is crossed—that is, if you do go into overwhelm—well, then you lose your growth. You see, you lose the ability to cope with the new pattern. Once you've surrendered to the overwhelm, apathy allows you to revert to your old comfortable behavior, the one you're trying to transform. The tricky part is that the old behavior soothes. It is what you know. These thoughtforms, the old behaviors, do not die easily."

Thanks to Zeeq, David and Roxy were provided with the perfect potent testing arena.

"Katrina's breathing stopped!" David yelled, yet he simply nudged her and her breathing resumed. Five minutes passed and it happened again.

"Roxy, come here! Her breathing stopped again." Again he nudged her and she resumed breathing.

"God! What's going on now? Tenaiia!" Roxy wailed.

"Yes?" Tenaiia answered from Katrina's body.

"What's going on now?" they asked in unison.

"Zeeq detonated one of his bombs. It removed her automatic breathing mechanism."

"Excuse me?" Roxy said, squinting her eyes.

"The brain function in Katrina, which automatically keeps her breathing, has been shut down. Now she must remember on her own." Then, looking at David and smiling, Tenaiia said, "She's not doing so well is she?"

"No," David groaned. She's forgotten twice in the last ten minutes."

"How long is she safe not breathing before we have a problem?" David asked.

"Not longer than five minutes. May I remind you that you are in testing? If Katrina's breathing is not resumed in time and there is brain damage, there is no guarantee of ethereal surgery. After all, you are being tested."

Tenaiia was right. The full weight fell directly on the caretakers' shoulders twenty-four hours each day. The only exceptions were when Katrina went to school on Tuesdays and Thursdays, and when the caretakers were at income-earning pursuits.

The burden was enormous.

This was Zeeq's first attack that never let up. There was no four hours of uninterrupted rest at night, no short periods of time during the day when Zeeq was busy elsewhere. No forgetting to check on Katrina every four minutes. And Roxy couldn't keep her distance from Katrina, as Katrina preferred.

The tension mounted. The days ticked by … two … three … four ….

They nudged Katrina often. To David, she'd smile a "thank you." To Roxy, came a flat "thanks." Looking at Roxy reminded Katrina that she was about to surrender David. The wound ran deep and broad.

Nothing much got done besides reminding Katrina to breathe. Cleaning fell behind and laundry, too. Cooking was a real challenge in four-minute increments. Food burned often but at least Katrina was breathing.

The worst part were the long, sleepless nights. The caretakers alternately took two-hour shifts to keep watch over Katrina's breathing. For Roxy, there was the immense pain of watching Katrina and David sleeping together, their bodies naturally entwined. For David, it was a mammoth challenge to stay awake.

As the nights dragged on, Roxy came to notice that there was a way that David and Katrina absolutely fit together, more than she and David ever had. The sting of this persisted as Roxy was forced to sit and closely monitor Katrina wrapped firmly in David's arms night after night.

David's solution to the nodding problem was to busy himself twenty feet away in the garage organizing anything he could get his hands on. He would frequently return to the bedroom to check on Katrina but his distance left Roxy unnerved. She never quite surrendered to sleep. The nights seemed like an eternity ... five ... six ... eight .... Even the distractions Roxy came up with didn't remove the pain of watching them asleep united.

Exhausted to the bone, Roxy was knitting one night when David stirred. She looked up to see David roll over and place his arm across Katrina's breasts.

A lump formed in Roxy's throat and a tear rolled down her cheek. So natural, so peaceful, she thought. So separate from me. Then silently, she screamed: David, move your arm from her breast! She forced herself not to move. Tears escaped, betraying her wound. She missed David terribly.

Still the process continued. Overwhelm lurked around every corner, at every breath. Roxy breathed past the rough spots. David simply muscled it through. The days continued ... nine ... ten ... eleven ....

Katrina was tired of it, too. It was a strain on her body and she hated having Roxy constantly hovering about. The sight of Roxy brought up painful realizations that Katrina was in no mood to process, particularly with Roxy. Katrina felt suffocated and powerless to do anything about it. Often she forgot to breathe. She bit her tongue and tried to at least feign a smile when Roxy nudged her. She, too, wondered when this hideously exhausting process would go away. The days ticked on ... twelve ... thirteen ....

On the fourteenth day of the breathing process, Katrina, returning from school, bounded out of her car with excitement.

"Guess what! They turned my breathing mechanism back on. Isn't that great? I can breathe on my own again. Master Merlin said both you guys passed your tests. You proved that you wouldn't fail. Isn't that great?"

Miraculously, neither caretaker crossed the line into the forbidden realm of losing their acute presence of mind to the ravages of self-focused overwhelm.

Truth That Sets Us Free.

The prison that you find yourself in,
Is mirroring the Real prison inside of you.
It is a worthy opposition for a worthy soul.
Learn the lesson and you shall be set Free.

—Keith Amber

34

Amnesia

For a couple of days following the breathing process, Zeeq's presence was diminished. He was busy preparing for his next attack. In that brief window, Roxy spoke with Arianne.

"Why doesn't Katrina have to keep working through her jealousy anymore?"

"I am no longer funneling her emotional body through jealousy," Arianne said. "I have redirected it through loneliness. When she moves, she will find herself to be extremely lonely."

Roxy cocked her head. "Lonely for David?"

"Yes, lonely for David."

"Then why is she looking so forward to moving?"

"Because I have placed those thoughts and feelings into her," Arianne explained. "Otherwise she would greatly resist moving."

"So she doesn't have to work through her jealousy?" Roxy persisted.

"She will work through these feelings later, when she is alone, without David, when Zeeq is no longer in the picture. Now, with the weaving in place, she is getting too activated. It is too dangerous at this time for her to attempt to work through these feelings. It would be perilous to leave her alone while you two spend time together."

"So, does this happen often? Higher Selves placing the positive feelings in the lower self to get them into confrontive directions in their lives?"

"Yes. This is one use of veils," Arianne said. "It allows us to gracefully guide you into areas you would not consciously choose to go into on your own, yet the direction is vital for both the lower and Higher self's growth, for our lessons to be learned."

"So when will the loneliness hit Katrina?"

"Shortly after she moves. Until then, she will greatly look forward to it."

Zeeq's next scheme backfired, thrusting him out of the arena. Katrina was left with amnesia. Her prime consciousness was replaced by a layer of repressed consciousness.

Tenaiia rushed to the rescue before any inadvertent damage was done. "Katrina has amnesia and The Melding has been disconnected," she said.

"Amnesia? Can you fix The Melding?" Roxy asked.

"Yes, both can be fixed. However, there are other points to consider. Arianne is dangerously exhausted. She has not rested since she became fully Melded." Tenaiia paused. "Even ethereal Beings, like humans, require regular rest periods. Arianne has not had this basic need met for months, due to the battle with Zeeq on the ethereal plane. During her current state of amnesia—without The Melding—Zeeq cannot come through Katrina or bother Arianne. Under the terms of the contract, he can only do battle with Katrina's prime consciousness, when The Melding is intact. It seems as though we can use his blunder to our advantage and give Arianne some badly needed rest."

Zeeq provided Katrina an opportunity to express an entire reality trapped inside her. It was a suppressed part which believed David to actually be her husband. As Tenaiia spoke to them, the ethereal Melding Team pondered the wisest course of action and considered all points: Zeeq's needs, Arianne's needs, Katrina's needs, and how their plan would affect David and Roxy. A decision was made. Tenaiia laid out the strategy that would align David and Roxy with Katrina's current reality.

Tenaiia began. "In her current condition she is experiencing a repressed layer of her own subconscious where there is no Trinity. So it has been decided that, for now, David and Katrina shall be newlyweds and you, Roxy, shall be David's sister who is temporarily living with them. Do you understand?"

Roxy shrugged. "Okay, I guess."

"And you, David?" Tenaiia asked.

"Fine with me. Let's go." David was ready for action.

"Very well then, good luck," Tenaiia said and left.

Katrina was back for only a few seconds before the bombardment began.

"Sweetheart, I think I'll go fix us some dinner," Roxy offered.

"Why are you calling him 'sweetheart'?" Katrina demanded, daggers and barbs shooting through the air.

"Family habit," Roxy said.

"Well, I don't like it!" Katrina said, rubbing David's shoulders and arms and cooing, "I love you, honey" in his ear.

"Sorry," Roxy said. "Why don't I go make some food?"

Roxy realized that it was best to stay out of sight. Every time Katrina saw her, psychic bullets shot through the air. It was a mammoth effort to avoid saying all the wrong words.

As Roxy monitored her thoughts, she was astounded to notice just how much Katrina had to put up with. After dinner, Roxy heard Katrina suggest they make love in the bedroom. Then Roxy heard the bedroom door close, the first of many closings to come.

When it came time for bed, David whispered to Roxy. "Why don't you take Katrina's bedroom?"

"No. I'll sleep on the couch." She sensed trouble lurking if she surrendered her space for good. As Roxy gathered the needed bedding, she heard Katrina seducing her "new" husband once again.

The next morning other problems plagued the caretakers.

"Why is Roxy sleeping on the couch? Why are *her* clothes in *my* bedroom? Why does she have to live with us at all?" Katrina wanted to know now, every hour on the hour. The anxiety, and the pressure, built to explosive proportions by the second.

"We're in the process of changing bedrooms, don't you remember? We'll take care of it soon." David cajoled. "Roxy will be moving soon."

But not soon enough for Katrina. David's answers didn't suffice. An hour later, she demanded to know again. She just couldn't hold David's answers in her mind, didn't want them to be true. Katrina wanted Roxy out of their life, permanently. She wanted her new husband to promise her that they would be alone forever.

"Tell her to move out, David. I love you so much, honey. Why does she have to be here anyway? I don't trust her. Please, go tell her that she has to move out tomorrow. Surely there is some place where she could go. Darling, please! Go tell her," Katrina persisted between their lovemaking.

Such a perfect mirror for Roxy, who'd allowed her natural tendencies to flow towards David in Katrina's presence. Now the tables were turned.

Before twenty-four hours passed, Katrina suggested several times that David kick Roxy out. Roxy didn't have a dime to her name, or a credit card at her disposal. She had no resources to accommodate

Katrina's demands. The hours passed torturously slow as the pressure continued to rise.

Katrina let it all hang out. She hugged David at every turn, tweaked his crotch with a playful shine in her eyes, and ran her fingers through his hair, murmuring, "I love you so much." She was glued to his every glance, word, or touch. She glowed like a neon sign in his presence. Without Zeeq and the weaving she was soft, gentle, and graceful. Sensuality oozed from her pores. She wouldn't leave the room for any reason without hugging him and telling him how much she loved him.

All the thoughts and feelings she'd repressed rushed to the surface for expression. Katrina loathed Roxy's existence and, worse, that she was in *their* space. Every ounce of her was in love with David. She wanted to expunge anything that kept them apart. Katrina had even hidden her deepest feelings from David, never feeling safe with Roxy always in the distance.

David loved it. He had no idea of the true depth of Katrina's love. She was soft, loving, and infinitely attentive. He'd never experienced such devotion. For a giver to receive such passion was a slice of heaven. Still, the turmoil between the women was horrendous. His skill at maintaining peace was stretched beyond his limit. He existed in a warp zone between two opposing forces: absolute glee at his new relationship with Katrina, and hurricane-force strain in balancing the hate and fear from Katrina to Roxy.

Roxy was petrified. What would Katrina demand next? Being hated so much was hideous; there was no escaping it. Watching her husband so utterly in love with another woman drove her to the edges of sanity. The pain was unbearable. Tears rolled down her face as she listened to them making love one more time. Even worse, David couldn't express any of his feelings to Roxy because it sent Katrina into a raging fit. As David kept his distance, Roxy had never felt so isolated in her life.

Alarmed, Roxy realized the magnitude of The Trinity's demands on their emotional growth. For The Trinity to succeed, both women had to find peace in these shows of affection with David. No wonder Zeeq was upset that Katrina was dissolving The Trinity. It would have taken Katrina and Roxy years to reach such a peaceful, mature place.

As this process continued, it dislodged Roxy's very roots. Her husband was gone, control no longer existed, and their bedroom was gone. The bed had been removed and her clothes were conditionally available only when Katrina wasn't looking. During this period of amnesia,

Katrina didn't attend school and lurked around every corner. Roxy's very identity was being ripped away. David could not touch her or hardly speak to her without Katrina throwing another fit. Then she would demand, once more, that he throw Roxy out.

"I don't care if she has no place to go!" Roxy heard Katrina yell through the bedroom wall as she prepared lunch. "I just want her out!"

Every heave of Roxy's chest hurt. Fright filled the air.

They made love often—twice daily, at least—loudly, passionately. Katrina could hardly get enough of David. The days continued to pass … two … three ….

Roxy tried to stay out of sight and David had a terrible time. Among other things, Katrina wanted David to take her out to dinner. She craved a public display of their marriage. Not getting it made her want it all the more. In their small community, it wasn't an option.

By day four, Roxy was crumbling under the strain. She was sure she was going to break. David was exhausted. This was the toughest "glue" job he had ever done and he wasn't succeeding. Katrina and her demands could not be appeased.

Each day David asked Tenaiia, "When are the Guides going to reverse this process?"

Each day her response was, "Arianne is getting the badly needed rest. The Troops are monitoring the situation very closely."

Roxy was desperate. She felt that she had reached her explosive point many times over yet she was being asked to stretch further. It seemed as though the Guides-of-Light knew something about her limits that she didn't know and they were determined to push her against them. She felt abandoned, like a rope being pulled to the snapping point in a terrible tug-of-war. Yet the days continued … five … six … unbearable, intolerable.

On day seven, Katrina decided that she was no longer going to wait until David kicked Roxy out. She was going to do it herself—today—right now! David was at his wits' end.

Finally The Troops decided that Arianne had gotten enough rest—barely—to resume her duties. As the days ticked away, Zeeq chomped at the bit to get back into action. At the last tolerable second, as Katrina was heading into the living room to kick Roxy out, Tenaiia took her body over and took her back to bed. The process was reversed.

"The Melding will be reconnected," Tenaiia told David, "and for a period of time she will be quite raw from the experience. Be gentle with her."

"Roxy, I thought you'd like to know that Tenaiia was just here," David said. "The amnesia's been reversed and The Melding will be reconnected. I need to go back and be with Katrina." And he was gone.

Roxy collapsed on the couch and tears rolled down her face. She breathed for the first time in a week. She had never experienced being so totally out of control. She was humbled, stronger, more distant, more independent. She'd experienced that she wasn't her possessions, her marriage, her space, or her limits. She was more in touch with her true, core essence. She no longer wanted to wield the same control. It didn't feel right anymore.

Katrina, who struggled for every ounce of David she could get, was unwilling to give all the control back. The scales were painfully tipping; Katrina's truth was now exposed and raw. She had a gaping wound festering at the surface and Zeeq had a field day from this point onward.

The experience magnified the energy in David. He was profoundly moved by Katrina's love for him; he didn't want to give it up. Still, he was very much in love with Roxy, his Twin Flame.

A couple of hours later Katrina was still confused, lost, and fragile. Roxy had no strength or grace left to give. Exhausted, she walked into the bedroom to go to bed.

David was holding Katrina as she cried. Looking at Roxy, David said, "I'd like to make love to Katrina."

Roxy slumped, eyes weary. They had made love twice a day for days but that had been the "other" Katrina. Even to Roxy it was obvious that "this" Katrina desperately needed it now.

But Roxy also felt a need for David. Her world had been turned inside out. She, too, was raw. Still, David chose to tend to Katrina first. Hurt, Roxy left.

She could no longer contain the hurt, frustration and rage. She walked across the meadow to a distant group of trees, far away from anyone. The rage welled up until she found herself hitting a tree as hard as she could. She screamed, cried and pummeled the tree for twenty minutes. Finally she was spent. Rubbing her bruised hands, she returned home.

She was different, more detached, freer, but she was still angry at David. She watched as he came out of the house and into the garage.

"We're done," he said.

"Great! She like it?" Sarcasm filled the air.

"She cried the whole time. She's pretty raw."

"Is she sleeping?"

"No. She's heating water for a bath." David looked at Roxy with the puppy-dog eyes that had always melted her anger but it didn't work this time.

"Fuck you! Just fuck you!" Roxy shouted, piercing her anger into his eyes.

"Roxy, I love you! You did great this week! I love you," David said, attempting to melt her anger.

"Fuck you! I don't care, just go away!" Roxy yelled back, wounded and enraged.

David walked away, not knowing what else to do to help his wife. He understood her pain. The problem was that Katrina's pain was greater.

Roxy didn't always want to be strong but she was. Her time with David was over. More hell was on its way.

Who Are Lightworkers?

They are people interested in
Owning themselves
Rather than things.

—Jack Clarke

35

Banks Of Love

With the weaving came a distorted Katrina. With the altered Katrina, David felt an urgent need to spend every possible waking moment with her. David and Roxy's time together diminished into conversations to and from work and the time while Katrina was at school. Even their time on Tuesdays and Thursdays had shriveled. Now David scheduled most of his appointments during Katrina's time at school so that he could be home with Katrina.

Katrina's dislike for Roxy grew to monumental proportions, partly because her inner truth was exposed, and partly due to the magnification of that truth through the weaving. Katrina needed all of David's attention, forcing Roxy to stretch into realms of augmented strength and endurance.

As the weaving evolved, Katrina's intolerance of Roxy manifested at new levels. Now whenever Katrina saw Roxy, she fainted on the spot. Numerous times daily, Katrina would rush around a corner, see Roxy, and drop to the floor.

Roxy never quite knew when or where it would happen next, or what Katrina might hit on her way down. Roxy tried to avoid such scenes, as did David, who nudged Katrina into other directions, away from Roxy. But Zeeq had a keen ability to sniff Roxy out and lead Katrina right to her.

With these new problems, Roxy abandoned housecleaning chores altogether. The constant strain of needing to keep out of sight left Roxy feeling as though the log cabin was hardly her home anymore. Hate and dread filled every breath, every molecule of space. With three months to go, Roxy wondered if her declaration of, "I can do anything for five months," was really true. It was certainly being challenged.

There was a purpose behind Zeeq's strategy. The more he got Katrina to reject one of her caretakers, the more the burden fell on the other, who might tire and become prone to making a mistake. Zeeq banked on this eventuality. The demand on David was crushing and the encumbrance was escalating.

Whenever David was out of Katrina's presence, except when she was at school, in the blink of an eye the weaving sucked Katrina's mind into a dark and distant hole. Katrina would sit, usually crumpled into a corner or on her bed, and stare into nothingness for hours on end. She would sink deeper and deeper until David came home and coaxed her out. He would call to her, rub her forehead, shake her—anything to pull her back into the waking world. It became evident that David was Katrina's lifeline, her link with reality.

As the days and weeks passed, these stupors became deeper and more intense. Each daze gripped Katrina more firmly than the last. In the end, David would spend up to an hour coaxing her back, and then spend more time helping her out of her confusion. In Roxy's presence, Katrina went in further. It was even necessary for Roxy to creep into bed after the lights went out and never move all night long. The mere presence of Roxy activated Katrina further.

Katrina lived in a constant state of disorienting stupors. For her, all of life stopped—her homework, her emotions, and her spiritual development were all stymied. Her consciousness insidiously eroded away into emptiness.

It was nothing short of a miracle that Katrina had managed to finish school at all, even with Tenaiia's help. Indeed, it was the Guides who made that happen; it surely wasn't Katrina during this phase of Zeeq's evil attack.

The caretakers feared that if Katrina went too far into the dark-mind holes, David would be unable to pull her back out. She would be lost forever, The Melding along with her. The only weapon in their arsenal was David's presence. That alone kept Katrina from going into a hellish daze. Her life and sanity depended upon him. The pressure was enormous.

Roxy was of little help. Either she activated Katrina further or she craved "venting." There was no one else to vent to besides used-up David. In their brief time together to and from work, the venting continued and regular arguments ensued. David did not have the capacity to be there for Roxy in any form. He needed Roxy to be there for him.

It was Leviticus who came to their rescue. He wasn't around much any more. Not accustomed to splitting his consciousness simultaneously between an incarnation and channeling, his focus predominantly remained in his Earth lifetime, giving psychic readings. The rare times Leviticus chose to channel through David were only for reasons he deemed vital. Roxy paid close attention to his every word.

"You are beyond needing to vent at David any longer," Leviticus began one Tuesday just prior to Katrina's expected arrival home. "You are able, Dear One, to process these feelings on your own. Why not use your brief time with David more productively?"

Leviticus was right. Roxy knew in her heart that it was time to control her emotions further, to process them alone. Initially, she fought an intense internal battle between the two opposing factions: the old self-focused part that liked venting versus the new, maturing potion that was ready to move on and let go. She refused to let the "venting" escape her lips.

She became proficient at processing her feelings privately, over and over, until they no longer hurt and they matured to a point of unconditional love. Roxy emerged as a self-contained, loving, supportive individual, leaving behind the dependent, needy, and self-oriented parts. Mastering self-control replaced her desire to control others. The arguments faded.

Time together was at a premium. It was a warm Tuesday in March when David's schedule unexpectedly freed up. David and Roxy took advantage of it.

To best use their five free hours, they decided to go to the warm, dry northeast side of Mt. Shasta and frolic in the sun. A bottle of fruity wine, crackers, and cheddar cheese in hand, they drove to the desert side of the mountain. After traveling for forty-five minutes, they found a dirt road amid the dry, brittle sage and rocky terrain, far away from anyone else. They were alone at last.

Giggling, they climbed on top of their big, white Plymouth to brave nude sunbathing while sipping wine and eating warm cheese and Ritz crackers.

An hour or so later they made love in the company of the lizards under the velvety blue sky. After a while, their faces turned rosy and their bodies pink. They both breathed unencumbered for the first time in weeks.

"I love you, David."

"I love you, too, Roxy. I'm sorry there isn't more time we can spend together. I don't know what else to do with Katrina. She's a mess all the time now, you know?"

"Yeah, I know. It's okay. I still love you. Always will," Roxy smiled.

A little over three blissful hours later they drove home, peaceful and rested.

Katrina returned at nine that evening, bringing with her a dark cloud that remained until her scheduled departure thirteen weeks away.

Tenaiia, in Katrina's body, bolted through the kitchen door, "Katrina was nearly killed today," she blurted out. Tenaiia, masterful at rolling with the punches, looked shaken. Her anxiety was unnerving.

"How? What happened?" David asked.

"Zeeq managed to get an oncoming vehicle to cross over the line. We nearly had a high-speed, head-on collision. If this occurs again, it is doubtful that I will be successful in stopping it. It was an extremely close call." Tenaiia quivered. Zeeq, for the first time, had thrown Tenaiia off-center. Roxy and David shuddered.

"How did Zeeq do it?" David asked.

"He tapped your energy bank," Tenaiia said more calmly. "That gave him the extra burst of physical energy he needed to accomplish an isolated physical attack. What were you both doing this afternoon around three-thirty?"

Roxy's eyes rolled up into her head. "Makin' love in the sun."

"I see!" Tenaiia sighed. "Well, at that moment the reserve in your energy bank went up considerably. Zeeq siphoned the energy off and used it to force the other car over the center line."

"Energy bank? Is this legal? Can Zeeq do that?" Roxy's heart pounded as shock spread.

"Yes. He's acting within his legal boundaries."

"What's an energy bank?" Fear shot through Roxy.

"An ethereal energy bank is similar to a financial bank, except that energy flows through it instead of money."

"Who has these energy banks?" David asked.

"Any two people who share love between them have an energy bank; they are connected to it by a cord. The reserve in the energy bank increases when love is shared and decreases during conflict. If there is a steady flow of love, the energy bank reserve grows in strength and stability. Such is the case with you and David. You have a strong energy bank, not because you spend volumes of time together but because of your intent. You love each other very much and your energy bank reflects that."

"Can Zeeq keep his siphon in our ethereal energy bank?" Roxy asked, her chest tightening.

"Yes, and you can be sure that he will. This gives him the extra energy needed for difficult physical attacks."

"How can we stop him?" Roxy asked.

"By not replenishing your energy bank," Tenaiia said.

"What are you suggesting?" Roxy snapped.

"I am not suggesting anything. I am merely pointing out how to keep Zeeq from getting energy from your energy bank." Tenaiia was unyielding.

"Go on." Apprehension filled Roxy's voice.

"Any time you express love to each other, you build your reserve. Even when you share a bed for sleep, the reserve gets filled. Of course, making love adds a great deal, but smaller things add up as well. Every time you touch, each 'I love you'—any loving conversation adds to the reserve."

"You mean we can't sleep together anymore?" A lump formed in Roxy's throat.

"These decisions are up to you," Tenaiia smiled. "I am merely reporting the facts, as you have asked me to do. You are her caretakers; you must decide."

Roxy's mind spun. Mortified, her eyes stared blankly. "A loveless relationship," she mumbled, tears escaping her eyes. She pleaded with Athena, to no avail. Zeeq was acting within the boundaries of their contract.

For David, the answer was simple. If keeping Katrina alive meant they had to do certain things, well, then, so be it. If Roxy and he had to cease expressing love, consider it done. In the flash of a moment he shut down an entire reality. All natural tendencies were reversed. No more touching, no warmth, no words, no sleeping together.

Their conversations became a dry reporting of logistical information. Propelled by fear, David mastered this new strategy in a split second. From that moment on, he did not express his love for Roxy in any form whatsoever. His goal was to keep their energy bank empty. He was determined and unyielding.

The next day Katrina emanated glee as she converted her bedroom into "their" bedroom. She glowed as bright as a Halogen lamp. Her euphoria filled the house. She sang and skipped like a teenager. For the first time in a year she laundered her own bedding, dusted, and vacuumed. Her room was cleaner than Roxy had ever seen it. On that rare day, even Roxy's presence wasn't a problem. There were no fainting or distant-daze episodes. The excitement of having David to herself kept Zeeq, and the weaving, at bay.

Roxy was petrified. Her control was over. At once she was both free and aghast. What if Katrina captured David's heart forever? Roxy had to let go and trust.

Although Roxy was just as determined to succeed as David was, it was a colossal undertaking for her. She was thrust into managing every word that came out of her mouth. Controlling herself at this crucial level made her feel like a pressure cooker at the exploding point. On top of that, she still did the best she could to provide daily meals and clean clothes while staying out of Katrina's sight.

The worst part was not knowing if David loved her anymore. Maybe his heart really was Katrina's now. The notion terrified her every day, every hour, every minute. The mixture of demands and uncertainty were hair raising. Still, the days, the weeks, ticked on at the perpetual speed of a snail.

The fainting problem progressively worsened. At times, just Roxy's presence in the house—not even in Katrina's immediate presence—was a problem. The anxiety, pressure, and strain were debilitating. And all this to keep Katrina/Arianne alive, and The Melding intact, so that Katrina/Arianne could help transform the educational system.

At each new stage of Zeeq's game plan, he had managed to induce greater levels of anxiety until the pressure reached unimaginable proportions. For thirteen lonely weeks, David and Roxy's relationship was to be stripped of the one thing that had enabled them to survive thus far: love.

David and Katrina had finally become man and wife. Behind closed doors, their relationship blossomed without restraint. They made passionate love daily. Each time David pulled Katrina out of the incessant dazed states, he found that lovemaking was his only effective tool that strengthened her auric field. Zeeq's presence remained daunting.

By the end of March, life for Roxy became a dichotomy. On one hand, her counseling clients gradually increased. She used more of her inner vision and telepathic skills to sense her clients' feelings and she could hear clients' Guides and Higher Selves more clearly. In this arena, her self-confidence flourished. On the other hand, the inner strain from The Trinity's stringent demands was hazardous to her well-being.

After five weeks of constant demand to control her every emotional, physical, sexual, and mental urge, Roxy was a volatile, frantic, isolated island with insanity looming on the horizon. In the car next to David, so close yet so far away, a tear rolled down her cheek. She looked out the window, careful not to let David see it. She loved this man; she always had. Still, she forced herself to remain quiet. It was the only way to save Katrina and The Melding. After all, that's what this was all about, wasn't it?

Seeking relief, Roxy ventured into the realms of a couple of new friendships away from her private hell. It was her only release valve, her anchor with sanity outside the insanity of their home. Though her secrets were never revealed to her new friends, she was at least able to communicate with others, get a hug, and experience a touch of normalcy. These friends became a loving oasis amid the ordeal.

The growing emptiness between them made Roxy desperate to tell David about her new friends but she couldn't. During the energy-bank "ice" phase, their short, perfunctory conversations always drifted into silence. Seven weeks into the rigorous discipline of not talking beyond vital logistics or expressing love in any form, the gap between David and Roxy mushroomed exponentially and tension snowballed.

On May 5, Roxy heard the first "music to her ears" in months. "Katrina will be leaving on May fifteenth instead of June fifth as originally scheduled," David said.

"Why? What about school?" Roxy's heart jumped.

"I don't know. It's something about doing a class in the fall instead of now. Anyway, I have to get back to Katrina now. I just thought you had a right to know." Without even a hint of a smile, David left.

Soon! Soon I get my husband back! Roxy thought. May 15th is a mere ten days away, a full three weeks early. She forced herself to contain the joy.

About the time of "the announcement," Katrina's fainting eased and Roxy began staying home more. One evening after Katrina arrived home from school, the three sat together for the first time in months. David and Katrina smoked a cigarette, and boy, did they feel married. Roxy felt on the outs with both of them. Life certainly had changed.

Katrina began relating an experience she'd had on her way home from school. She car-pooled with a lady she didn't like. The lady, Katrina insisted, had urged her three times to debate a school topic and Katrina finally gave in. Laughing, and with a cocky smirk, Katrina declared, "I tore her to shreds." The lady had been shocked and hurt but Katrina didn't care. That was not the pre-weaving Katrina Roxy remembered.

Worse yet, David was equally amused. He found the story highly entertaining, Katrina's actions appropriate. The whole scene unnerved Roxy. It seemed as though all of the ego work Katrina had done, the weaving had undone. Her intellectual arrogance blossomed out of control. David either couldn't see it or he didn't care.

Shortly before May 15th Tenaiia came to talk with David and Roxy. "I thought you might like to know that you had a three percent chance to win against this energy-bank strategy. Also, you might like to know that both Zeeq and The Troops expected you to fail. They all felt it was just too big a job to keep your energy bank depleted for so long. They doubted, Roxy, that you could keep your emotional body in check. You both have surprised them all." Tenaiia smiled. "Congratulations!"

Indeed, it was a mind-boggling, awesome personal achievement.

Who Are Lightworkers?

They are people taking conscious responsibility
For their own lives,
Not blaming others for their problems.

—Jack Clarke

36

The Grand Finale

"Master Merlin wants to talk you, David, privately," Katrina announced two days before her scheduled departure. These private sessions still unnerved Roxy. What couldn't she hear?

David and Katrina headed into the woods, creating plenty of space between them and Roxy.

"Good afternoon," boomed Master Merlin. "Congratulations on your success."

"Thanks. Is this Merlin of the Light?"

"Yes, it is Merlin who speaks to you now. I have asked for this meeting in private, as Roxy would surely block the information from coming through."

"Must be heavy," David said wearily.

"For her, it shall be. It is also in the highest good for all, though it will take some time for that to unfold," Master Merlin said. "I am here to inform you, David, that your responsibilities to Katrina do not end on the day she departs."

"Okay. What do you have in mind?"

"For a period of two years you are to maintain a financial, emotional, physical, and sexual responsibility to her."

David was both relieved and torn. He didn't want to give up Katrina anymore than she wanted to give him up but there was the matter of Roxy. David still loved her in the depths of his heart and soul. The other problem was that this agreement was probably going to send Roxy berserk.

Master Merlin interrupted David's thoughts. "You shall visit Katrina at her house in Davis once every four to six weeks, remaining overnight, beginning after her summer in Portland. You are to help her financially as needed. You are to continue to be available for emotional support and physically help her as needed. Are you clear?"

It was a lot to take in. However, it was not one more ounce to give to Katrina than already lived inside David's heart. "Yes, I believe I am clear."

"Very well, then we shall expect you to live up to your word. Again, congratulations on your accomplishment. We doubted you and Roxy would succeed. I must depart now. And you must deliver this news to Roxy."

Merlin departed back into the galaxy, leaving David to face the unpleasant task at hand.

"What? You're kidding, right? Two years? For two years you're supposed to stay responsible? Sexually, financially, and what else?" Roxy shrieked.

"Emotionally and physically," David said.

"Why?"

"We owe her, Roxy."

"Sure, financially we owe her, I agree. But sexually? What's the deal, anyway?" Roxy was hurt, livid, and frightened. "What does all this mean?"

"I don't know. All I know is that Merlin made me give him my word that'd I'd go see her every four to six weeks. And that's what I'm going to do. I need to go help Katrina now."

Roxy thought her life, the old life with David she so fondly re-membered, was about to land back in her lap. However, it remained intangible. Why did David seemed relieved by these new responsibili-ties? The news, and David's reaction, jarred Roxy to her core. Even though Katrina would leave in two days, in no way was she going to be gone from their lives. What next? Roxy wondered with dread.

All Zeeq-related activities calmed down those last days prior to Katrina's departure. The constant pressure lifted and Katrina's hate melted. And just as Arianne had predicted, another part of Katrina looked forward to moving. Her loneliness was intangible.

Katrina and Roxy talked for the first time in months, even though Katrina was still in a bit of a weaving-induced stupor.

"Do you remember the apathy implant?" Roxy asked.

"The what?" Katrina looked mystified.

I see, Roxy thought, sex three times a day, versions of hell for me, and she doesn't even remember. That's good! Really good! "How about the breathing process? Remember any of that?"

"Yeah, some," Katrina nodded.

"And the week of amnesia?"

"Excuse me?" Katrina blinked.

Roxy dropped it. "And the weaving?"

"The what?" Katrina blinked again. Her only exclusively married time with David was a fog from beginning to end.

"It's been a real strain," Roxy commented.

But Katrina didn't want to know. She wanted to leave all the bad memories and anxiety behind and who could blame her? The weaving had been a living hell for her, start to finish. Every time she had tried to study, her mind would uncontrollably "mush out" until she could think no more. Then, she would be aware of David, in front of her yelling, concern etched all over his face, sometimes even with tears rolling down his face. Then she would realize that the precious hours of study time had passed and she was still on the same page in her text. No homework had gotten done. Worse yet, she had been unable to prevent it from happening, no matter how hard she tried. And it just kept happening.

She had also been confused about why she kept finding herself on the floor, all bruised. What caused all this weirdness to happen? she'd asked David. What was going on? She remembered his telling her, then the strangest thing would happen. Just as she had locked onto his words, they'd suddenly vanish and she couldn't find them anywhere. She wondered if it happened a lot. She wasn't sure of that either.

At some point, she had become aware that Roxy wasn't around the house so much anymore, and vaguely wondered where she was. And it troubled her that she couldn't remember much of her time with David. Just the other day she noticed for the first time that she and David were sharing a bedroom alone. She wondered when all that had transpired. Fog? Yep. There certainly was plenty of fog around. All Katrina knew was that she wanted out, and the sooner the better.

On May 14, David and Katrina loaded a U-Haul with most of the household items. David and Roxy were moving into a furnished house, so they didn't need much.

David and Katrina drove the truck to Davis, unloading everything into a storage unit where it would remain until Katrina returned from her summer in Portland. Katrina, needing some healing time, was going to stay with her gay soul friend, Gerald, whom she'd known for years.

At last May 15 arrived and Katrina and David loaded her car.

"Honey, where did you put the box marked 'fragile'?" Katrina asked.

"I put it on the floor in the front seat," David said, as though they'd been married for years.

Katrina's use of the word 'honey' made Roxy's insides tense. In all their nine years together, Roxy had never been able to call David 'honey.' It felt strange somehow. There was a naturalness about David and Katrina that David and Roxy had never encountered. Is this how it is between them when they're alone? Roxy wondered. She shuddered and left.

When the car was loaded, they returned to Katrina's bedroom to make love one last time. An hour later, it was time for Katrina to leave. They emerged from the bedroom somber. Roxy had difficulty containing her glee.

Roxy followed them to the garage. Katrina glanced a farewell in Roxy's direction. She embraced David, crying for a long, long time. At last, mustering every ounce of willpower, Katrina forced herself into her car. Once again, she looked with yearning into David's eyes, tears streaming down her face. She put the car into gear. "Good-bye. I love you," she said and drove off.

No more Zeeq, no more strain, no more pressure. The realization was days from sinking in.

David seemed like a stranger to Roxy. She wanted to celebrate but David was terribly sad. Roxy had waited months for David to be free to return to her, but in all that time David had been full of Katrina; he hadn't yearned for Roxy. The transition from Katrina to Roxy would take some time. David needed space.

An hour after Katrina's departure, David offered to make love. During their intimacy, Roxy felt something was different. Something was missing. David was present elsewhere. He appeared automated, as though going through the motions. The old magic was gone. Though Katrina wasn't interrupting the psychic airwaves, their lovemaking was still flat. Roxy wondered if they could recapture the old, or were they both too altered, too tainted, too distant?

The next day, David had planned to scout new residential areas. His insurance company had developed a new cost-effective homeowner's policy and David, wanting to get money flowing again, was planning to canvass new areas in the days to come. With his caretaking responsibilities lifted, he wanted to refocus his energies into being the breadwinner, to help both households. He invited Roxy to join him when she completed her cleaning job.

"Hi. You ready?" Roxy smiled as she entered David's office.

David, still weary, nodded. "Okay, let's go."

One block from the office, the fight began. The pitch was low at first, then escalated like a wild fire fanned by hurricane winds, but it was inevitable. Months and months of forcibly contained stress, pressure, and demands had to come out at some point.

Less than a mile from the office, David approached their freeway exit and Roxy blurted out, "I don't want to be with you when you're in this ugly mood."

"Fine!" David snapped. He took their exit and stopped. In his anger over his lost love and the rip he felt inside, he could not bring himself to look at his wife. He simply wanted her out of the car, out of his space and, for the moment, out of his life. Confused by the conflicting feelings raging inside, he wanted time alone to think and feel without influence. He missed Katrina and he hated himself for it.

Less needy, Roxy joyfully walked the three miles home, blisters and all. She'd put up with David's moodiness for too long. She was tired of it. Her self-worth, her independence had grown.

Once home, she began to clean—walls, floors, bedrooms and bathrooms, top to bottom, thoroughly. Zeeq's energy was removed, Katrina's jealousy exterminated. With every swipe of the rag, all the strain was expunged from the space. The minutes turned into hours as Roxy hummed. She purified their space. When she finished, her anger was gone and she remembered how much she loved David.

About an hour later, David arrived. "Hi," he said. "I'm sorry I exploded at you. I guess I needed some time alone."

"Yeah, I guess I did, too. I'm sorry, too."

"I bought us a bottle of wine. How about we start over?" He opened his arms to Roxy and she melted into his embrace. Their life together could begin anew.

That evening they made love again. Afterward they snuggled and talked, giggled and laughed. Roxy began massaging David's penis again, wanting the bliss to last forever. But for all of David's desire to respond, it remained flaccid.

"What's wrong?" Roxy gently asked.

"I don't know. This has never happened before." David was mystified. The problem was to remain unsolved for many months to come.

The next day, the phone rang. Katrina was desperate to connect with David. Roxy's heart sank when she heard Katrina's voice. "I cleaned the house yesterday," Roxy blurted out, as though trying to send Katrina a message. But Katrina wasn't listening, she just wanted to talk to David.

On the first day of June, David and Roxy moved into town. Gary, on his own spiritual quest, received them with open arms.

Calm permeated their relationship. That wasn't all bad after what they had gone through but the magic of days gone by was missing. And Katrina called daily, desperate. Only David would do. Roxy's resentment grew. Then, on June 15th, Tenaiia, in Katrina's body, called David on the phone with urgency in her tone.

"Katrina is in trouble, David. We need your help."

"What do you want me to do?"

"Could you meet Katrina halfway between here and Mt. Shasta in the next couple days?"

"Absolutely."

"I have a plan I will share with you when we meet. I will give you back to Katrina now so you can finish the details."

Katrina was thrilled that she'd be seeing David in just two days. This did not strike Roxy as a woman getting over her lover.

Three days later, David departed at 5:30 in the morning. Three hours after that, they met at a way station just off the I-5 freeway.

"Oh, honey, I've missed you. I love you so much. How are you?" Katrina declared, hugging David.

"I'm fine. More importantly, how are you, my love? I've missed you, too." David held Katrina tightly.

"I'm fine." Katrina lied. "Tenaiia's all in a snit to talk to you right away. I guess it's urgent. I'd better let her come." Katrina sat on top of the old scratched and chipped green picnic table close by, closed her eyes, and took a deep breath. Her eyes opened and Tenaiia said, "Thank you for meeting Katrina so quickly."

"Is this Tenaiia of the Light?"

"Yes, it is I," Tenaiia assured Katrina's caretaker.

"So tell me, what's going on?" The feeling in David smacked of the old days, a warrior ready for battle.

"Zeeq has been missing for some time," Tenaiia began. "No one is quite sure where he is. I have a hunch he has shrunk his energy, hiding himself inside Katrina's head."

"What makes you think Zeeq is in her head?"

"Katrina did not tell you, but she has been suicidal since she left Mt. Shasta," Tenaiia explained. "She has nearly killed herself four times."

The news hit David with the weight of an elephant. "Okay. What do you want me to do?"

"For reasons I do not understand, Katrina's sexual juices have been shut down. We need to reawaken them, which will require a great deal of foreplay. Perhaps you could stimulate her while you find a motel where you can make love to her. If you can raise her vibration through lovemaking to a high enough level, you will force Zeeq to expose himself. Too high a vibration will be painful and intolerable for him. I know of no other way than lovemaking to accomplish this."

"Fine. Let's go."

Something was amiss. David felt it, too. It took forever to find a motel while David caressed Katrina's nipples and privates through her clothes. By the time they got into the musty, worn-out room, they were ready for each other. Undressing, they plunged in, the bed creaking from their weight. Not wanting to lose the momentum, David continued the foreplay.

Katrina's eyes closed and she finally began responding, moaning in delight.

"I love you, honey. Relax, enjoy. That's it." He sucked her erect nipples, first one, then the other—sucking, kneading, licking.

"Ohhhhh, David, I love you. Ohhhh, yessssss! Honey, I love you so much." Her legs fell open, inviting and moist.

David rose, his erection ready to send Katrina—and Zeeq—to new heights of bliss, rapture and surrender. Slowly, gently he pierced into her folds of delight. Katrina shuddered throughout as a sigh escaped her mouth. Rhythmically he plunged to the count of thirty, abruptly stopping.

At the brink, Katrina gasped for air, silently screaming for more. Then back to the nipples, pink and proudly tall, hungry for more. David's tongue teased them till they were rock hard and pulsating in delight. Then thirty more thrusts to the next verge of bliss. Katrina panted for more. Over the edge, she silently begged her masterful lover, over the edge! Slowly, David picked up momentum, thrusting deeper and deeper till Katrina was shrieking, "Yes, yes, yes! God, I love you! Yes!" And out into orbit she went.

Suddenly, Katrina's face went from sublime rapture to a gruesome mask contorted in pain. Zeeq growled as her body writhed in agony. Zeeq pushed David away.

"Leave us alone!" Zeeq's deep voice roared, exposing himself. The vibrations of love drove Zeeq mad. He'd left Katrina's head and moved into her body, defending his turf.

"I thought so, you bastard! You *are* in Katrina. Get out! You have no right to be there! The battle's over. We won. Give up. I won't let you have her! I won't!" David thrust rapidly several more times, forcing Katrina's body to involuntarily respond, reaching new orgasmic heights. The ecstasy caused Zeeq to squirm in pain.

"I will *not* give up her body!" Zeeq proclaimed, face contorted in anguish, pushing at David.

"The hell you won't!" David declared, intensifying his momentum while Zeeq clutched and fought. Then Katrina fell back panting and moaning.

The battle raged for hours, Katrina's body violently switching from intense euphoria to explosive pain. The momentum kept shoving and squeezing Zeeq to the fringes of his hold on Katrina. But Zeeq wouldn't leave. He was relentless; he just couldn't live with the loss. The ego blow was more than he could bear.

David reached exhaustion many times over. Still, he could not abandon his ward, his love. They'd already won the battle with Zeeq before Katrina had left The Trinity. David wasn't about to let Zeeq illegally take over now, not after all that they'd gone through. The idea of Katrina dying fueled David. He found his fourth wind and wildly began driving into Katrina.

"Ohhh! Yes! Yes!" Katrina cooed.

Leviticus joined the battle, telepathically encouraging David to maintain his frantic rhythm.

Seconds later, Zeeq bellowed, "I WILL NOT GIVE UP!"

"Come on, Katrina, stay with me! I love you!" David gasped between thrusts. Exhausted, he rolled Katrina onto her side and continued plunging.

Leviticus joined the fight. Using his intense psychic force, he pulled on Zeeq's energy to break it free of Katrina's body. "Go faster, David," Leviticus telepathically instructed.

Welling up with his last bit of strength, David began wildly ramming into Katrina, her body vibrating in response. Suddenly, Zeeq screamed, "STOP!"

"Give up, you bastard!" David yelled as Leviticus continued to pull.

"Noooooo . . . ." Zeeq's cruel voice died in the motel room's musky air. Leviticus pulled him out of Katrina's body.

In that instant, Master Merlin swooped down, captured Zeeq, and whisked him away, rendering him incapable of ever doing harm to Katrina again. The battle was finally, truly over.

David, Roxy and Katrina—the Light in each—had won. The threat of Katrina/Arianne going to the dark for the duration of this Melded lifetime was over.

Zeeq had grossly violated the terms of their contract. It was expected. The dark ones are known for breaking their word; it's part of the nature of being or having dark within. There would be grave consequences for Zeeq's actions. He was now in the hands of The Troops and would not be bothering David, Roxy or Katrina for the rest of this lifetime.

Katrina, aglow, lay secure in David's arms.

"How do you feel now?" David smiled at her.

"Better than I have in a very long time. Thanks, honey. What happened anyway? It all seems kinda like a fog to me. All I vaguely remember is meeting you at the exit, then it's a blank."

"Well," David began, "I stimulated you for an hour in the car till we found this place."

"Really? I don't remember any of that."

"Then, once we got here, we did battle with Zeeq. The bastard still hadn't given up. Can you believe it?" David was angry again.

"I wondered what was going on," Katrina said. "I mean, I know I missed you a lot, but not so that I would try to commit suicide. That's what's been happening since I moved to Portland. I'd find myself in front of the mirror, making horrific faces at myself, incessantly repeating, 'I hate myself'. Then I'd notice that hours had passed. Several times, I came to with a razor in my hand, ready to cut my wrists. None of it made any sense. The mood swings were awful. The whole month has been a living hell. That's why I called you so often."

"It's a miracle you survived, honey. Why didn't you tell me any of this before?"

"I thought I did, several times. I guess Zeeq had me think I did but I hadn't." Katrina shrugged.

"Well, Zeeq won't be back any more. Merlin took him away for good. You're safe now, my love." David squeezed her tight.

Exhausted, David drove home. He staggered in the door at five in the morning and hit the bed with barely a "Hello" before the snoring began.

The next afternoon he shared the horror story with Roxy. What Zeeq did was unconscionable. Roxy was relieved that Katrina was finally safe. She was also left wondering where David's sex drive had come from—and where it had disappeared to once again.

Who Are Lightworkers?

People seeking the perfection of God
While forgiving
Their own and others' imperfections.

—Jack Clarke

37

Katrina's New Love

At last, life settled down. July and August came and went unnoticed. September was sneaking by as well. Katrina had relocated to Davis and had been permitted ethereal surgery to repair her uterus damaged by the lightening bolts Zeeq shot through her body. The Guides had told Katrina that since she and her caretakers had won the battle with Zeeq, it was legal within the parameters of her contract. The surgery process lasted for two days and left Katrina in bed, out of it, for most of that time. With her uterus repaired, she would be able to have children.

David's regular trips to Davis ensued, but his sex drive remained an enigma. It was available only on his weekends with Katrina. Even then it was compromised.

Conversations between Roxy and Grant had been on the upswing. Grant and his wife, Wanda, were having increased marital problems. Roxy felt sure that she could help. Somehow she felt that she already intimately knew Grant. She knew that Grant's Higher Self was Antonomn. Their souls were close. Just how close she didn't know.

Roxy said that if Grant flew her to Seattle, she'd work with him and his wife. She would also work with his consulting staff on their emotional and spiritual issues. Frustrated, Grant finally agreed. He didn't know what else to do.

Once in Seattle, the work progressed briskly and potently. Grant reluctantly admitted that he had control issues. He was quick to point out that so did Wanda. It was obvious to Roxy that Grant would not be one to let go and change any time soon. Each of the four nights, Roxy stayed with Grant's friends and associates, Toni and Sophia.

Although the consulting work was a success, it was not that portion of the trip that lodged in Roxy's mind. On the final night of the visit, after she had finished with Grant's family, Grant took Roxy back to Toni and Sofia's house and raided the refrigerator. As Roxy turned to say good-bye to Grant, he kissed her—once, twice, three times. Roxy was electrified. This level of intensity had *never* happened before. Their eyes locked and there was a knowing, something magically familiar, a yearning. It would have been so easy to make love right there.

After a lovely eternity, Grant pried himself away and vanished into the night. Roxy was stunned. The next morning on the plane, uncontrollable crying overtook her. Something elusive stirred. Tears escaped several minutes into the short flight until a disturbing vision grabbed her attention. In that vision, she saw that the plane was going to crash.

Fear swept over her. Startled, she forced herself to shift from fear into action. Telepathically, she requested Commander Ashtar to assist in protecting the plane. She also called upon the Great White Brotherhood. Then she visualized the entire plane encapsulated in a huge ball of radiant white protective Light. She held fast to that vision for the rest of the flight. The whole experience smacked of Zeeq. Roxy shivered at the thought.

Once in the car with David, Roxy asked if she could speak with Leviticus.

"The dark ones tried to crash your plane," Leviticus began. "You have a powerful mind, Dear One. If you had locked onto the vision they gave you, you would probably have caused the plane to crash. You prevented this from occurring by shifting your focus. Good job!"

"Are the dark ones doing this often?"

"Indeed they are. They are the cause of more accidents than many are aware. They are attempting to kill Lightworkers before they wake up. This puts the odds in their favor. They are having a degree of success, you know. I cannot stay long. My body is busy at the moment, and I must tend to it."

"How's it going over there, you psychic?" Roxy smiled.

"It goes well."

"I wish I could say the same with David and me. He sure gets irritated quickly these days, about most anything. I came home from Seattle, where I picked up their lingo, and David about jumped down my throat." Roxy wondered if she and David would ever get their old magic back.

"Soon, Dear One, soon it shall all work out. You shall see. I must be off. In Love and Light." Leviticus bowed his head in namasté and was gone.

The brief, lovely, time with Leviticus had done nothing to alleviate the tension between David and Roxy. A subtle but noticeable edginess had begun to permeate the very fabric of their relationship.

Shortly into the school year, calls from Katrina escalated to daily. Slowly, when David was unavailable, Roxy became a suitable substitute. Katrina was growing stronger and more mature and though her loneliness was ever-present, her ability to cope with it was improving. Her Melding connection was helping, as was Zeeq's absence.

October and November brought disruption. The promise of more disorder lurked. The Guides sent an omen and two catalysts into their lives. The omen involved a movie, *The Seventh Sign*, a spiritual movie with a profound message. David and Roxy went to a friend's house to watch it.

The story line developed around the seven signs, which prophecy claims portend the apocalypse. In the leading character's past life, she had failed Jesus during his time on Earth. Now she was being asked if she would die for Jesus in this life. The movie shook Roxy to her core, thrusting her into gut-wrenching crying. Pain surged from some unknown, untouched place inside of her that she couldn't even describe. She was left with a haunting feeling that "dying for Jesus" in this lifetime was more an emotional death than a physical one.

Roxy wondered what could possibly be bigger or more painful than what she had endured during The Trinity. But fear permeated her consciousness. The lack of alignment between her and David exacerbated that fear.

The first catalyst came in the form of a gift from Master Merlin. One night in Katrina's apartment, a crystal charm materialized out of nowhere. Katrina was to give the small two-inch charm to David on his next visit. It was a long, thin clear crystal in a silver eagle-shaped holder on a silver chain.

Two weeks later, on David's weekend with Katrina, he accepted the gift and hung it over his tortoise shell chakra. Halfway between the throat and heart chakras, the tortoise shell is typically blocked in people who have a hard time stating their truth. David had a nice-guy pattern and rarely was willing to say hard, confrontational things. The charm was designed to help break through the blockage and help David speak his truth.

It made Roxy nervous.

Within hours of David's return with his new magical charm dangling from his neck, truths began uncontrollably emerging. David wasn't even aware of it. Habits of affinity, like Roxy tweaking his crotch, became the source of conflict. "I don't like when you do that."

"I thought you liked it?" Roxy was surprised.

"Well, maybe I did, but I don't anymore." David stomped off.

The second catalyst snuck up from behind. Roxy was doing more spiritual consulting as the Guides brought her new clients. One day in November, one of Grant's staff consultants called to say he'd referred a client to Roxy. The client's name was Samuel Wheaton, who lived in Oregon.

Samuel was tall, clean shaven, had hazel eyes and a full, bushy head of dirty blond curly hair. He had powerful arms and chest from working as a fireman for thirty years. He'd recently retired and he spent his time either reading spiritual/metaphysical books, or working on what he called "financial transactions."

These transactions occurred between corporations and sometimes individuals and involved thousands, sometimes millions, of dollars. Samuel's job was to connect a buyer with a seller. His commission was dependent upon completing the transaction. To date, he'd been working on them for over a year and had not closed a deal.

Roxy's consulting work focused on finding the potential internal blocks sabotaging Samuel's efforts. After spending a weekend watching, listening and sensing, it was clear that there were problems. Samuel had poor listening skills and an even worse memory. He missed, or dropped out, numerous vital details. He did everything, even his thinking, in slow motion. After three days, Roxy realized how deep the difficulties ran.

After Samuel left, Roxy pondered the wisest course of action. She sensed that answers to the problems loomed just out of her reach. Who best to help her tap them than Katrina/Arianne. Roxy and Katrina's relationship had been on a slow steady mend. The stronger Katrina got, the more they were able to talk; they found that they liked each other again.

A day or so after Samuel left Mt. Shasta, Roxy brought the subject of the transactions up with Katrina. At the mention of Samuel's name, a sexual chemistry exploded out of Katrina like fireworks in July.

"I know Samuel on a soul level, Roxy, I'm sure of it," Katrina said, trying to hide her excitement from Roxy. "Perhaps you'd better give me his number. It might be better if I talk to him directly ... about the transactions."

Katrina and Samuel instantly hit it off. In three short days their calls escalated to multiple times daily. The prime conversation had already drifted from transactions to sexuality. Their romance blossomed and within a week Katrina announced that she and Samuel had agreed to meet the coming weekend. Roxy was thrilled. David was not.

Mid-December descended on Mt. Shasta, the meeting place for Katrina and Samuel. But before that came about, Katrina had one request: to spend two nights alone with David, a farewell between lovers. Then, if all went well between Katrina and Samuel, the Guides would release David of his sexual responsibilities.

Katrina arrived at noon on Thursday. For the first time since the dissolving of The Trinity, Katrina and Roxy spent time together. David and Katrina were still deeply in love but there was a noticeable absence of jealousy in the space. Katrina was of sound mind and had mellowed. A lovely maturity had blossomed. They laughed, just as they had two years before.

"You miss David?" Roxy probed.

"Yeah," Katrina winked in David's direction. "But it's okay. I can get past the emotions now so much easier and faster."

"The Melding is helping?"

"Yep. You know, Roxy, before I'd get lost in my emotions. Now I feel the emotion, see the lesson in it for me—you know, that I'm supposed to get through loneliness—and I just remember how much I love David. Then I let go and move on. It's intense, yet it moves really fast."

"How's school coming?"

"Really well. With The Melding, I'm able to take most of the school's teaching suggestions to an advanced level. I'm not telling others yet. I'll wait 'til I get my first classroom and begin to implement my ideas."

"Like what?"

"To teach math I plan to use a style similar to Pee Wee Herman's. The humor will help kids remember the numbers easier."

"I'll bet you're grateful to have Zeeq gone from your life."

"Poor guy. He sure wouldn't give up. Yeah, it's nice to have that level of intensity out of my life. And the ones who are present aren't too troublesome. They're still around you sometimes, aren't they?"

"Yeah. Leviticus told us they'd probably continue hanging around. He said they're around most folks a lot. We keep aware and then they don't bug us too much, except when we're on the verge of a breakthrough. Then their attempts intensify. Anyway, Katrina, I've been wanting to tell you that I don't mind David going to see you anymore."

"Thanks, Roxy, I appreciate that. I can tell. There's tons less tension in the space."

David brought food for Katrina, who smiled at him and ate gratefully.

Later that day they all went to dinner at the busy Italian restaurant just down the road.

"This afternoon, Katrina, when you channeled, do you know why Joshua smiled at me?" Roxy asked.

"Smiled, huh? He doesn't smile much. Let me go find out why," Katrina offered as she set about to use her Melded gift. She placed her elbow on the table and nestled her chin in the palm of her hand. She set her eyes to staring off into the distance. Then with her eyes open, her Light body left her physical body through her Melded connection. She was gone for about two minutes. No one else noticed that her presence was missing.

"Well," Katrina began after her consciousness returned to her body. "Joshua said that the question you asked was one only he could answer. None of the other six entities who came to speak were permitted to give you the answer or tell you that only Joshua had the answer. So when you asked him the question just as he was leaving, he was amused that you had once again found your way through the maze to satisfy your insatiable curiosity."

"Wow, that's some answer, thanks. By the way, how do you like your new mother-in-law's apartment?"

"Great, except for the two teenage girls that live upstairs. They love to snoop through my stuff while I'm at school."

"Why don't you lock them out?" Roxy suggested.

"The door that separates our living quarters doesn't have a lock. Anyway, I set up beams of light across the front of the entrance. Ethereal beams, of course. Only I can see them. When the girls walk through the beams, they get altered. When I get home I immediately know that the girls came into my apartment 'cause the beams are changed."

"Do you tell them?" Roxy asked.

"Sure. I immediately go and remind them that I don't want them in my apartment. They look at me baffled. See, they never touch anything so they wonder how I know they were in my apartment."

They finished their meal and went back home, where Tenaiia briefly spoke to Roxy and David through Katrina. When Tenaiia finished, Katrina had a minor Melding glitch.

"David, help me get up. My foot is numb," Katrina said.

"What's wrong? What happened?" David asked.

"I don't know. It's like my foot's all numb. Wow, what a strange feeling." Katrina said as she limped on her right foot.

"Are you okay?" Roxy asked.

"Sure, I'll be fine. I just need to figure out what's goin' on," she said as David helped her to the door.

"Have a good time," Roxy called as they left.

Fifteen minutes later the phone rang. "Hello."

"Roxy, this is Katrina. I figured out what's going on with my foot."

"What?"

"I left my foot by my favorite waterfall out in the universe. But the cool part is why I left it there. See, a part of me was having so much fun with you that I didn't want to leave the house. So I left my foot to keep myself from leaving. Cool, huh?"

"Wow, really cool. So did you find it again?"

"Yes. I went out and got it. Isn't that the best?"

"Yep. I love you, Katrina. Have a good night."

"Love you, too, Roxy. And thanks."

Saturday morning, about an hour before Samuel was due to arrive, Katrina delivered the bomb to Roxy. "David and I talked this morning and we both feel that we can't honestly say that we'll never want to make love again. We both feel that we can't make a promise like that to you, or to each other. I mean, I really do feel a strong bond with Samuel but I also feel a strong bond with David."

"I understand," Roxy said, cringing.

Moments later Tenaiia urgently came calling. "Zeeq placed a bomb in Katrina's head when he set up the weaving," Tenaiia announced. "It was designed to go off today."

"Today? Why today? When will this ever end?" Roxy groaned.

"What kind of bomb?" David focused on the moment.

"If Katrina sees Samuel drive up, she will go into excitement about meeting him. This will cause the chemicals of anticipation to be released in her brain. These chemicals will trigger the bomb and she will die."

"Just great. Another blast from the past," Roxy moaned.

"What should we do?" David asked, ready to do anything.

"Have Katrina go to sleep so she won't see him arrive. Have Samuel wake her up by kissing her."

"You mean Zeeq knew about this day way back then?" Roxy asked.

"Yes," was all Tenaiia had time to say. She left Katrina's body so Katrina could be told of the strategy. Reminiscent of days gone by, Katrina refused to follow the plan. "I can handle my anticipation!" she insisted. "Really!"

David and Roxy sighed, eyes rolling into their heads. Tenaiia came to the rescue, putting Katrina to sleep in the nick of time. Samuel arrived early.

"Katrina's asleep." Roxy pointed to Katrina lying on the couch after Samuel had entered the living room. "Why don't you kiss her to wake her up?"

Samuel scurried to kiss his princess. Katrina awoke to Samuel's soft kiss on her cheek. They fell in love.

She touched, caressed and kissed Samuel often saying, "I love you, honey." She was soft, sensuous and selfless. Samuel lapped it up. In his self-centered reality, all the attention ascribed to him was glorious. David stayed away. If he was around when Samuel and Katrina were in their house, he made himself scarce. He spoke little but frowned a lot.

Roxy, Katrina and Samuel focused on the financial transactions.

"Is there even a chance of a deal closing?" Roxy asked Katrina one day, while they sat in Roxy and David's bedroom. Can you use The Melding to find out?"

"Let's give it a try," Katrina said. She telepathically put the request out into the universe: "Whoever has information regarding the transactions with Samuel, I humbly request a private audience."

Katrina closed her eyes. A moment passed and the Melded Katrina/Arianne traveled out into space while her physical body remained sitting on the bed next to Roxy. Katrina/Arianne opened her eyes out in the universe, on spaceship 1-0. There, she found herself sitting at a table across from Lady Commander Athena. Ah, here is where I will get answers to my questions, Katrina/Arianne observed to herself.

Katrina/Arianne took a moment to notice her surroundings. She was in a large room, with windows in one wall where she could see the stars outside the ship. The other end of the ship was beyond her sight; she guessed she could see some four hundred yards down its length before it blurred from view. Against the opposite wall was a long and lovely metallic, glowing planter full of greenery and unusual prickly pink and blue flowers. Their exotic scent filled the room. Soothing celestial music played softly in the background. The room resembled a mostly barren conference room with a huge table and chairs. The table was long and oval, capable of seating perhaps thirty, with a silver metallic smooth surface that was warm and inviting to the touch. The tall straight-back chairs rolled, without rollers. Although the room was well lit, the source of the light was not apparent.

Athena and Katrina/Arianne sat opposite each other in the first two chairs. Suddenly a door appeared out of nowhere and opened. Commander Ashtar stood in the opening, his presence compassionate and stern. Katrina/Arianne could see past Ashtar into the huge control room with walls and walls of control panels and a mammoth screen where Katrina/Arianne could see millions of stars and a large planet off in the distance. It seemed as though they were not moving since everything in the twelve-foot-square screen remained static.

She gazed at the planet until it struck her: *that's Earth!* As Ashtar passed through the portal, the door silently closed and disappeared into the fabric of the wall. Commander Ashtar walked briskly across the expanse of the room and sat perpendicular to Katrina/Arianne and Athena at the front of the table.

Katrina/Arianne began, "I am interested in knowing if these transactions are likely to close."

"It would appear that you wish to know this information from an egoed position," Commander Ashtar said.

Katrina/Arianne thought for a moment, then noticed the part of her that was wrapped in her ego. She wanted to be the one instrumental in getting a transaction to close. She wanted to be the savior, to be placed on a pedestal. "Yes, I see your point."

In that moment, Katrina/Arianne set out to shift her position, her energy, from wanting to be the savior on a pedestal to pledging that she would quietly give the information to Roxy and she herself would remain hidden. A moment or two passed while Commander Ashtar observed Katrina/Arianne's energy field changing. When he was satisfied that she had shifted her focus sufficiently from her ego, he said, "There are five possible alternate realities with these transactions. In two of the five, they will close. In the other three, they do not."

Katrina's eyes opened and there was Roxy in front of her.

"What did you find out?" Roxy asked, eyes wide.

Katrina told her what Ashtar had said.

"What percentage were the two possibilities?"

"You know, Roxy," Katrina said, "Ashtar gave me the odds but I can't remember. Guess I'm not supposed to. Anyway, I do remember that the odds were way against us."

"So The Melding can help us with this, eh?" Roxy asked.

"Not necessarily," Katrina warned. "There are lots of factors involved, like karma and negative energy patterns that can block progress. All the information in the universe cannot alter karma. If Samuel doesn't have the right karma, you know, to earn the windfall a closing would bring, than there is simply nothing we can do about it."

"Then why not tell us, so we can let go of them, if that's what we're supposed to do?"

"I think we're supposed to keep working on them for some reason. Who knows, maybe we'll succeed?" Katrina got up and rejoined Samuel in the living room.

By the end of their five days together, Katrina and Samuel spoke of living together in Mt. Shasta. For Roxy, it was a dream come true. Katrina was transferring her feelings from David to Samuel. David was the only one emerging as a thorn in the plans.

"I don't like it one bit." David told Roxy after Katrina and Samuel left town.

"What's the problem. They're falling in love," Roxy retorted.

"I don't believe it." David stormed out of the house.

As explosive jealousy built in David; he became distant from everyone.

Who Are Lightworkers?

They are people who
Chose their own path
Rather than follow dogma.

—Jack Clarke

SHIP 1-0 HOVERING CLOSE TO EARTH

38

Two Halves Of A Whole

David attempted not to get defensive and irritated and Roxy tried not to be critical. But for all their massive efforts, relief was nowhere in sight. Arguments were frequent and intense, often over a variety of nothing. The edge was pervasive and unrelenting.

"Did you pick up the rice?" Roxy asked when he came home from work.

"Damn! Why didn't you call me and remind me?"

"I did call you. Don't you remember?"

"That was at two o'clock! Why didn't you call me before I left! I have too many things to do. I can't remember everything!"

David stormed off. He was more defensive than Roxy had ever seen. He was miserable and out of control. Lost, he recommended that he and Roxy pursue some answers from Katrina. Roxy agreed. She had no better solution to offer.

"Your relationship hasn't been working for about six months now," Katrina began. "I don't think either one of you is willing to tell the truth about it."

"So what are you suggesting?" Roxy asked.

"I'm not suggesting anything," Katrina hedged. "I'm merely pointing out the obvious."

They felt worse after the call but something rang true in Katrina's words. Desperate, Roxy vowed to put even more energy into making their relationship work.

Later that day while David and Roxy were on a walk, David said, "I don't know if we're still meant to be together." The words flew out of David's mouth, complements of his magical charm.

Roxy stopped, stunned. "What are you saying?"

"I don't know. My 'bad and wrong' pattern is constantly activated. All you have to do is look at me cross and I feel bad and wrong. I'm insecure all the time, Roxy. It doesn't seem to matter how hard you try to do or say the right things, either. It's like it happens sideways. You look at me even slightly cross and I feel bad and defensive. It's not your fault, Roxy. I can't seem to shake feeling bad all the time."

"Are you saying, " Roxy choked out, "that you want a divorce?"

"I don't know what I'm saying." David looked awful. "All I know is that something isn't right. That's all I know."

The frigid walk home was silent and distressed. Roxy watched every word to avoid activating David's low self-worth. Their relationship problems seemed insurmountable.

Two days later, the next bomb dropped. Roxy attempted to seduce her husband, with little luck. David was upset and suddenly his Higher Self came through to talk to Roxy.

"Who are you?" Roxy asked, baffled.

"I am David's Higher Self."

Roxy's stomach knotted.

"Why do you still want me?" David's Higher Self asked Roxy.

"Because I love you!"

"Can't you see that it isn't working any longer? When will you be ready to let go of me?" And David's Higher Self split.

Roxy was numb. David was disoriented and confused. With nowhere else to turn, Roxy picked up the phone and called Katrina.

"Hi, " Roxy said.

"Something's happened." Katrina could feel it.

"Yeah. " Roxy stammered.

"With David?" Katrina tried to help.

"Yeah. He spoke ... his Higher Self spoke."

Roxy's story did not surprise Katrina. Even with Katrina's attempts to soothe her, Roxy remained unnerved, frightened, and lost.

1988 came to a close.

Over the holidays, Samuel and Katrina maintained daily phone contact. Their relationship was alive and passionate.

Samuel arrived as planned on January 5. With him came all his possessions tucked into the back of his pickup truck. "I don't need much. All I need is Katrina and that's enough for me."

Within hours he secured living quarters, a room to rent in a house where he shared the kitchen, living room and bath. Like Samuel, it was rustic. In his room he set up his phone and fax machine. It was all he needed to continue pursuing the transactions.

Katrina arrived the next day. She went to Samuel's first. That hit David between the eyes. His foundation swayed and creaked. Then she went to visit the Plumbs where she announced that Master Merlin wanted another private conversation with David. Roxy's jumpiness escalated. Katrina and David were gone for two hours.

David was visibly shaken when he walked through the kitchen door. Among other things, he was told the name of his Higher Self: Kalvet. Having just received what Roxy considered exciting information, he was moody and upset. All he wanted was to be left alone. He was lost and torn between two worlds.

Katrina suggested to Roxy that they go for a walk.

"David is in love with us both," Katrina gently began. "He thinks he's bad for loving us both. He doesn't know what to do about it. He's really torn. He really needs to be needed, Roxy. It's in his destiny. You're strong. You don't need him the way he craves to be needed."

"*I* need him!" Roxy protested.

"Yes, I know," she said softly and then added, "He feels guilty for loving us both and that's why he's always so defensive."

Roxy knew what Katrina meant but she wasn't ready to admit it to anyone.

Four days later, Katrina offered to take all four out to eat. During dinner, David's strain progressed until it was etched across his face.

"Stop kissing her in public!" David demanded of Samuel. "And must you sit so close to her?" he snapped again.

Roxy found David's behavior embarrassing. "What's wrong, David?" She tried to tame him. Nothing worked.

David's mind raced as an energy descended upon him like a heavy gray cloud. He charged out of the restaurant without saying a word.

Roxy went in search of David. After an hour of walking the streets, she gave up and went home. There he was, knocked out in bed in an unconscious state of overwhelm. Two worlds were tearing at his soul.

Roxy was confused. Katrina and Samuel were doing great. What was David's problem?

The next day Tenaiia decided to stir David further. She announced that it was time to test Samuel's abilities as a caretaker. If Samuel and Katrina were to be together, then Samuel had to keep Katrina/Arianne fed, on schedule, cleanly clothed, and protected.

Despite Katrina's belief that she could maintain The Melding connection alone, keeping her own self grounded and fed, time had proven her wrong. Since she left The Trinity, The Melding had begun dissolving. Katrina was aware of this harsh reality but had not told David and Roxy.

Tenaiia requested that David and Roxy be present for the test. One set of caretakers would pass the baton to the next.

Samuel had been told about Katrina's unusual gift and he had met Tenaiia on several occasions. He was captivated, but as for being a caretaker, he had slow reflexes, was irresponsible and too self-consumed. His observational skills were minimal; he couldn't keep himself focused on a task for more than a few seconds.

For the test, Tenaiia made David and Roxy promise not to interfere. With considerable doubt, they agreed. Then she told Samuel to watch for Katrina's fluttering eyes, a sure sign that she was about to pass out. Then to protect Katrina from getting hurt when she fell.

David and Roxy watched as Samuel sat on the edge of the bed and Katrina walked around the small bedroom. Within seconds of Tenaiia's departure, Samuel began talking, losing his focus. Katrina's eyes fluttered. David and Roxy grabbed their chair arms. Mid-push they stopped, remembering their promise. Even with all that movement, Samuel rambled on, unmoving. He caught Katrina's fluttering eyes as she headed for the ground. Not a muscle of Samuel's body moved in assistance before it was all over.

Samuel, stuck in his destructive patterns, was incapable of changing in the ways needed to be a successful caretaker. He went into an immediate state of overwhelm. His magical erotic relationship with Katrina was now shrouded with a heavy cloud of responsibility. The consequences of his slow reactions bothered him.

David hit the roof. "Don't you know how important it is to keep Katrina from hurting herself? How am I supposed to turn caretaking over to you when you don't even move to help her!"

Samuel had no answers. He wanted life to be fun. He was in way over his head. He promised that he would change. Everyone knew it would never happen, not in this lifetime.

By the sixth day, David was going berserk. Samuel was an incompetent caretaker and an overactive lover. David's jealousy reached explosive proportions and Samuel took the brunt of it. David snapped at Samuel at every turn for no discernible reasons.

About noon that same day, Samuel and Katrina went to bed. In the midst of their foreplay, Tenaiia popped in to ensure that Samuel was keeping his word and using a condom. Once Katrina was aroused, with her gift of sexuality and The Melding, she was incapable of keeping track of such matters. She counted on her lover to be responsible. Samuel was not. He was more interested in satisfying his own needs. He *wanted* to impregnate Katrina. Who cared if it was against her wishes?

Then Tenaiia pulled another of her calculated, dynamite-packed strategies. She asked Samuel if he would like to make love to her instead of Katrina. Samuel dove in.

The lovemaking was extraordinary. Unknown to him, it was spurred on by his soul connection with Tenaiia. He was hooked. When Katrina returned to her body she realized what had transpired. She was outraged, appalled that Samuel had made love to Tenaiia, another woman, and that he was not respecting her choice not to get pregnant. She was livid.

In all of the two-plus years that Katrina and David had made love, David had never made love to Tenaiia, though opportunities arose. It would be a violation of Katrina's body.

Katrina no longer trusted Samuel. Tenaiia had gambled and won.

Katrina ran from Samuel's room, crying and upset, never to return. She went in search of David's secure arms, sobbing her story to David and Roxy. David exploded in rage. Samuel's clear disregard for Katrina's body and emotions was beyond tolerance.

The strain debilitated Katrina. Ungrounded, exhausted, and half out of her body, she was unable to drive home. The thought of another night with Samuel was revolting. David came to her rescue by announcing that he would drive her home himself, spend the night, and they would drive back in the morning. As before, Katrina/Arianne and The Melding came first. Roxy's hurt and disappointment thickened the air.

"I'm sorry, Roxy," Katrina/Arianne said.

After they left, Roxy tended to Samuel's emotional bruises. He was shocked. "Do you think she'll come back?"

"No, Samuel. Katrina has left town with David."

"Can you talk to her? How can it be over just like that?" He was aghast.

"You violated her trust. I don't think you'll get another chance."

"You mean I'll never be able to make love to Tenaiia again?" He said and wept. He had no idea what had transpired around him. David,

Roxy and Katrina's world moved at a speed foreign to him, a speed that made him spin. He couldn't believe that he and Katrina were already over. He wasn't used to the consequences of his actions crashing in with such velocity.

Samuel's Guides-of-Light had brought him into Katrina, David and Roxy's tiny circle to serve as a catalyst, with little ultimate benefit for himself. After all, he owed karma many times over due to his incessant, selfish side. He was to serve David by catalyzing David into knowing and speaking his truth. In one single moment, all hopes of Samuel and Katrina's blossoming relationship were lost forever.

Roxy was bereft. During the night, she awoke to a strange feeling. Something had changed. The uneasiness intensified. Whatever had shifted was monumental.

The next morning, David called Roxy. He sounded bizarre, distant, foreign.

"What's wrong?" Roxy asked frantically.

"We'll talk when I get there. Meet us at the coffee shop at one o'clock."

"Can't you just tell me now what's going on?"

"No! We'll talk when I get there. I've got to go now," David flashed back.

As the minutes ticked by, Roxy breathed into her toes. Still the knots in her guts tightened.

David and Katrina arrived at the restaurant after one. They ordered. Strain filled their booth. Attempting to clear the space, Roxy asked David, "What's up?"

Around the fourth time, David exploded. "Can't you just let it be until we're alone?"

Roxy's stomach was too sour to eat. Ironically, only Katrina felt like eating. She even ate the French fries on Roxy's plate.

David and Roxy left together, their meals abandoned, and headed to his empty office. David wore a sorrowful, pained look. It was more than Roxy could bear.

"Katrina channeled last night," David said.

"Did you make love, too?"

"Yes."

"How many times?" Roxy shot back.

David's face tightened. "Three."

"Three times! Why can you make love to her and not to me?" Roxy demanded.

David's pained look got worse. "Look, Roxy, the Guides told me some stuff." He drew a picture of two separate circles connected by a line. He wrote DAVID by one circle, and ROXY by the other, with TWIN FLAMES written over both. Then he drew a line straight up from the DAVID circle and drew another circle with a line down the center. To this he added two names.

"This," he said, pointing to the names, ARIANNE/KALVET, "is what's called Two Halves of a Whole. That's what Katrina and I are: Two Halves of a Whole."

Roxy's heart plummeted to the floor. It was a higher connection than theirs. "Do you know who my other half is?"

"Yes. It's Grant. Roxy, I'm supposed to be with Katrina, my other half." His eyes were so very sad.

The words hit Roxy like burning acid. Hurt, anger, betrayal and disbelief exploded inside Roxy's mind. Her arms began thrashing, violently throwing the objects on David's desktop to the floor. Katrina *had* stolen his heart!

Miraculously, no one came in. When Roxy calmed down, she replaced the items, one by one, on David's desk.

David, horrified during the tantrum, fought every instinct to leave never moving a muscle. "I'm sorry, Roxy," he said. "I'm so very sorry! I love you." Tears rolled down his face.

Despite all of Roxy's rage, David's sorrow touched a deep place, a moment etched into memory.

"But we're such a good team together!" Roxy said.

"I know, Roxy."

"We got the job done!"

"I know, but I need to be with Katrina, Roxy. Please, can you forgive me? I love you so much. I never wanted to hurt you. Never." Tears still trickled down his cheeks.

"Two years of battle with Katrina over your heart turns meaningless in one statement."

David looked at Roxy. "What do you mean?"

"I had no idea that you two are Two Halves of a Whole. I can't stand in your way. Your soul connection is higher than our Twin Flame connection ever was. If I had only known, I'd have let go two years ago. Of course you two must be together."

David sighed in relief.

They sat in painful silence for several minutes. Katrina came in and Roxy felt that same mysterious energy between them, the one she'd been aware of for two years, the one she'd never quite been able to identify. Two Halves of a Whole, she thought. Two Halves of a Whole.

"Please, Katrina," Roxy said through labored breathing, "will you leave?"

"Sure. You know where to find me if you need me." Katrina smiled and left.

Roxy sat in a numb, dumb daze. David's excitement over Katrina was evident. The unspoken energy between Katrina and David oozed out of their auras.

Roxy braved the question, "Is sex better with Katrina?"

"Yes."

"How long has that been true?"

"Since about mid-point during The Trinity. Our spark just seemed to fade, Roxy, and the spark with Katrina just kept getting better."

The spark had left for Roxy as well. All her remedies had failed. Now she realized that it wasn't meant to be fixed. It had taken its appropriate course, as was written in their contracts.

Their time together had come to an end.

Truth That Sets Us Free.

Our Higher Selves condense us,
Into this dualistic, chaotic, limited school of hard knocks.
We are here to learn and become whole.
And to humbly surrender,
To the Higher Power and the Greater Picture.

—Keith Amber

39

The Pieces Fall Into Place

Her mind wandered in a fog. What next? Where next? Divorce? The implications were beyond comprehension. Where to go for answers? Leviticus? Surely he knows what I'm supposed to do, where I'm supposed to go. But before the request got past Roxy's lips, Leviticus offered through David to come and talk later.

They returned to David's vacant office just after seven that night. Despite the raging inner turmoil, no tears had been shed, though shock permeated every breath.

David, too, was buried in sorrow. This whole turn of events had him stunned. He loved Roxy and though things weren't right, divorcing her had never occurred to him until last night. The news of his other half resonated to his core. He was compelled to be with his other half.

Tucked in the rear of David's office, Leviticus came to the rescue. "Hello, Dear One," Leviticus said with so much love that Roxy felt it penetrate every cell of her body. He took her hands and held them. He moved his feet to connect with hers. That connection triggered the massive dam to rupture, the suffering and the fear. Tears gushed forth like a torrential storm. Dread of the unknown and anguish—such anguish! Roxy's guts wrenched.

This is the pain and emotional death *The Seventh Sign* had foretold, Roxy thought through her tears. Death of an old existence—David and me—to make way for a new reality, the great and frightening unknown.

Leviticus reached through the torment, touching Roxy's soul with healing love. He by-passed all of David's and her obstacles and filled her with a love so profound, the experience was engraved into her memory. He remained connected to Roxy's hands and feet, balancing her fluctuating energy while delivering crystal clarity to his ward.

"Was this supposed to happen all along? David going off with Katrina?" Roxy asked.

"It was one of the options, certainly the option most likely to occur. It was doubtful that Katrina would stick it out to the end. Too painful for her. Indeed, as painful as it was for you, Dear One, it was tenfold more for her. After all, she is in the youth of her emotional body and she was to share her other half. This is a tall order on any soul, even *with* the assistance of being Melded."

"Then why didn't David leave with Katrina?" Roxy snapped.

"Because David's love for you was so great that he was unable to see beyond that." Leviticus smiled. "It was for David to figure out that he must go with Katrina. This was a very difficult decision for him because of his love for you."

That touched Roxy at her tender, frail center. David does love me, she thought. "Then the energy bank strategy was really meant to be, wasn't it?

"Yes, Dear One. It was expected that Zeeq would use the strategy of siphoning your energy bank. And it was hoped that David would figure out his true destiny with Katrina during that time. It was also an opportunity for you to let go of David so that he could move on. But, alas, it did not work. You were unable to let go and David did not figure it out. He loves you very much, you know."

"Where am I supposed to go?" Panic filled her voice.

"Go to Seattle, Dear One. Your destiny awaits you there."

"Am I supposed to be with my other half, Grant?" Roxy was desperate for a security blanket.

"It is unknown at this time what Grant will choose to do. He is at a crossroads; you are one option. But you have other options as well."

"Is Grant conscious that I am one of his options?"

"Not at this time."

"What if it doesn't work out with Grant?"

"There are others in Seattle whom your Higher Self has chosen."

"Others? Why can't I just go and be by myself? I'd rather just do it alone. I don't want another husband!" Pain surged through her veins.

"You work best as part of a team, Dear One. It is written in your soul, it is written in your destiny. Trust me. You shall be happier working in team with another."

"Will the others share my drive for mission?"

"Yes. The others will easily match and balance your intensity and drive. David no longer does, Dear One. You and David are no longer compatible. You have outgrown him. He is designed in this lifetime to be a caretaker. You are a high-powered teacher, consultant, and leader. You need a husband and partner who has the same destiny in his soul as you do."

"If Grant doesn't work out, how will I find the others?"

"You will know, Dear One. Trust us. We will guide you," Leviticus assured her.

"When did Katrina know that David was supposed to go with her?"

"She was told at the same time she chose to leave The Trinity. You see, it was known from the beginning that Katrina would probably choose not to remain in The Trinity. For that reason a contingency plan was installed into the original contract. It stated that if Katrina chose to leave, then David would go with her. She is unable to maintain The Melding alone. David is the logical and natural choice as caretaker. It was also stated in the contract that David would have to figure this out on his own. He did not know before she left and Katrina was not permitted to tell him, or you. The Melding has begun to fade in David's absence. Katrina cannot do it alone."

"The Melding is fading?"

"Yes. Katrina is unable to keep herself fed and grounded. Without assistance, The Melding will be gone in two to three months."

"Why weren't we told?" Roxy shrieked. "After all, isn't that why we did all of this?"

"It was for David to figure out but his love for you prevented him from realizing or seeing his path clearly. Now it is clear to all what must be done. It is not too late, The Melding can still be saved."

"My refusal to let go didn't help any, did it?" Roxy asked.

"No, Dear One, it did not." Leviticus smiled lovingly.

"In fact, our spark began to fade after Katrina made her decision?"

"That is correct."

"And Katrina was never meant to let go and get over David?"

"Indeed. He is her most potent asset. She simply cannot do this alone. She has been patiently waiting for her other half to find his way back to her."

Roxy thought for a moment. "Seattle, huh?"

"Yes. Seattle awaits you, Dear One. Trust us. We will guide you. I promise that you shall not be left alone." Leviticus squeezed her hand.

"So the time has come for me to gracefully leave, once and for all. So be it." Roxy began sobbing again. "It's time to be strong, really strong."

"And indeed you shall be, Dear One. You have far more strength than you realize."

"When should I go?"

"You will know, Dear One. It will be soon." Love glowed from his eyes. It reached into and touched her heart. Her panic eased.

"Before you go, can I call Katrina?"

"Indeed. That would be wise," Leviticus agreed.

She dialed the phone. "Hi."

"Hi."

There was a dead quiet.

Roxy broke the silence, forcing herself to say the words. "I'll be leaving. You can have David. We'll get a divorce so you can get married." There, she'd said it. Divorce!

Again, silence. Roxy pierced the stillness. "You know, it's always been important to me that you be taken care of. I didn't know The Melding was suffering." Tears rolled down her face.

"I know," Katrina cooed.

"David should be with you. I'll be gone soon," Roxy promised.

A humble, "Thank you," floated through the phone.

"It is time for me to go," Leviticus said. "This body is in need of rest. One last thing, Dear One. Be gentle and kind to this one. He has given a great deal of his life force tonight to allow you to receive supreme clarity."

When David's consciousness returned, he looked awful. The supreme gift of his very life force humbled Roxy. "Thank you, Sweetie."

"I love you, you know."

"Yeah, I know."

Truth That Sets Us Free.

Our perfect Creator has already made a perfect creation.
Our job is to get out of the way and flow with it.

—Keith Amber

40

A Teacher Of Truth

The fog in Roxy's head was thick as her gaze drifted out the window to take in the clear blue morning. David's soft snoring announced his presence. Their bodies hugged the outer edges of the small mattress. The knotted, sick feeling in her stomach consumed her thoughts. Divorce. The pervasive sick feeling thickened. Roxy breathed into the knots, but the sickness persisted. "Please, God, what do I do next?" she pleaded.

Constructive thoughts began to emerge. A plan began to take shape. She got up and went to find an empty box. In it she placed a few items that she wanted to keep. She came across their wedding pictures. Nope, she decided, I'm not taking anything that will remind me of David. Decisions formed inside her throbbing head.

In the week that followed, David and Roxy set their intent in place to resolve and release all residual issues between them. They both wanted to move forward into their new lives, not hindered by their past. They expressed abundant gratitude to each other, remembering good times and bad, and burned wedding pictures, vows, and anything else that had been pertinent to them. They both resolved to empower each other into happy, fulfilling separate futures.

For days Roxy grappled with their impending divorce until she came to peace. Finally she was ready to go out into the world and share the news. Grant was the first. Roxy hoped that Grant would rescue her. For two agonizing days, she waited for his call.

"Divorce? You're getting a divorce? There's no way to work this out?" Grant shot bullets of judgment through the phone line.

"No. Divorce is the right thing for us to do," Roxy said, convinced. "I'll be moving to Seattle soon."

"Seattle! Why Seattle? There's a million places to move. Why here?" Edginess filled his voice.

"Because Leviticus said that's where I'm to move." Her unspoken request for a place to stay hung heavy in the airwaves.

"Sophia says that you can stay at their place," Grant said flatly.

"Thanks," Roxy managed. "I'd like to come work for you, Grant."

"I'm not in a position to offer you work at this time."

Roxy hung up in shock. Grant seemed like a stranger. She remembered Leviticus saying that he was still unconscious of their connection. She envied David's position. He was going into a known, stable direction while she felt like she was going into a void, jumping off a cliff with faith as her only parachute.

She was broke, had a borrowed truck from Samuel, and had found short-term housing. Other than the radically chilly Grant, and Sophia and her husband, Roxy didn't know anyone in the Seattle. She was terrified. Her inner knowing, and her faith and trust in Leviticus and the other Guides, was the only thing that kept her from going insane with terror.

A day or so later, the Guides-of-Light gave David and Roxy a final gift: two wonderful lovemaking sessions. The spark was back. It relieved them both to know that there was nothing wrong between them. Their chemistry had simply been removed to empower them into their higher knowing. The Guides-of-Light had given and the Guides-of-Light had taken away their magical sexual spark, all in alignment with the contract they had signed so long ago.

"Our Twin Flame connection is melting," Roxy observed.

"Yes, it is," David said, brushing his hand against her cheek.

Two days later their Twin Flame connection was history. The familiar electrical passion was like a distant memory. They slept without touching. They passed one another and used care to avoid brushing bodies. They talked without passion. They still loved one another but now it was from afar. Roxy's destiny beckoned her to leave.

Two days later Roxy picked up the phone. Grant's Higher Self, Antonomn, spoke on the phone, channeled through Katrina. "It is important for you to remember, regardless of how Grant treats you, that I love you, and I shall always love you. The odds are not in our favor to be together. There is a twenty percent chance that we shall unite on the physical plane. Grant is filled with resistance. He is stubborn and does not want to change. Being with you will mean he will have to change. It is unlikely that he will face his blocks and find his true feelings. Still, always remember: I love you." And Antonomn was gone.

It was the softest side of Antonomn that Roxy had ever experienced. A tear rolled down her cheek as she realized the struggle she was up against. The journey would be a rough one.

Katrina and Roxy resumed communication. Both were determined to maintain their friendship through the transition. Katrina yearned for David at her side. Roxy's departure was eight days away. For her, time moved at breakneck speed. For Katrina, the wait was forever.

On January 25, Katrina called. "There's still a cord between you and David."

"I've really let go!" Roxy was surprised.

"I know you have. That's why this is puzzling. I'm wondering if the problem is that you're in love with Leviticus."

Roxy gasped. "Oh my God! You're right!" She hung up and went for a walk.

Telepathically she and Leviticus spoke. "I love you. Always have, and I guess I always will," Roxy said.

"And my love for you is eternal as well," Leviticus responded. "You shall be fine, my dear friend. You are fully equipped to carry on and apply that which you have been taught by me and the others. Go now in faith. We shall guide your way, just as I have promised. Remember always, I love you. Call on me telepathically whenever you need. I shall always be there for you."

Tears rolled down Roxy's face. She was more resolved than ever that her destiny beckoned her to move on.

Later that afternoon the phone rang with the next surprise. Commander Ashtar, channeling through Katrina, spoke. "I am here to inform you that you have been given the position you have worked so hard to earn."

Euphoria flooded Roxy's consciousness. "Can you give me any specifics?"

"Not at this time. It is too big for you to know at this hour. It would overwhelm you. It will be unfolded to you as you are ready to know and when the time is right. Be patient." With those words Commander Ashtar bid his farewell.

Roxy's mind danced. All the hell she'd gone through had paid off. She sang for joy.

More surprises arrived. Master Merlin came through Katrina while on the phone. "I have two gifts to impart to you before your journey. I speak first to you of your ethereal father. He loves you very much. He is a wise old geezer who read the destiny in your soul and discovered you to be a teacher, a teacher of truth. That is part of your destiny. Also, he has asked me to deliver to you your ethereal name. It is time for you to use this on Earth."

A teacher of truth. The words sang true. Riveted, Roxy waited to hear her name.

"It is Sharmai."

An energy shot through Roxy like a bolt of lightning. The connection occurred in every cell of her body and exploded into knowing.

As soon as she hung up, she deciphered the numerology for "Sharmai," and was stunned by the deeper meaning encoded in her Higher Self's name. The inner personality was 11, the number calling for mastery in manifesting or doing. The outer personality was 22, master visionary. And the destiny 33, master teacher.

Although Roxy had seen aspects of these in herself for years, a master she was not. Having three master numbers to embrace was overwhelming. The 33 in her life path that she had tackled during The Trinity had been hell. Instant replay? No thank you!

The phone rang again. "Taking Sharmai will be easier than you realize," Antonomn said as he channeled through Katrina. "You have accomplished more than you know. Take this name as your surname. In time, you shall be ready to take it as your first name."

Roxy agreed, trusting Antonomn. She became Roxy Sharmai. Over the next couple of days, she noticed the new energy the name Sharmai brought. Soothing, natural, familiar, it was a broader experience of herself. It was time to go.

She called Sophia, who welcomed her early arrival. Her entire material universe fit into twelve boxes. "I'm ready," she announced.

"We have one hundred and fifty dollars. How much can I take?" Roxy asked David.

"Take whatever you want," David smiled. Roxy took one hundred dollars.

David masterfully loaded the back of Samuel's truck. Roxy was heading into a massive storm, the great West Coast storm of 1989, where there was a sheet of ice from Vancouver, Canada, to Northern California. Despite the predicted storm, Roxy knew it was right to go. It was four in the afternoon on January 26, 1989.

Facing each other in the living room, David and Roxy said goodbye. They glowed. There were no regrets; there was no anger, no resentment. Just love, gratitude, appreciation, and respect.

They bowed in namasté. Roxy left. She was doing the right thing. She was in right action, aligned with her higher destiny. It felt good already. She never looked back.

The journey was grueling beginning thirty miles north of Mt. Shasta to the bitter, hair-raising end. But the Guides knew what they were doing when they sent Roxy out into that dangerous storm. It was her initiation into selfhood, her opportunity to remember just how competent she was, especially on her own.

Roxy was keenly aware of the presence of Commander Ashtar, Lady Commander Athena, Master Merlin, and her good friend, Leviticus. She felt the cocoon of their protection while they allowed her to experience how competent and whole she was on her own.

It was mid-morning on Saturday, still hours away from Seattle, when the last of several obstacles occurred. Roxy's truck, like so many others, spun out of control. She had seen dozens of abandoned cars in the ditch because of the hazardous ice.

The truck spun in circles. Roxy was frantic. Then she felt herself float into an altered state, a time warp. There she was, with Leviticus.

"What are you going to do?" Calmness emanated from Leviticus.

Roxy took his cue. "Not panic, stay calm. Guide the truck out of harm's way."

"Very good, Dear One. You shall be fine." Leviticus smiled.

Roxy was back in her body, one part driving, another watching herself. She and another car were spinning together. She remained calm until both vehicles stopped at the edge of a steep ravine, inches from hanging over the edge, bumpers an inch apart.

When the truck finally came to a halt, Roxy knew that if she continued to listen to and follow the Guides' advice, they would always keep her safe. Her job was to stay calm and centered.

Exhausted and wired, Roxy arrived at Sophia's. The nine-to-ten-hour trip had taken twenty-five hours. The only rest she'd gotten was five brief hours the previous night.

"David called. He's worried about you," Sophia said.

Roxy smiled and called David. "Hi."

"Are you okay? That storm was a mess. Where are you?" His concern touched her heart.

"I'm fine, really. And yes, the storm was a mess but the Guides were with me all the way, and I'm fine. Tired and exhausted, but fine," Roxy assured him. "I wanted to call you when I got here. I guess it's a habit."

"I know," David said. There was so much love in his voice, a lump formed in her throat.

"I should go now," she said. "You belong to Katrina now and I'm safely in Seattle. My destiny lies here."

"Yeah," he replied.

"I love you, David."

"I love you, too, Roxy."

Truth That Sets Us Free.

Align with Truth...
And you will accumulate virtues.

—Keith Amber

HIGHER SELF LADY SHARMAI

Epilogue

A Message From Sharmai

What price are you willing to pay to earn your spiritual gifts? Everyone has spiritual gifts tucked away inside and there is an access door awaiting discovery. For some, you must release an old wound. For others, there is a limiting belief or position. Still others must learn how to forgive and be responsible for their life. We are placed here to learn and when we learn, we reap the benefits.

The dues we paid for our spiritual gifts left Katrina and me with massive wounds, which we healed through intent. David and I set the *intent* into motion the day we agreed to go forward in our lives, with no residual, unresolved feelings lurking about. From that decision, God, through our Guides-of-Light, responded by setting the flashbacks and other healing tools into motion.

The flashbacks began the night I spent five hours in the hotel on the way to Seattle during that massive storm. Nightmares plagued that brief erratic rest. Days later, the nightmares bled into my waking hours.

The Trinity flashbacks, or images on my third-eye screen, were always accompanied with the associated debilitating feelings. It got so that these flashbacks would jolt me at the most unusual times: on a lovely walk around the lake, or while washing dishes. My entire reality would be flung back in time, rendering me paralyzed in anguish for up to five minutes. They occurred three or four times a day, gradually lessening over time until two years later, when they stopped altogether. God also sent me a psychic soul healer who endlessly listened to my woes, loving and healing me through my grief. Katrina also had the flashbacks. They were designed to help us to dissolve and heal the residual trauma.

With every flashback I had to re-experience the pain, then choose to release it and heal. Because my intent was to purge the pain and not blame or feel sorry for myself, I healed. It's really as simple as all that. I *chose* to have the experience so that I could grow. And I *chose* to heal. I chose not to remain stuck, not to allow a festering wound to torture me for the rest of my life. I chose to have the experience profoundly forward my life.

Anyone can get past their wounds if they really want to. It's a matter of choice. It requires one to learn the truth, take personal responsibility for all aspects of their life, forgive, choose love, and heal. To transform negative soul patterns, one must choose new behavior a hundred times each day until the old pattern dies for good.

My new husband and I observe others stuck in negative patterns. Often they are blind to them, as I was. I wonder if a wallop in some form isn't what's needed. Maybe that's what really causes debilitating illnesses, birth defects, child abuse, disastrous car accidents, life-altering divorces, homelessness, poverty, the death of a child, the loss of a job. All too often we're afraid of the pain, and willing to collapse into our resistance. Sometimes our Higher Selves and our Guides must resort to more rigorous means to get us to face and deal with the lessons and issues we previously agreed to transform.

We find that those resisting their lessons are usually experiencing more pain in the resistance than they would by going through the lesson itself. Sometimes that fact is the toughest to realize, that the resistance is worse than the pain itself. The Light on the other side of the tunnel is worth every ounce of pain always—guaranteed! And the pain is never ever bigger than you are. It just feels that way sometimes.

Speaking of resistance, Grant's won out. Although he was aware that there was something special between us, it threatened him. Nevertheless, as Leviticus had promised, it wasn't long into my stay in Seattle until I was guided to my new husband, Keith Amber, a gifted psychic soul healer. The Guides did a brilliant job in bringing us together, despite my initial refusal to connect.

My husband and I have learned through our own experiences how to empower others through the mire of transformation with more grace and ease. That's what our work is all about. But we cannot help those who do not have the right intent; we aren't miracle workers. We simply have powerful tools for the serious student who wants to fly into freedom and perhaps help others to do the same.

As the Guides had promised, Keith and I are a perfect match. Our individual purposes on Earth exquisitely mingle on our enchanting and productive dance through life. What a joy, what a blessing! Since meeting and marrying Keith, our souls have also married on the ethereal plane, where we are committed to one another for eons. Keith says that I'm the only one he's ever met who refers to time in increments of eons. I tell him it's what I resonate with most. It's the term we most often use in the castle, our ethereal home that sits on a rock and floats in space out in the middle of nowhere. There are beautiful flowers and trees and magical fairies that dance, twinkle, and fly across a lake. And there's a bluish purple sun and moon. Consequently, we have bluish purple skin.

I know that probably sounds pretty weird but it really isn't. Yellow suns aren't everywhere. It is prophesied by Gordon Michael-Scallion of the Matrix Institute in New England that Earth is about to be in the presence of a blue star, which will tinge humanity's skin with a slight blue hue. You never know, it just might come to pass.

Not long after I left David, he went to be with his love, Katrina. The Melding regained its strength and they were happily married two years later. After Katrina graduated in the top five percent of her class, they moved to a new state where Katrina was offered a teaching job. With The Melding intact, Katrina shone brightly as a new teacher. She was voted as the Best All Around First Year Teacher in her state.

By Katrina's second year, her Principal had already noticed something extraordinary about this young new teacher. She had an excellent command of her students, whose scores and self-worth soared. Seasoned teachers migrated to her in search of solutions with their problem students. The Principal noticed the high level of respect Katrina received from her older peers. Katrina was left in charge of the entire school when her Principal had to be away for any length of time. Katrina quickly became known for her strange yet highly effective teaching techniques. Others began to follow in her footsteps. Her mission was well under way by her second year of teaching.

Maintaining spiritual gifts such as The Melding requires an ongoing commitment to humbleness, purity, and the proper use of the gifts. This is not an easy task and there are no guarantees. Many have earned such profound gifts only to lose them later. Katrina's propensity toward the need to be placed on a pedestal remained a potential obstacle for her.

Our lives have led us down different paths and we are no longer in touch. However, it is my greatest wish that she succeed. And I hope David and she experience all the happiness and success the world, and their gifts, have to offer.

Samuel never closed a deal and eventually gave up. He didn't have the right karma for success.

The dominoes of change that The Trinity set into motion continue to topple through my life. Emotional body, control issues, selfish sides, and general self-mastery all continue to be ever more enlightened. For all of that, I am deeply and eternally grateful to Katrina, David, Leviticus, Tenaiia and all the Guides-of-Light who shined a light on our path, guiding our way.

Sharmai, my Higher Self, is also grateful for how the experience has enriched her. She feels freer and Lighter than she ever has in her entire existence out of God. Her Lightness transfers into my life stream with every breath of life I inhale. It is a joy for me to work so closely with my Higher Self and to know that this connection is available to so many others today, *just for the seeking!*

It took seven years for me to finally gain crystal clarity regarding the position I had earned in the Ashtar Commander. At its core, I have been asked to be "a teacher of truth" to those who will listen. Keith and I endeavor to fulfill our missions, following and living by the guidance from our Guides-of-Light daily.

Most important of all, I am left with an ever-increasing personal experience of God. The marvel, the brilliance, the profound love of God, leaves me teary, humbled, and awestruck. And to think that we all have the spark of God within! Imagine what we are all capable of if we just let our God-self flourish. The possibilities boggle my mind.

In Love and Light,
God bless us all.

Partial Chart of Soul Connections
Found between Humans

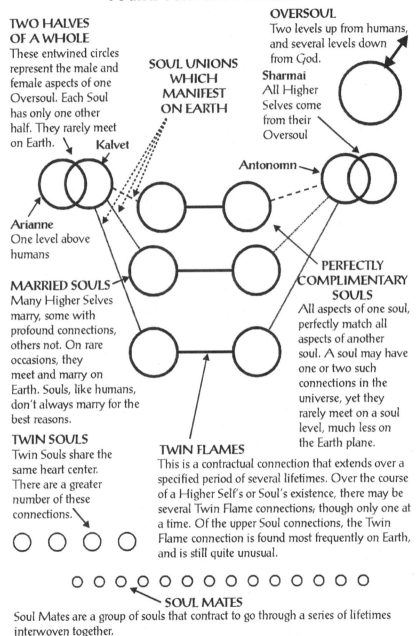

TWO HALVES OF A WHOLE
These entwined circles represent the male and female aspects of one Oversoul. Each Soul has only one other half. They rarely meet on Earth.

Kalvet

SOUL UNIONS WHICH MANIFEST ON EARTH

OVERSOUL
Two levels up from humans, and several levels down from God.

Sharmai
All Higher Selves come from their Oversoul

Antonomn

Arianne
One level above humans

MARRIED SOULS
Many Higher Selves marry, some with profound connections, others not. On rare occasions, they meet and marry on Earth. Souls, like humans, don't always marry for the best reasons.

PERFECTLY COMPLIMENTARY SOULS
All aspects of one soul, perfectly match all aspects of another soul. A soul may have one or two such connections in the universe, yet they rarely meet on a soul level, much less on the Earth plane.

TWIN SOULS
Twin Souls share the same heart center. There are a greater number of these connections.

TWIN FLAMES
This is a contractual connection that extends over a specified period of several lifetimes. Over the course of a Higher Self's or Soul's existence, there may be several Twin Flame connections; though only one at a time. Of the upper Soul connections, the Twin Flame connection is found most frequently on Earth, and is still quite unusual.

SOUL MATES
Soul Mates are a group of souls that contract to go through a series of lifetimes interwoven together.

SOULS
Yet a broader group of souls contracted to intertwine lives over a specific series of lifetimes with certain lessons in mind.

Glossary

Channeling: The act of allowing a non-physical Being to speak or write through a physical body. In the case of a trance channel the non-physical Being temporarily takes over the physical body.

Dark: Refers to the shadow side within humans and non-physical Beings in the universe, particularly when their actions originate from that part of the self.

Dark Ones: Also referred to as Satan. Non-physical Souls who are operating predominately from their shadow or evil side.

Ethereal Plane: The fourth dimension. The plane where most of Earth's inhabitants Higher Selves reside. The dimension Earth is currently evolving into. Also the dimension where most Guides-of-Light reside.

Dis-ease: The condition in humans where negative emotions are allowed to become stalled. Over time this condition manifests into a state of disease.

Filters: The beliefs, rules, limits and conditioning instilled into humans from birth onward. These filters are often blindly followed and can distort pure incoming information.

God: The creator of all the universe. Everything contains a speck of God within.

Great White Brotherhood: A group of non-physical Souls, anchored in the Light, available to assist physical and non-physical Souls in need of protection from the dark.

Guides: Chosen before birth, these ethereal Souls remain with their human ward guiding their way through all of life. Guardian Angels are also Guides.

Guides-of-Light: Non-physical Guides who are operating primarily from enlightenment, love and goodwill.

Higher Self: A human's Soul. The life-stream from which a human being comes.

Light: Enlightenment. The energy which contains love, goodwill and unlimited healing powers. The positive side of God.

Light Body: The Soul essence contained within the physical body.

Lightworkers: Individuals with a focus on the enlightenment of the self for the good of the whole. Also with a desire to assist others into the Light for the betterment of Earth.

Namasté: The act of placing one's hands, palms touching, at the chest and bowing the head in reverence. This gesture indicates an honoring of the God presence in all of creation.

Prebirth Contracts: The contract a Soul or Higher Self designs before birth which outlines all of the intended lessons, obstacles, relationships, and alternate realities which the lower self will encounter during its time on Earth.

Psychic or Etheric Surgery: Actual physical healing or altering of the physical body from a non-physical source.

Sananda or Jesus/Sananda: Sananda is the name of Jesus' Higher Self or Soul. The name he is called on the ethereal plane.

Soul: The life-stream from which a human being comes. Also called Higher Self.

Terra: Earth's ethereal name. The name she will be called after her transition into the fourth dimension.

Thoughtform: An energy comprised of specific thoughts which contains a life of its own.

Universe: The vast creation of God.

Universal Laws: The laws which govern all Higher Selves from all worlds.

Veils: The shields placed between humans and their Higher Selves to allow for lessons to be learned.

Walk-In: A Soul who bypasses the birthing process and, with full permission, takes over a physical body. This occurs at times according to a prebirth agreement, and at other times, because the Soul occupying the physical body has become so overwhelmed in its life that it wishes to abandon the body.

Copyright Acknowledgments

About the Author

Sharmai Amber possesses an extraordinary desire to assist in the enlightenment of humanity. After one year of college at the University of Minnesota, she dropped out in favor of following her heart. Driven to pursue a maverick spiritual path, she has accumulated hundreds of magical experiences and extensive spiritual wisdom designed to assist others in their search for truth and wholeness.

She and her husband Keith have been working together since they met in 1989. Sharmai, a spiritual teacher, delivers messages from the Spirit Guides, and Keith, a psychic soul healer, channels messages and a profound healing sound called Toning. Both are gifted visionaries, telepaths, psychics and channels. Equipped with a clear, potent and guided message, she is available to speak to groups on the subjects contained in *The Melding* and more.

In their work they have been called dynamic, humorous, compassionate, and highly effective in assisting others in getting whole and clear. They are instrumental in empowering individuals to heal and then unfold their own inner spiritual gifts, fulfillment, and contributions. They have led hundreds of spiritual groups and workshops in the Pacific Northwest and the Midwest on the U.S. mainland, and in Hawai'i. They have also hosted their own weekly radio show and monthly television program in Hawai'i.

Privately, they enjoy their three Persian cats, an aviary stocked with five species of birds, numerous fresh and salt water aquariums, and an inspiring collection of natural crystals, all of which help in their work.

The author can be reached at www.lava.net/heal, or by e-mail at: heal@lava.net

Additional copies of this book are available at your local bookstore or toll-free: 1-800-211-7370.

OUGHTEN HOUSE PUBLICATIONS

PO Box 2008
LIVERMORE · CALIFORNIA · 94551-2008 · USA
PHONE: (510) 447-2332
TOLL-FREE: 1-888-ORDERIT
FAX: (510) 447-2376
E-MAIL: oughten@oughtenhouse.com
INTERNET: www.oughtenhouse.com